NEVER RAN,
NEVER WILL

NEVER RAN, NEVER WILL

Boyhood *and* Football
in a Changing
American Inner City

Albert Samaha

PUBLICAFFAIRS
NEW YORK

PublicAffairs
Hachette Book Group
1290 Avenue of the Americas, New York, NY 10104
www.publicaffairsbooks.com
@Public_Affairs

Printed in the United States of America
First Edition: September 2018
Published by PublicAffairs, an imprint of Perseus Books, LLC, a subsidiary
of Hachette Book Group, Inc. The PublicAffairs name and logo is a trademark
of the Hachette Book Group.

The publisher is not responsible for websites (or their content) that are not
owned by the publisher.

Print book interior design by Linda Mark.

Library of Congress Cataloging-in-Publication Data
Names: Samaha, Albert, author.
Title: Never ran, never will: boyhood and football in a changing American inner
  city / Albert Samaha.
Description: First edition. | New York: PublicAffairs, 2018. | Includes
  bibliographical references and index.
Identifiers: LCCN 2018000983| ISBN 9781610398688 (hardcover) |
  ISBN 9781541767867 (ebook)
Subjects: LCSH: Mo Better Jaguars (Football team) | Football—Social aspects—
  New York (State)—New York. | Brownsville (New York, N.Y.)—Social conditions.
Classification: LCC GV956.M6 S34 2018 | DDC 796.332/6209747/1—dc23
LC record available at https://lccn.loc.gov/2018000983

ISBNs: 978-1-61039-868-8 (hardcover), 978-1-54176-786-7 (ebook)

LSC-C
10 9 8 7 6 5 4 3 2 1

For my mother, Lucy Concepcion

Maybe it's better to have the terrible times first. I don't know. Maybe, then, you can have, if you live, a better life, a real life, because you had to fight so hard to get it away— you know?—from the mad dog who held it in his teeth. But then your life has all those tooth marks, too, all those tatters, and all that blood.

—JAMES BALDWIN,
"This Morning, This Evening, So Soon"

Contents

Characters

2013 Mo Better Jaguars

Junior Midgets (ages 10 to 13):

Chris Legree—program director, coach in charge of Junior Midget age group
Gary Gravenhise—assistant coach

Gio—offensive lineman, defensive lineman
Isaiah—running back, defensive back

Junior Pee Wees (ages 8 to 11):

Muhammad Esau—coach in charge of Junior Pee Wee age group
Andrell—assistant coach

Oomz—running back, linebacker
Hart—offensive lineman, defensive lineman
Chaka—wide receiver, defensive back
Naz—quarterback, defensive back
Time Out—running back, defensive lineman
Dorian—offensive lineman, linebacker
Lamont—offensive lineman, defensive lineman

Mitey Mites (ages 7 to 9):

    Vick Davis—coach in charge of Mitey Mite age group
    Elsie—assistant coach
    James—assistant coach
    Oscar—assistant coach

    Puerto Rico—offensive lineman, defensive lineman

2014 Mo Better Jaguars

Pee Wees (ages 9 to 12):

    Muhammad Esau—coach in charge of Junior Pee Wee age group
    Andrell—assistant coach

    Oomz—running back, linebacker
    Hart—offensive lineman, defensive lineman
    Isaiah—running back, linebacker
    Donnie—offensive lineman, defensive lineman
    Chaka—wide receiver, defensive back
    Naz—quarterback, defensive back
    Time Out—tight end, defensive lineman
    Dorian—offensive lineman, linebacker
    Lamont—offensive lineman, defensive lineman

Junior Pee Wees (age 8 to 11):

    Chris Legree—program director, coach in charge of Junior Pee Wee age group
    Gary Gravenhise—assistant coach

Mitey Mites (ages 7 to 9):

    Vick Davis—coach in charge of Mitey Mite age group
    Elsie—assistant coach
    James—assistant coach
    Oscar—assistant coach

    Puerto Rico—offensive lineman, defensive lineman
    Tarell—wide receiver, defensive back

Author's Note

I BEGAN REPORTING THIS BOOK IN THE SUMMER OF 2013. Over the next two years, I spent many hours with the players of the Mo Better Jaguars, their coaches, their parents, and other current and former neighborhood residents. I went to nearly every practice and game, and spent time with them at the park, at their homes, on the phone, in their cars, walking around, on buses to New Jersey, and anyplace else they'd let me shadow them.

This book is based on interviews, conversations, and observations from four and a half years of reporting in and around Brooklyn's Brownsville neighborhood, as well as outside research. It's filtered through my own interpretations of what I saw, heard, read, concluded, and believed.

One of the harder decisions was over what to call a neighborhood like Brownsville. I went with "inner city" because it's what most of the locals used and, I guess, the clearest way to put it at the moment. The word is loaded because it has been misused so often, especially in efforts to deny the forces of systemic oppression that batter black and brown neighborhoods.

I wrote this book because I wanted to explore why some kids made it out and some didn't. What were the factors that made the difference? And did escaping tough circumstances also have to mean turning your back on the neighborhood? In my reporting on disenfranchised communities across the country, I repeatedly came across people who'd dealt with the fear of poverty or crime, learned lessons from their circumstances that helped them grow into successful adults, and then found themselves drawn back to their homes. This book is entirely from a third-person perspective because I wanted to present this world as it looked—and as it continued to look in the moments I wasn't there. This story belongs to the people who allowed me to peek into their lives, and my primary goal is to do them justice, while answering the questions I'd become focused on.

While I do not appear in the book as a character, the story I chose to tell is undoubtedly personal, a journey to better understand tensions that have discomforted me. I was part of the wave of gentrifiers moving into Flatbush, Brooklyn, in the early 2010s, and I still live there as of this writing. My apartment is two and half miles from Betsy Head Park, an easy walk on a nice day. I go to bars and brunch spots that replaced longtime local businesses. There's no escaping the knowledge of the benefits I've gained at the expense of families with deep roots in a place I only recently started calling home.

I began reporting this book around the time I'd started grappling with my feelings about football, the sport that dominated much of my childhood. I had NFL aspirations and played until my second year in college. I love the game and still believe that the virtues I learned from playing it were critical to whatever success I have been able to find. Like many, the more I learned about the brain research, the more I cringed at the big hits, wondered about the sport's future, and questioned the morality of supporting it. In reporting this book, I hoped to cultivate some sort of understanding—in myself, at least—of what football's place in American society is, will be, and should be.

Albert Samaha
January 27, 2018
Flatbush, Brooklyn

PART I

BOYHOOD

GIO'S ARRIVAL
July 2013

THE BOYS CAME TO THE PARK FOR FOOTBALL PRACTICE on Saturday mornings in the summer. Some of them would be lost by winter; Coach Chris Legree couldn't yet say which ones. It was early July 2013, and Chris was hopeful. Despite years of evidence to the contrary, he still held on to the dream that this would be the year he saved all the boys gathered around him at the park.

There were more than 50 of them lined up across the hard dirt field in the Brownsville neighborhood, deep in east Brooklyn. The youngest boys were 7; the oldest, 12. Most wore T-shirts and basketball shorts, though a few, the newcomers who didn't know better, were in jeans. In a few weeks, they'd all be in helmets and shoulder pads, and Chris would learn "who was really a football player" and who wasn't cut out for the game. But for now, in the thick heat of peak summer, their only tasks were to learn the plays and get in shape.

"Set! Go!" shouted Chris, who was 57, built like a bouncer, and had the robust, commanding voice of a former quarterback. "Let's go! All the way through!"

The boys sprinted across the field, their sneakers and cleats kicking up dust. Yes, Chris knew some would be lost, but he was just as certain that within this pack, too, were future stars. Every boy had aspirations beyond professional football dreams. Isaiah, a rail-thin 11-year-old who ran with easy strides, his slender frame almost gliding with the dust, wanted to start his own business. Oomz, a mercurial and solidly built 10-year-old jogging in the middle of the pack, wanted to become a doctor. Hart, a big 10-year-old lumbering near the back, wanted to practice law.

It was hard to tell, at this point, whose childhood struggles were prologues to against-all-odds stories of upward mobility and whose foreshadowed tragedy. Who would make it out and who wouldn't. To Chris, it sometimes felt arbitrary. He'd coached boys at this park for nearly two decades, and over those years he'd seen promising kids, from stable households and decent schools, fall into the streets, and he'd seen troubled kids, with poor grades and juvenile records, get on track. The adolescent years were fickle in this neighborhood. One push this way or that could make all the difference, erasing every move that came before. It was both a reason to hope and to despair.

"Keep going!" Chris shouted. "Don't slow down! When they see us they gon' know what Brownsville's about!"

Within minutes, some boys were hunched over, out of breath, wilting in the sticky heat. Chris called for a water break. His eight assistant coaches, posted at various points on the field, reminded the boys that walking wasn't allowed during practice. As the boys dispersed, to their backpacks piled at the base of a tall cement light post or to the water fountain behind the baseball diamond, Chris spotted an older boy watching them from behind the fence.

Chris always scanned the park during practice. A five-block patch of dried grass and cracked pavement in the center of Brownsville, Betsy Head Park was his domain. He'd grown up in the housing projects down the street, the Brownsville Houses, and his Mo Better Jaguars youth football program had practiced on this dusty field for years. Anybody looking for Chris knew to find him at the park. He waved at friends, greeted parents and former players, scouted for new recruits, and kept an eye out for any older kids who might tempt his boys onto the streets. Chris couldn't protect his boys once they left Betsy Head Park, but as long as they were under his watch on this field, nothing could touch them.

The boy behind the fence wore a dark T-shirt, shiny basketball shorts, and unremarkable sneakers. He had close-cut hair, high cheekbones, and big, down-turned eyes that lent him an air of vulnerability despite the ridges of muscle visible on his calves and forearms. Chris didn't recognize the boy, but the boy began walking toward him.

"Hey, how ya doing?" Chris said warmly.

"Hi," the boy said. "I was wondering how I could join the team."

Now that they stood toe-to-toe, Chris saw that the boy did not wear the hard face he'd seen on so many of the older boys around the neighborhood. His voice, too, was soft, hesitant.

"How old are you?"

"Twelve."

The boy's name was Gio. The first thing Chris noticed about him was that he was big for his age. The second was how politely he spoke even without a parent present. Later, after seeing him move on the field for the first time, Chris told his fellow coaches: "This kid got a chance to be a star."

∞∞∞

GIO HAD ALWAYS wanted to play football. He hadn't gotten much of a chance to try the sport growing up in Saint Lucia, in the Caribbean, where his friends mostly played soccer. Gio was good at soccer, faster and more coordinated than the other boys his age. But the complexity and collisions of football appealed to him, and he watched the game as often as possible. His favorite team was the New York Giants.

By the time Gio was in grade school, his mother and older brother had moved to New York City, where they lived in a big brick apartment building in Brownsville. Gio stayed behind with his father in Saint Lucia while his mother settled into the new home. The boy enjoyed life on the island. It was comfortable. He had many friends. They often spent their afternoons on the beach, kicking a soccer ball, swimming, running races, and roughhousing. But it was a small place, and Gio grew bored of the beach. "It gets old if it's the only thing you do every day," Gio said. He welcomed his mother's decision to bring him to America.

To his eyes, the country was full of wonders. Tall buildings blocked the horizon. Cars filled every driveway and lined every curb. Large flat-screen televisions glowed through living-room windows. A few days after he arrived in the summer of 2013, his mother took him to Coney Island, eight miles south of Brownsville, where the beach was thronging, far busier than any he'd seen. Wide-eyed, he took in the roller coasters, ice cream parlors, carnival games, and the hundreds of people strolling along the boardwalk and crammed towel-to-towel on the sand. There was abundance all around him. Within his own neighborhood, he saw big shops that sold many versions of any kind of item you could want. On a single block there might be a place for Chinese food, a place for burgers, and a place for deli sandwiches. Across the street from his apartment building, a block down from a halfway house, stood a Dunkin' Donuts, a T-Mobile branch, a Dollar Tree, a fried chicken joint, and two pizza chains. Several blocks farther north, on Pitkin Avenue, the neighborhood's main commercial thoroughfare, the shops lined up, one after the next, as far as his eyes could see— selling sneakers, suits, hair products, discount jeans, fresh fruit, liquor, video games, tattoos, and more. "It's like you can get anything you want," Gio said. He liked to go for walks along Pitkin Avenue, dropping into shops and people watching. He wondered if all of America was like this.

One Saturday, a month after his arrival, Gio cut through Betsy Head on his way home from Pitkin and saw kids playing football. The park teemed with summer life. Sweaty guys played pickup basketball on blacktops. Small children splashed in the pool. Joggers looped the red rubber track. Teenagers lounged on the jungle gym. Old-timers played cards on chipped picnic tables. Young men and women chatted on cell phones and ate greasy takeout on the red cement steps that served as bleachers behind the baseball diamond. Somewhere, a boom box was blasting hip-hop. And, in the center of it all, 50 or so boys kicked up dust.

Gio was taller than all of the boys, and as he watched them, he figured he was stronger too. He imagined himself running with the ball and knocking opponents to the ground, the big hits that made the crowd go *ooooh!* on TV. He thought about how popular football was in this country and the riches that came from being good at it. He began to dream.

ooooo

Gio's mother didn't know much about football, but she supported his interest. Though she came to the country with high hopes for the future, she worried about her son's transition into American life. It was not the glittering paradise some of her relatives in the Caribbean pictured, and she'd hesitated to move Gio to the States. There were more opportunities here than anywhere else, she still believed, but soon after arriving she realized that those opportunities were more distant than she expected—especially for boys Gio's age, especially in working-class neighborhoods like Brownsville, where she landed because rent was cheap. She learned that many of the schools in her neighborhood were notorious for hallway fights and low test scores. She read news articles declaring that Brownsville's crime rate was among the highest in the city. She heard stories of young people falling in with local gangs.

Before her 12-year-old son could go off to college, start a career, and buy a house, he had to make it out of the neighborhood, avoiding the traps along the way. Gio had grown up in an insulated, safe environment, where he'd had the same friends all his life and saw the same people every day. His mother worried he'd be unable to handle the negative influences she saw around the neighborhood, the older boys on the corners late at night who pulled younger boys into their circle. She worked all day and so did Gio's 20-year-old brother, and she worried how Gio would spend his free time. It calmed her to know that he would be at the park, learning from coaches and meeting new friends, for so many hours each week.

She met Coach Chris, liked his enthusiasm, and felt blessed to have another adult looking after her son. She hadn't really considered how football could shape Gio's future until she talked to Chris. The coach was telling her that her son might be good enough to go to college for free. Within days of their first meeting, Gio had become Chris's prized prospect. Not only was he fast and strong, but he could kick the ball 40 yards and throw it nearly as far. He had a sharp mind, quickly picking up the plays and the rules, and he showed up to every practice. Chris bragged to high school coaches about him. When old friends dropped by the field to see Chris, he pointed to Gio and said, "Watch this kid right here. This kid could be a star." He worked with Gio on kicking and blocking drills before practice and during water breaks. "Just imagine what this kid can do when he actually knows how to play," Chris said.

The other boys were just as impressed. It wasn't long before many of them looked up to Gio. He was funny and warm and, even though he was older and more athletic than the others, he never acted like he was too cool. One night, after a Tuesday evening practice in mid-August, a group of them stayed on the field with Gio to see how far he could kick the ball. The sun was setting. Lights on tall cement posts around the park illuminated the field, where, on the other side, a group of mostly West Indian men were playing soccer. Gio launched the football high into the darkening blue sky. As it barreled down, the other boys jockeyed to get underneath, but it hit the dirt before anybody could snag it, and it bounced around the way footballs do. The boys raced after it, pushing one another away until finally somebody dove on the ball.

"My ball!" shouted Oomz, as he hopped to his feet, his white shirt stained with dirt. He threw the ball to Gio, then got back in position for the next round. But before the kick, he heard somebody calling his name: "Yo, Oomz!" He turned and saw Hart standing by the side of the field with his parents, who were folding up the lawn chairs they'd sat on during practice.

"I'll let y'all get the next one," Oomz said to the other boys before jogging off toward Hart and greeting his parents.

"Oomz, you wanna come over tonight?" Hart said. "My mom and dad said it's cool."

"I wish I could, but I gotta ask my mom first," Oomz said. "Next practice, though?"

"You're welcome at our place anytime," Hart's mother chimed in.

The boys slapped hands and parted ways. As Oomz sprinted back to the middle of the field, Hart and his parents headed for their car, bound for a quiet block of nice houses in southeastern Queens. While a majority of boys on the team lived in Brownsville, some commuted to practice from middle-class pockets of the city, where white people lived and parks had lush grass. Several boys waited at the park entrance for their rides. Others took off on bikes or caught the bus or subway. A few stood with their parents talking to coaches, their conversations punctuated every minute or so by the thud of Gio's booming kicks.

Coach Muhammad Esau, at 24 the second-youngest coach on the staff, stayed at the park with the boys waiting out front. Once they'd all been picked up, he turned his attention to the field, where the game of kick and catch continued. Esau had been a team captain during Mo Better's glory years, a sure-tackling cornerback. Even back then, Chris thought Esau would make a good coach. In Chris's ideal world, Esau would one day run the program. For now, he was deputy in charge of the Junior Pee Wee age group, which included Oomz and Hart.

"Yo, what y'all still doing out here?" Esau said to the boys on the field. "Y'all should be headed home."

The summer had been violent. Tensions between the two dominant crews of the neighborhood, the Hood Starz and the Wave Gang, had thickened. On some nights, teenagers opened fire on one another on Rockaway Avenue, the boundary between their territories, three blocks from the park. The coaches recalled at least six shootings on the avenue this summer. Other nights, boys traded shots in the cluster of housing projects across the street from the park.

The coaches were familiar with the rivalry. Less than a decade earlier, a group of former Mo Better players had formed the Hood Starz. Some of those players got locked up after a police gang sweep in the late 2000s. Others were killed in the conflict with the Wave Gang. Hakeem, the 16-year-old alleged leader of the Hood Starz, had been murdered in 2010. And as the older boys went away, to prisons and cemeteries, younger boys stepped up to replace them and avenge their deaths, keeping alive a rivalry whose origins many of them did not know. Now Hakeem's younger brother Poppa, once a star quarterback and team captain on Mo Better, was said to be among the crew's leaders. Coach Chris didn't believe this was true. "Just rumors," he said. But he also knew that, for an adolescent boy, the neighborhood was a tinderbox of social pressures, street politics, and the directionless anger that blooms from the daily struggle of poverty. These were the same factors battering boys in working-class black neighborhoods all over America. In most ways, Brownsville had more in common with blocks in south Chicago, north St. Louis, west Baltimore, and east Oakland than it did with the increasingly gentrified stretches of north and central Brooklyn, much less any place in Manhattan. While crime rates dropped across America—most dramatically in New York City—in the 1990s and 2000s, violence became increasingly concentrated in these neighborhoods. Dreams of upward mobility still felt remote. Coach Chris had lost scores of boys to the streets over the program's 18 years. Esau had played with some of them.

Hearing Esau's orders, the boys left the field and headed home. Gio went south, down Livonia Avenue, to his building on Kings Highway five minutes away. Oomz went north, up Strauss Street, where his grandmother's house was a block down. He lived on the same block as Poppa, whom he'd known for as long as he could remember. Poppa's final year on Mo Better, when he was 15, was Oomz's first year, when he was 7, in the Mitey Mite age group, which was headed by Coach Vick Davis, the most respected and feared coach in the program. When Oomz was 8, he and Hart led the Mitey Mites to a North Jersey Pop Warner League championship. "We was some pretty bad dudes," said Hart. By now, they were veterans of the program, the two best players on the Junior Pee Wee team. At practice, they stood out from the boys whose muscles had yet to memorize the technical movements of football. Oomz and Hart had mastered the sport's dance—hips twisting, backs flat, balls of their feet chopping the ground. Just as their bodies had internalized the sport's mechanics, their minds were synchronized to the seasonal routines that had structured their lives for years. For Oomz and Hart, the summer was about to reach its crescendo—that narrow stretch of time every year between the first day in football pads and the first day of school, when the hours feel shorter and reality sets in.

ooooo

THE DOOR TO the building was open when Gio arrived. The lock had been broken for at least as long as he'd lived there, in the massive brick structure locals called the Castle because it looked like one from the outside. The lobby was long and wide, and during the day it was filled with little kids playing, sometimes bouncing a red rubber kickball across the linoleum. Paper plates, empty cans, and broken glass littered the elevator floor. The building's hallways were loud, echoing pattering footsteps, distant shouting, and thudding music. Gio liked many things about New York City, but one thing he hadn't gotten used to was the constant noise. Cars blasting heavy bass waited at stoplights. Sirens whined. Gio entered his front door, shuffled down the long hallway of the railroad-style apartment, and collapsed onto his bed. The subway rumbled by on the elevated tracks a few dozen yards from his window, a long, low thunder that shook the bare walls of his room all day and all night. Some nights, too, he heard gunshots.

Still, he felt like he was adjusting well to the new environment. He hung around the park on most days and began recognizing familiar faces from the neighborhood. When the helmets and shoulder pads came on in late August, he quickly got comfortable with the equipment. At first, the gear had felt heavy and suffocating. The helmet blocked peripheral vision. The shoulder pads limited arm mobility. The tight pants lined with protective cushions slowed his strides. But by the end of his first week of practice in pads, Gio's movements had become smooth and casual, as if the armor were nothing more than a hoodie and basketball shorts. What had initially felt oppressive now felt freeing. Stripped of fear and physical inhibitions, Gio ran full speed into the game's maelstrom of collisions. Football, it turned out, came easily to him. It was the rest of his American life he had to worry about.

– 2 –

LOOKING FOR THESE BETTER DAYS
August 2013

THE DUST CLOUDS FORMED AFTER THE HITTING BEGAN. Several collisions in, the dust hung like a fog over Betsy Head Park. There was not much grass on the field, and so the dust rose from the ground. It drifted toward the housing projects to the east and the elevated subway tracks hanging over the park's southern edge. The August evening was warm and humid and the dust stuck to everybody. It stuck to the legs and feet of the mothers sitting along the green benches near the park's entrance. It stuck to the necks and foreheads of the fathers leaning against the waist-high fence to watch the hitting. It stained the yellow bills of the ball caps worn by the coaches spread across the field. It covered the purple mesh jerseys of the boys, who stood in two lines, facing each other, forming a stage for the tackling drill.

Crack!

Ooohhhh!

Oomz had just run through another defender. Oomz had gripped the football in his right arm, faked to the right, then cut to the left in a burst and knocked the boy trying to tackle him on his back for the second straight time. The boy turned onto his stomach and slowly pushed himself up.

"Come on! I want you nasty!" said Coach Chris. "This is Brownsville! This is not Flatbush! Or Sheepshead Bay! This is Brownsville! Get aggressive! Who gon' be nasty?"

At first, no boy stepped forward. Oomz's teammates knew he wouldn't ease up. It wasn't that Oomz was fighting to earn more playing time. He had been a star running back and team captain since his first season at Mo Better. And it wasn't that he was showing off. Oomz wasn't interested in attention. He didn't count how many touchdowns he scored and he didn't pout when his coach asked him to block for another ballcarrier. It wasn't even that Oomz took football so seriously. He usually took his time to get to practice and often arrived late, and once at practice he rarely gave full effort on footwork drills and wind sprints. Simply, Oomz wouldn't ease up because he loved to hit. He felt a thrill in the seconds before contact and a deep satisfaction in the seconds after it. It felt natural.

"Come on, who gon' be nasty?"

Another 10-year-old hopped out of the line and onto the stage.

"There we go! Let's see what you got!"

Oomz jogged to the opposite end, 10 yards from the boy. He stood casually, his head tilted to the side, the football at his waist, a look of indifference on his face, and he watched the boy. The boy bent his knees and leaned forward. Dug his cleats into the rock-hard, weedy, dusty field. Checked the straps on his purple and yellow helmet.

"Set!" shouted a couch.

The boy was a bit smaller than Oomz, and Oomz decided he would not make a cut but run straight at the boy. He took pride in his strength. He was not particularly big, but he was built sturdy, with compact legs and a solid chest. Oomz watched the boy bite down on his mouthpiece, and he believed the boy was scared. He also believed fear didn't belong on a football field.

"Go!"

The boy shuffled forward, reading Oomz's movement, toes chopping the ground. Oomz ran forward, two slow steps then a burst. The boy cocked his arms back and lunged toward Oomz's waist. Oomz crouched at the moment of impact and the boys' helmets went *thwack!*

More *ooohs* from the teammates and fathers.

The boy fell backward, onto his butt, but grabbed two handfuls of Oomz's jersey on the way down. Oomz trudged on for three strides then fell forward, stretching his arms over the imaginary goal line.

"Wooo!" howled one of the coaches.

"He run just like his daddy!" shouted another.

Oomz loved hearing that, and he heard it all the time. His father had played at Mo Better in the '90s. His father was the original "Oomz," but some now called him "Big Oomz." He was one of the fastest kids to ever come through the program, and one of the roughest too. He would run over three defenders and break away for an 80-yard touchdown, then jog to the sidelines struggling to breathe. In his effort to suck in air, he would wheeze: *ooooommz oomz . . . ooooommzz . . . oomz . . .*, which is how he got his nickname. A parent would rush over with his inhaler. He'd take two big puffs then run back onto the field for defense and deliver the biggest hit of the game. Longtime coaches around the regional youth football league still talked about the block Big Oomz laid on some poor 12-year-old during a teammate's interception return. Most of them couldn't tell you who the opponent was or exactly what year it happened, but they could tell you that the hit knocked the buckles off the kid's helmet and left him writhing on the ground. The teammate went 104 yards for a touchdown, but all anyone could talk about was the block. Most vicious block in league history, everyone who saw it agreed.

Those were the days when Mo Better was dominant. The pride of Brownsville. The younger Oomz had heard the stories. All five age groups, from 5 years old to 15, made the playoffs every year, and a few made it to Florida for the Pop Warner Super Bowl. Youth football coaches across the mid-Atlantic respected, feared, and admired this hard-nosed powerhouse from the zip code with the highest concentration of housing projects in America and the highest murder rate in New York City. Mo Better's coaches recruited players almost exclusively from the projects in Brownsville and neighboring East New York back then. Those teams were strong, disciplined, and played with an edge. They simply overpowered opponents.

The Mo Better teams were not as good these days. They still won more than they lost, and some years one age group might showcase the talent common in years past. But the program was smaller. Oomz's father had played football with many of his friends from around the neighborhood. Few of Oomz's friends played, though. With all the new concerns about concussions and brain injuries, their parents wouldn't let them. Once, more than 100 kids came out to play; less than half that number signed up for the 2013 season. Now Mo Better fielded only three age groups: 7-to-9-year-old Mitey Mites, 8-to-11-year-old Junior Pee Wees, and 10-to-13-year-old Junior Midgets.

Oomz's Junior Pee Wee team reminded some coaches of the '90s-era squads. This was an athletic and physical team. Many of its players had been together for three years now, and they'd rarely lost a game. Oomz believed he could restore the glory of his father's days. He wanted to live up to his name and build on it. He wanted to reach the dream his father had failed to reach. "I came to this team to represent my father," he said. "Ever since he was little he played, but he didn't get to finish playing football because he got caught up in something, and he didn't want me to do what he did." Big Oomz had been a hustler. He caught his first drug conviction when Oomz was a baby, and he spent nearly a decade in prison. He served his time, but then was arrested again shortly after his release. He was in jail now, on Rikers Island awaiting trial, and Oomz feared his father would be locked up for many more years. Oomz wanted nothing more than for his dad to see him play and hear the coaches shout, "He run just like his daddy!" He was angry that his dad was in jail, and he ran like his daddy because he was angry like him. His favorite part of football, he said, was "the impact of pads on somebody else."

His face was solemn even as his teammates slapped him on the shoulder pads and his coaches patted him on the helmet.

"That's what I'm talkin''bout!"

"There you go, baby!"

"That's a Mo Better football player right there!"

○○○○○

THE HITTING AND the dust and the rush of early season excitement sent a shiver of nostalgia through the coaches. But Mo Better had, over the past year or so, stepped into a new and worrisome era. These days, Coach Chris wasn't sure how many more seasons his program could survive. He'd begun to see teams around the region fold. It was a national trend: Pop Warner, the largest youth football league in the country, lost around 10 percent of its players from 2010 to 2012, the first stretch of decline in the organization's 84-year history. While Mo Better's turnout was solid in 2012, Chris was troubled that the gradual decline in participation had accelerated in 2013. He kept his concerns to himself—the last thing Mo Better needed was an exodus of players to programs that seemed more stable. But also, he didn't have to say anything. The struggle was obvious to every coach and parent, and nowhere was it clearer than on Gio's Junior Midget team.

Before the season had even started, the number of 12- and 13-year-old boys showing up to practice had dwindled to 14. To meet the Pop Warner requirement of 16 players, Chris had to bump up two 11-year-olds from the Junior Pee Wee group. One of them, Isaiah, had never played tackle football before. So much lighter was Isaiah than the other Junior Midgets on the field that Chris hesitated to give him the ball despite his speed. Instead, he turned to a strategy of brutal simplicity: the team's biggest runners would plow forward behind Gio's bulldozing blocks. Usually, Mo Better's oldest team was its best, a machine crafted to precision over years of work, the group Coach Chris devoted the most attention to while leaving his assistants to manage the younger divisions—Coach Vick called the shots for the Mitey Mites, Coach Esau the Junior Pee Wees. But this year's Junior Midgets were an inexperienced bunch. The cohort had shrunk over the years. Unlike the Junior Pee Wees, the Junior Midgets had few boys—three, to be exact—who had joined the program as Mitey Mites. It wasn't just that the other boys had to catch up on developing their skills. The main value of those Mitey Mite years was tutelage under the jurisdiction of Coach Vick Davis.

Every boy who passed through the Mitey Mites had stories he liked to tell about Coach Vick. Gio had heard some of the stories but hadn't spoken to the coach until a few days before the season's first game. He was slightly intimidated when Vick approached him before practice. At 43, Vick looked 10 years younger, and his pointy beard and raspy delivery gave off a vaguely menacing air that suited his reputation.

"I seen you around the park and on that playground a lot," Vick said once the official introductions were complete.

"Uh huh," Gio replied.

"Everything OK? Any problems you dealing with?"

"Nah, everything's cool," Gio said, his voice low.

"OK. OK. Just checking," Vick said, nodding slowly, a hint of skepticism in his eyes. "You ever need to talk to somebody, you got Coach Vick here for you. Remember that."

That Sunday, Gio's mother drove him to Fort Hamilton High School, the location of the game. It was 40 minutes away, in southwest Brooklyn, further than his mother expected, a frustrating surprise for the morning of her day off from her job as a receptionist. When they arrived, the Mitey Mite game had just finished and the Junior Pee Wees were taking the field. Gio's Junior Midgets would play last. His heart raced. Veteran players had told him that the hits came faster and harder in games than they did at practice.

He joined his teammates, who were watching the games from under the shade of an oak tree behind one of the end zones. He took a seat on the grass as the Mitey Mites made their way toward their parents in the bleachers. A few of the small boys were crying. At the edge of the field, Coach Vick crouched down beside one of those boys and put a hand on his shoulder.

"We gotta take our losses like men," he said, his voice calm but firm. "You gotta toughen up."

The boy nodded, his fingers wiping the tears from his cheek.

"Losing's part of life. Don't like how it feels, you gotta do something about it. You gon' do something about it?"

"Yes, sir," said the boy, no longer crying.

ooooo

VICK DIDN'T SMOKE cigarettes in front of the kids. So, with the Mitey Mite game finished, a tough loss, and the postgame speech done, he walked to the track around the field and pulled out his pack of Newports. He had coached at Mo Better for 17 years, and for 17 years he coached the Mitey Mites. Much of the credit for Mo Better's reputation for discipline fell on Vick. "Military man," one parent called him. Vick ran hard practices and spoke to his 7-, 8-, and 9-year-olds like they were grown men. He ordered push-ups if a boy left his helmet on the ground. Push-ups for a bad report card. Push-ups for talking back and sucking teeth. Push-ups for looking away when he was speaking to the team. Push-ups if a boy stepped out of the single-file line they had to keep as they walked off the field after practice. His boys spoke his name with reverence. "They don't respond to nobody else like they respond to Vick," Coach Esau said. Vick was known to show up to a kid's school without him knowing and sit in the back of the class. "Their eyes get big as fifty-cent pieces when they see him," said Miss Elsie, Vick's assistant coach and mother. And if the kid misbehaved, he'd order him to do 10 or 25 push-ups right there beside his desk. The way Vick saw his role, he was the first father figure in many kids' lives and one of the last guiding voices they heard before adolescence.

He didn't have any interest in coaching older boys. His tactics, he found, wouldn't be as effective. When he screamed at his Mitey Mites, they looked up at him wide-eyed, terrified, eager to please. Older boys shot back a cold, indifferent stare, fully aware that all he could do to them was yell. He couldn't hit them or ground them or take away their PlayStations. As he circled the track at Fort Hamilton, he saw those changes all around. The three age groups played on the same day on the same field in successive games, the youngest first and the oldest last, and to Vick's eyes the effect was like watching a time-lapse of every boy

who'd ever passed through the program. There, in front of the bleachers, were his Mitey Mites giggling, sipping on juice boxes, playing tag.
There, on the field, were the Junior Pee Wees, scowling at the ref after
a bad call, wearing colorful armbands and flashy cleats. There, strapping
on their pads under a tree, were the Junior Midgets, with hard faces and
a certain kind of walk. "That bop in their step," said Vick. "Swagger.
They're more conscious of their hair, sneakers, their appearance. Their
attitude changes. You can't reach 'em the same way."

And it was at that age that he and the other coaches risked losing
them. He'd seen it many times. He'd seen it in his own adolescence as
the kids he grew up with in Brownsville got sucked up into the street
life. He'd seen it with his former players, seen them on the corners after
dark or in a mug shot on the local news. He remembered one night
some years back when he walked through the Seth Low housing projects on the way home and five young men tried to rob him.

"Don't move," one said. Two nine-millimeter handguns were trained
at his head.

A few seconds of silence.

"Awww," one of the young men suddenly whined. "Come on, Coach
Vick, whatchu doin', man?"

Then Vick recognized three of the faces. They'd played for Mo Better. The young man leading the group, nicknamed Pup, had been one of
the program's best players in his day.

"Come on, man, get outta here, Coach!" Pup said. "We was 'bout to
get you."

Vick had been relieved at first. He would get home safe. Then he
was saddened at the thought that his boys had fallen through the cracks.
Whenever he saw his former players on the streets, he treated them with
a chilly respect. He didn't lecture them. He slapped hands with them,
told them it was good to see them, and went on his way. They were out
of his control now. There was nothing more he could do but hope. He
never gave up hope.

Before that time came, before a boy was beyond his command, there
was urgency. He'd seen signs for concern in Gio. Although he had not

coached the boy, he had observed him from afar, intrigued by his talent. He noticed that Gio was funny and confident around other boys—the type of kid who'd have no trouble making new friends. Yet his mature disposition veiled an underlying innocence, an inquisitive interest in the world without a deep understanding of how to navigate it. Maybe naïve was the right word. Maybe "being a kid" was a more accurate description. But naïveté was a trait many kids in Brownsville had shed early on. Vick considered the case of one his current players, a smiley eight-year-old he had nicknamed Puerto Rico.

One day when Puerto Rico was five, sitting in the back seat of the car as his mother was pulling into a parking spot, he saw a man shoot another man in the head in front of a barbershop. By the time he was seven, he knew that lampposts covered with flowers, teddy bears, ribbons, and hand-written notes were memorials for people who'd been killed. By the age of eight, he'd memorized the routine for what to do when he heard gunshots outside his second-floor window: crouch down, hustle to the windowless living room, shut the bedroom door. Sometimes, his cousins from out of town would be over at his house and they would think people were lighting fireworks outside. Puerto Rico would calmly correct them.

Vick feared what this exposure to violence did to a kid—how it stunted childhood, eroded innocence, burrowed deep, and shaped whatever worldview was blooming inside a young mind. And yet, perversely, there was a way in which this hardened mind-set helped protect youngsters from the environment they would face in adolescence, instilling an early onset world-weariness that kept them attuned to the neighborhood's minefields. Vick sensed it in local boys like Oomz and Isaiah. Not Gio, though—which is why he felt uneasy seeing Gio out at the park so often.

Vick stubbed out his cigarette and walked to the concession stand beside the bleachers. Under the tent, a 20-something man, wrist-deep in batter, was frying catfish, shrimp, and chicken. The batches made a loud sizzle.

"Smells good," Vick said.

The man under the tent looked up, grinned, and wiped his hands off on his apron.

"Wassup, Coach Vick!"

"Sup, Pup!"

The men hugged. Pup was careful not to get grease on his former coach.

ooooo

The Junior Midgets lost badly. Gio maintained proper decorum, his face somber as he left the field, but he had reason to feel good. His first official football game had bolstered his love for the sport. There's a certain thrill when the clock is on and the coaches are on the sidelines. The pre-snap chess match in the long seconds between plays—anticipating what will come and how to proceed—gets the mind running, coils the muscles, sharpens the senses before the built-up energy springs forward in the short seconds of hand-to-hand combat, a personal mission within the chaos of 22 bodies chasing and crashing.

Gio hoped to play running back one day, but because he was the biggest kid on the team—and because the team had few sizeable players to begin with—Chris saw no choice but to put him on the offensive line. He embraced the role, which further heightened his standing in Chris's mind, and whatever yardage the offense managed to get was thanks to his bullying blocking. He moved opponents as if they weren't resisting, driving defenders straight back, opening space for his runners to follow. On defense, he threw blockers off of him and engulfed the ballcarrier anytime he was in reach. He was tall and muscular and moved so gracefully that it was easy to miss how unrefined his fundamentals were. His footwork was sloppy, he stood too high on blocks, he grabbed at the ballcarrier's shoulder pads and whipped him down instead of squaring up and wrapping his arms around him. But even with those rookie blemishes, it was clear he was the best player on the field.

Gio's performance gave Chris something positive to think about, but his mood was down. While he had accepted that the Junior Midgets weren't going to be great this year, he didn't expect lopsided games. Chris gathered the boys, who each took a knee and stared at the ground. Parents stood in a row behind them.

"There's a thing in this life called being resilient," Chris said, his tone measured. "Being resilient is a father losing his job and worrying about how he gon' feed his family. He gotta do something. Can he stay home and cry about what happened?"

"No, sir," a handful of boys answered.

"He gotta get off his rear end and find a what? A job. Resilient people are people who don't quit, right? And they keep coming back. They keep coming back. Some of your ancestors was slaves. Whatever hardships they had, you think they said, 'Well I ain't gon' pick no cotton today?'"

"Tell 'em, coach!" shouted a parent.

"They ain't have a choice," Chris said. "What hardships we got? Losing a game?"

"There you go!" shouted the parent.

"Come on, man," Chris said to the boys. "We all right."

"Tell 'em, coach! Tell 'em!"

When the gathering broke, Gio stood up and saw a tall white guy walking toward him.

"Hey Gio, it's great to meet you," he said. "I've heard a lot about you." The man wore a cap bearing Fort Hamilton's logo. He introduced himself as the school's head football coach. "Have you thought at all about what high school you want to go to?"

Eavesdropping behind Gio, Chris beamed. He took great pride in his role as a conduit between promising players and high school football programs. Just as he boasted of his players to high school coaches, he gushed to parents about the top-notch schools he could help get their sons into. While he liked to send his most ambitious players, with the best grades and work ethic, to Poly Prep Country Day School, he recommended many of his talented prospects to Fort Hamilton, where his Mo Better pipeline had helped build a city powerhouse. The way Chris saw it, the pipeline kept going past high school, through college, and into professional life. It was a pipeline out of the neighborhood he loved, sending his boys away from the pain that filled Brownsville's air more often than he wanted to remember.

That night, after Gio and Oomz and Isaiah returned home, the familiar echo of gunshots carried across the neighborhood. Three blocks from Betsy Head Park, a one-year-old boy named Antiq Hennis was shot to death.

– 3 –

DIRECTED TOWARD DECAY
September 2013

"Sad what happened to that little boy," Coach Chris said to Coach Gary Gravenhise two days later. They stood by the Betsy Head field on the red rubber track, which was ragged with divots and cracks.

Gary, who had a shaved head and the body of an offensive lineman, nodded solemnly. The men had grown up together in Brownsville. The Sunday night shooting had been a big story for the local papers and TV news. The boy's father had been pushing him in a stroller through the Marcus Garvey housing projects when a gang rival opened fire. The shooter was going after the father but missed and hit the boy. Police sources quoted in newspapers said that the father refused to identify the shooter. Reporters went to the father's house, but he declined to speak more than a few words. "I've got to keep my family safe," he told the *New York Daily News*. "I got to get them out of this neighborhood."

He asked the reporters to leave, unless they were willing to pay him for an interview. Two photographers snapped photos of the father, and the next morning the *Daily News* and *New York Post* each featured a large picture of the scowling man. The caption beneath the *Daily News* image read: "Anthony Hennis—father of murdered baby Antiq—is angry with the media and begins attacking camera crews." The *Post*'s story began: "He won't lift a finger to help cops nail the low-life who gunned down his baby boy, but the father who was the likely target of the shooting doesn't mind profiting from his son's murder."

Gary and Chris knew the boy. The mother was Chris's wife's cousin and Gary's niece. Gary told Chris that his niece's family blamed the boy's father for the tragedy and demanded that he cooperate with the police. But Gary, as always, was working to calm everybody down.

"There's a lot of tension amongst the families," he said. "Our side is feeling that their side is at fault, you know what I'm saying? And I'm trying to tell 'em, why that man can't feel like he feel? Why he can't be in silence? Why he can't grieve? Why he can't feel whatever it is that he feels?"

"People grieve in different ways," said Chris.

"Exactly."

Chris left the park and headed up Saratoga Avenue. He liked to maintain a regular presence around the neighborhood. He checked in with the locals who kept eyes out for him. Subway workers informed him when one of his players ducked under a turnstile. Shop owners told him when one of his kids got jumped, or when one of them did the jumping. Neighborhood OGs told him who'd been staying out late at night.

On Saratoga, he passed the brick row houses, with driveways and iron fences, that had gone up within the last 20 years, replacing the empty lots that once surrounded the park. Now the lots, weedy and littered with trash, were only to the south of the park. On Strauss Street, he passed neat two-story houses with shingled roofs and barred windows and rocking chairs and potted plants on porches. He passed abandoned houses with overgrown front yards and caved-in doors and crumbling stoops and gutters that sagged like loose teeth.

He passed a church every few blocks, storefront churches: Seventh-day Adventist and AME Zion and Baptist and First Baptist and Missionary Baptist. In front of a liquor store, several men sat on folding chairs drinking bottles from brown paper bags, bobbing their heads to the '80s hip-hop crackling through an old boom box, slapping domino tiles on a plastic table at the edge of the sidewalk. Chris stepped around them. "What kinda example that set?" he said, still in their earshot.

He saw similar scenes across the neighborhood, if not in front of liquor stores, then on picnic benches in parks or in housing project courtyards. He passed through many housing projects on his walks through the neighborhood. There were 18 of them packed into Brownsville's 1.16 square miles, and they came in every form. Marcus Garvey Village: an open expanse of squat cement buildings, with wide pathways in between, the "suburb of the projects," as one local described it. Seth Low and Tilden: brick high-rises that towered over the neighborhood's low skyline. Van Dyke: a sprawling 22-acres of fat brick towers. Brownsville Houses: a dense cluster of more than two dozen six- and seven-story buildings.

Chris recognized a boy walking out of one of those buildings. He wore a gray polo shirt and he jogged over when Chris called out to him.

"How you doin'?" said Chris.

"Good," said the boy, who was 13.

"Whatchu doin', you playin' this year?"

"I wanted to."

"You wanted to," Chris repeated. "Why you didn't come back?"

The boy looked down nervously, shifted his feet. He didn't have an answer.

"Why don't you come by tomorrow night if you still wanna play? All right. OK?"

"All right."

"Good seeing you."

The boy then went and joined two other boys who were swinging on a milk crate hanging from a rope between two trees in the courtyard. He would not come by tomorrow night.

Chris grew up in the Brownsville Houses. The playgrounds of his youth had been all around where he now stood. Those playgrounds had helped shape him into one of Brownsville's legendary athletes. But they were gone now. The courtyard where he played stickball, now covered with scaffolding. The yard where he played touch football, now fenced in. Public School 125 and the blacktop where he played basketball, boarded up for more than three decades.

He turned up a pathway that snaked through the buildings and led back out to the street. Just then, a young man in green shorts sprinted by, looking back every few steps. Five seconds later, two police officers ran past in pursuit. Eight more uniformed officers followed at a jog. Sirens whooped in the distance. Suddenly dozens of youngsters, from first graders to college-age, filled the courtyard, popping out of doors and alleys, hustling toward the commotion.

"Yo, what are you running to?" Chris shouted at one of the packs. "You ain't got no business here! Why y'all run to it? For what?"

He shook his head. They hadn't learned to run away from trouble.

∞∞∞

THE WRITER ALFRED Kazin described his native Brownsville as "a place that measured all success by our skill in getting away from it." The neighborhood was born into poverty. Geography stunted its development: it was landlocked, filled with marshes, vulnerable to flooding, and far from Manhattan. For most of the nineteenth century, the area was sparsely populated, dotted with Dutch farms and small cottages, many of which were built by developer Charles S. Brown, the neighborhood's namesake. Near the end of the century, manufacturers settled in—producing steel, syrup, garments, processed food, staples, paper boxes. They built factories and then tenements to house the workers. Thousands of families poured in from lower Manhattan's slums: working class and poor, Italian and Irish and Russian, but mostly immigrants and mostly Jewish. The construction of two bridges, the Williamsburg in 1903 and the Manhattan in 1909, accelerated the migration into Brooklyn. From 1905 to 1920, Brownsville's population soared from around 38,000 to 101,000.

There was a bit more space in Brownsville, and more jobs. It was a better situation than the Manhattan slums, but that was a low bar to meet. This was incremental progress. Smokestacks dotted the skyline and stretches of open land became garbage dumps. More than 90 percent of residents lived in tenements. Writer Jacob Riis called Brownsville "that nasty little slum." Murder Incorporated, a gang of enforcers who carried out hundreds of hits for the Mafia during the Great Depression, based its headquarters inside a candy shop a block from Betsy Head Park. The neighborhood earned a reputation for violence and struggle. "Every New York Jew could feel certain about one thing," writer William Poster said. "He was superior to anybody living in Brownsville."

Chris Legree's grandfather, Fred Evans, came up with his family from Georgia in the mid-1930s. His parents had been sharecroppers and had heard that New York City offered a better life. They rented a big, cheap house near Betsy Head Park. The neighborhood was more than 85 percent white then. They were the only black family on their block for some years, but after World War II, many more arrived. Those families found that they faced the same oppressive forces in Brownsville as anywhere else in America.

Most restaurants on Pitkin Avenue were for whites only. Landlords often charged black tenants double the average rent, and police officers regularly harassed and beat black residents. In one high-profile incident in 1948, officers approached two black couples packing things into a car for a trip and accused them of stealing the items. The officers argued with the four locals. They knocked one of the men unconscious and shoved his pregnant wife to the ground. Outraged by this incident and a string of similar ones, Brownsville's black residents held a rally to protest police brutality. "Respect cannot be demanded if it is not practiced," a *New York Amsterdam News* editorial declared to the police department.

Though the neighborhood's blocks were mostly segregated, everybody hung out at Betsy Head Park, which looked bright and new in those days after a 1936 renovation financed by the New Deal and organized by New York City parks commissioner Robert Moses. An Olympic-size swimming pool and a brick bathhouse with glass block windows were constructed on the eastern half of the park. On the western side, soft grass stretched from fence to fence, interrupted only by a freshly laid baseball diamond on the far corner. Because there was only one diamond, Evans and his friends had to wait for the white people to finish before they could start a game.

Neither Evans nor his brothers had completed grade school, but they all found solid employment. Evans got a job with the city, in water sanitation. One brother worked at the post office, another in the parks department, and two at the lumberyards. Evans rented a house on Bristol Street, and he took good care of it. Years later, when the landlord decided to sell it, he offered it first to Evans, who accepted. It was a timely opportunity because private property was getting harder to come by in Brownsville.

In the 1940s, Moses chose Brownsville for a grand experiment in public housing. To make room for new highways, new bridges, new apartment buildings, and other "urban renewal" projects, he was knocking down homes across the city, mostly in black and Latino neighborhoods, and he needed places for all those displaced people to go. The city also needed more places to house the growing population of black families migrating north. Options were limited—landlords in most white neighborhoods refused to rent to black tenants, developers refused to sell to black buyers, and much of the city remained segregated. To Moses, Brownsville seemed a promising answer: the neighborhood's population was mostly poor and working-class Jewish people who were relatively progressive on race and had little political power to push back; it was filled with dilapidated, cheaply constructed buildings; and it sat beside Bedford-Stuyvesant, a mostly black neighborhood that was becoming increasingly crowded. "Moses and his staff viewed places like Brownsville as the most likely location for future expansion of the black ghetto," historian Wendell Pritchett wrote in *Brownsville, Brooklyn: Blacks, Jews, and the Changing Face of the Ghetto*.

Moses's interests happened to align with the interests of Brownsville's most powerful residents, a small but vocal group. This subsidized housing plan was a progressive idea. Advocates for the poor had for years called on the government to build housing for low-income families to replace the grimy and cramped tenements that for decades had symbolized the horrors of America's urban poverty. The Brownsville Neighborhood Council, a coalition of community leaders and business owners, led the campaign in 1940, releasing a pamphlet called *Brownsville Must Have Public Housing*. Many in the coalition envisioned these government-funded buildings serving as models for interracial living in a neighborhood filled with both poor white and poor black people. "Neither the white people nor the Negroes dwelling in the housing zone can afford to pay for adequate private housing," the pamphlet stated, declaring that it was "the duty of our democratic society to help provide housing for those in the lowest income brackets." The powerful parks commissioner sold his proposals to these well-meaning advocates.

Moses and other officials selected sites across the city for a wave of new public housing projects, with the biggest share of them in Brownsville. Advocates for the poor, in Brownsville and elsewhere, had envisioned the buildings surrounded by blocks of working-class or middle-income households—singular additions to be absorbed into the community in place. They objected to Moses's plan to build sprawling, multibuilding facilities within a few blocks of one another, creating dense, isolated pockets of poverty. Many of these advocates, including leaders of the Citizens Housing and Planning Council, lobbied for the city to build middle-income public housing in Brownsville to ensure "a wide range of incomes among tenants in the various projects in the area," the *Brooklyn Eagle* reported at the time. These objections would continue over the coming years. In a 1965 *New York Recorder* column, Bill Marley, a Brownsville Community Council board member, said, "Low-income housing is needed, yes, but there is only so much that one community can reasonably absorb."

But in a memo to the New York City Housing Authority, Moses countered that he saw "no other way" to improve conditions in Brownsville. City officials backed him. They argued that the neighborhood was too dilapidated to draw middle-income people and that local residents were too poor to afford middle-income housing. "Great care has been taken in the selection of the sites," Mayor Fiorello La Guardia said in a radio announcement. "All are in undesirable areas where there is not the slightest possibility of rehabilitation through private enterprise."

The city bought and demolished private properties and then began construction. The Brownsville Houses went up first, in 1948, standing as one of the city's few racially integrated projects: around half of its residents were white and half were black. Glenmore opened two years later. Then Howard and Van Dyke I in 1955, Tilden in 1960, Van Dyke II in 1964, Seth Low in 1967, Hughes in 1968, Woodson in 1970, Tapscott in 1972, and Prospect Plaza in 1974. To make room for Marcus Garvey Village, which opened in 1975, the city tore down the house on Bristol Street that had once belonged to Fred Evans. Eight more complexes went up over the next two decades, and by the turn of the twenty-first century, around 20,000 people lived in Brownsville subsidized housing, more than a third of the neighborhood's households.

After the projects started going up and black people, with few places to go, started moving into them, white people fled. The neighborhood's population shrank by 30,000 in the two decades following World War II. The low-income Jewish families that had occupied Brownsville for many years headed off to Canarsie and East Flatbush. Baptist churches replaced old synagogues. Public and private funding dried up for Brownsville's biggest community groups, in part because their support for integration had become too politically contentious; white people were migrating away from brown people, not mixing with them. And as the neighborhood became less white, residents suspected that housing officials began ignoring the maintenance problems piling up in the projects, which were already showing "marked deterioration," according to Rae Glauber's 1963 survey of Brownsville.

The only people who moved to the neighborhood were those unable to land anywhere else. According to historian Pritchett, the way most white people and wealthier black people saw it, "Why would they choose Brownsville, an area that the city had so clearly directed toward decay?" By 1970, following decades of citywide redlining—the practice of giving preference to white rental or mortgage applicants, famously practiced by Donald Trump, among others—the neighborhood was 70 percent black and 25 percent Puerto Rican.

This was Chris Legree's Brownsville. It was a tight-knit community, he would often tell people decades later. But it was also a community convulsed by the changes of the era and convinced that its city's institutions cared little about the neighborhood. In 1967, when Chris was 11, a police officer shot and killed an 11-year-old local boy named Richard Ross. Residents took to the streets in outrage. Some threw bottles at officers and lit police cars on fire with Molotov cocktails. According to the *New York Times'* report that week, one teenager taunted the cops by jeering, "Why don't you shoot me? I don't have a gun. This is not Mississippi. You can shoot me." The riot calmed only after city officials called in Sonny Carson and other local black activists to help clear the streets.

The following year, the city granted the local community board, a majority of whose members now were black, control over the Ocean Hill-Brownsville school district. The community board, frustrated by the poor quality of education, dismissed 19 teachers and administrators from Junior High School 271. All 19 were white, most of them Jewish. Albert Shanker, president of the city's teachers' union, deemed the decision "a kind of vigilante activity." Mayor John Lindsay called it "anarchy and lawlessness." The American Jewish Congress denounced the community board's actions, and the Board of Education ordered the 19 educators to show up to the school anyway. Tensions between the neighborhood's black and Jewish residents had existed for decades, thickening as the area's racial demographics and political power base shifted. Now, the uneasy truce seemed to be shattering. When the dismissed educators returned to the school one May morning, hundreds of Brownsville residents blocked the entrance. Police arrived to prevent possible violence.

At the start of the next school year that fall, teachers across New York City went on strike to protest. The strike lasted three months, until the state stepped in and stripped the community board of its authority over the school district. The 19 dismissed educators got their jobs back, but the dispute had exposed a lasting divide. Shanker captured the mind-set of many white people of the era when he later reflected to the *New York Times* that "the whole alliance of liberals, blacks, and Jews broke apart on this issue. It was a turning point in this way. It was a fact in the late 1960s that the African-American community was moving from the idea of integration toward the idea of black power, toward organizations like Rap Brown or the Black Panthers. Was it civil rights for minorities or civil rights for everybody?"

In June 1970, two Brownsville residents, angry that the city's sanitation department allowed garbage to pile up for days in the neighborhood without pickup, lit a mound of trash on fire. Police arrested the men, and riots started soon after. For two days, some locals lit more trash on fire, shattered windows, and looted stores. A year later, Brownsville residents marched through the neighborhood to protest social service cuts in the state's budget. The rally turned violent when police tried to disperse the crowd. Residents and officers fought. Some people lit buildings and cars on fire and then threw rocks and bottles at the fire fighters. By the end of 1970, around 700 abandoned buildings dotted the neighborhood. After visiting in 1971, Boston mayor John White said that Brownsville "may be the first tangible sign of the collapse of our civilization."

The following decade was rough on New York City, and Brownsville was hit hardest. Factories, which had fueled Brownsville's economy for decades, closed down. Landlords cut their losses and abandoned properties. The most cynical among them lit the buildings on fire for insurance money. Facing bankruptcy, the city cut more services, and housing projects fell into disrepair, becoming dark, towering caverns of heroin addiction and violence. All across the city and country, housing projects had begun to emerge as monuments to failed public policy, a policy that warehoused a high concentration of poor people into cramped blocks outside the view of wealthy and middle-class residents. Brownsville was at the heart of this failure. Around 25,000 people, more than a third of Brownsville's population, fled the neighborhood during the decade. By 1980, a fifth of the neighborhood's men were unemployed and more than 40 percent of families lived in poverty. Brownsville historian Pritchett concluded, "Public housing and urban renewal 'failed' because they were not designed to address the root causes of the slum—economic inequality and racial discrimination." At a time when many of America's neighborhoods were turning increasingly poor and violent, Brownsville was among the poorest and most violent.

And, many would speculate years later, maybe it was this struggle, this nothing-to-lose environment, this breeding ground for grit that explained why so many great athletes came out of Brownsville. Chris Legree knew many of them. He played baseball with Willie Randolph. He played basketball with World B. Free, and his brother hooped with Pearl Washington. He saw Fly Williams hanging around the blacktops with his girlfriend Pam Grier. And then there was the quiet little boy in torn and dirty clothes who sometimes dropped by the Legrees' apartment. He went by "Little Mike" and he kicked it with Chris's cousin Kenny back then.

"Lemme tell you what we used to do with Mike Tyson," Kenny said to Chris one day many years later, as the two men stood in front of the Brownsville Houses. "Me and my brothers, we used to take him on the bus. We used to ride on the back of the buses back then."

"Hitchhike," Chris added.

"A couple blocks up here, they had a store called Woolworths. We'd kick it in the Woolworths, you know, steal and stuff like that. Come on out, get back in the bus. Ride Tyson to Brownsville. Beat him up!"

He paused to chuckle at the irony.

"We was a little older than him," Kenny continued, "but mainly my brothers, they used to beat him up, take his stuff, man. Send him back to Amboy Street."

"He wasn't no star then," said Chris, joining in the laughter.

"Yeah, he wasn't no star," said Kenny. Then his face got serious and he added, "But that's how he got so tough. Then once he went to jail, went upstate, when he came back it was a different ball game."

"He was ripped," said Chris.

When Tyson gained fame as a boxer, Chris still saw the little kid who first started flying pigeons on a roof on Amboy Street. The kid who seemed to have it harder than the rest of them.

"Mike, he was just like us, man," said Kenny. "But, you know, Mike was a little more messed up than what we were. 'Cause we used to have a mother and a father that we could run to. Mike's mom, she was like in the drug game. He had no father. So Mike, he was always running around, here and there, seeing where he could get a plate of food. Used to come to my house sometimes, and sleep, eat, stuff like that."

"When you look at a grown man and his behavior," said Chris, "all that stuff in his childhood come into play."

Chris grew up in a stable household with 10 siblings. His mother worked as a public-school receptionist for some years, before enrolling in college to get a degree and becoming a police officer. She kept all her children on track without Chris's father around. He was an Air Force veteran and spent most of Chris's childhood in prison. Chris didn't hear from him until his senior year of high school. It was Chris's grandfather Fred Evans who handled the discipline. The backbone of the family, Chris called him. He beat them for any disobedience. He never used a belt or a switch or an extension cord; just his hands. "He had big hands, too," Chris said. "His philosophy was: If I don't beat them, someone else gon' beat 'em. Better them get beat here than out on the street." And he retained this role until the day he died. A stroke left him partially paralyzed and he was unable to escape when his house caught on fire.

Chris's childhood was filled with praise and victories. He dominated Little League and racked up Punt, Pass & Kick trophies. During his senior year at South Shore High, he quarterbacked the football team to the city championship game, then a few months later took the mound as the starting pitcher in the baseball title game. South Shore lost both—"Heartbreakers," his younger brother Jeff said. Chris accepted a football scholarship to the University of Pittsburgh, where Tony Dorsett played, but Pitt was stacked at QB and Chris rode the bench for two years. Frustrated, he transferred to Fordham. He played well but didn't make the NFL. So, he came home to Brownsville and joined a semipro team called the Brooklyn Golden Knights. They traveled around the region and played their home games at Betsy Head. Players earned up to $50 a contest, usually less. Chris played for seven years, paying the bills with a Consolidated Edison job his coach helped him land. "Everywhere I walked, everybody wanted to know what was going on," Chris said. "I was the guy who was supposed to make it, to really be a star." He felt like he'd let Brownsville down. He'd been so blessed—with athletic talent, with an active mother, with a team of uncles and brothers loving

NEVER RAN, NEVER WILL — 37

and supporting him, with coaches and teachers invested in him. "I felt like I needed to make amends," he said.

By then, crack cocaine had arrived in Brownsville. More potent and much cheaper than the powdered version, the drug induced a nation-wide epidemic, provoking tough-on-crime policies that played an equal role in tearing families apart. Fathers went to prison. Mothers spent paychecks to feed their addiction. Addicts robbed. Kids fell in with the gangs who controlled the neighborhood, using force to ward off competitors in a highly profitable market—anybody could buy a chunk of coke, turn it to rock, and double their money. Death was all around. "The crack epidemic has precipitated an explosion of violent crime, unlike anything we've ever experienced," Lee Brown, the city's police commissioner in the early '90s, told the *Harvard Business Review* in 1991.

In 1990, Brownsville's 73rd Precinct averaged eight reported robberies, four reported assaults, and three reported stolen cars a day. In 1993, the neighborhood averaged a murder every five days. Even kids from other rough patches of Brooklyn, like Bed-Stuy and Flatbush and East New York, knew not to fuck with Brownsville kids. "Notorious cats in Brownsville," said Parrish Johnson, who grew up in Bed-Stuy. "If you were talking to a girl from Brownsville and you wanted to go visit her, you better bring a crew. Those folks were fierce." And the Brownsville kids knew they were fierce. The attitude, as Brownsville native Erica Mateo put it, was, "I'm from Brownsville and I don't give a fuck where you from."

This mind-set of toughness and pride had inspired a neighborhood motto, though nobody was sure who said it first: "I'm from the 'Ville—never ran, never will." Some residents traced the line to the late '60s. Richard Swinson, a community activist who mentored a young Chris Legree back in the day, recalled uttering the phrase in his teenage years, and in the decades that followed "it picked up steam." By 2013, it was mostly just older adults who still said it, or younger folks using it ironically, or local businesses attaching it to their brands. But "I remember when cats were saying it all the time," said Nelson Urraca, a longtime barber in Flatbush. "They wanted you to know they were from there. We all knew guys from there didn't back down from nothing." In 1993, Riddick Bowe, the heavyweight champion boxer from Brownsville, had carried the refrain into wider culture when he told *New York Magazine*, "I'm not ducking anybody. I'm from the 'Ville—never ran, never will."

In October 1995, Chris and his childhood friend Erv Roberson drove down to DC for the Million Man March. They returned to Brownsville energized. They decided they would create something to help the community, and football was what they knew best. Chris liked Spike Lee's film *Mo' Better Blues*, so they decided to name their program the Mo Better Jaguars. "I just thought it sounded nice," he said. "Jaguar's a smart, fierce animal. And Spike's from Brooklyn so it pays respect to where we come from." All winter and spring they passed out fliers in the neighborhood and spread the word. Two kids showed up to their first practice, and one of them was Erv's son. But soon more came, and by the time fall arrived they had enough kids for two teams: 10-to-13-year-old Junior Midgets and 12-to-15-year-old Midgets. The Midgets won a league championship that first year. Two years later, Mo Better's Midgets won the eastern regional title. Three years after that, the 2001 Midgets won league, then regionals, and then went down to Florida for the national finals and won the Pop Warner Super Bowl.

∞∞∞∞

CHRIS HAD THOUGHT last year's 2012 Midget team would bring Mo Better its first national championship since 2001. The team had seemed unbeatable, rolling to a North Jersey Pop Warner League title, before losing in the regional championship game in Maryland by six points. That was a talented group of 14- and 15-year-olds. Chris's nephew, Sharif, was the star quarterback, and now, just a year later, the sophomore was starting varsity quarterback at Fort Hamilton High. He would make his debut on this September Saturday afternoon, and Chris was excited for the game.

More than a dozen of those 2012 Midgets were making varsity debuts. Though Mo Better had practice scheduled until 1 p.m., any player or coach who wanted to watch a loved one's high school game was excused to leave early. Chris walked across the Betsy Head field, checking to see who was going to which game.

Vick's son was making his debut for Tottenville High School, which was playing Erasmus Hall High School in a rematch of the previous season's city championship game. Chris had considered it one of the best city championship games he had ever seen. Tottenville played well, but Erasmus's junior running back Curtis Samuel was too dominant a force. He rushed for 117 yards. Tottenville took a 14–7 lead in the second half, before an Erasmus touchdown cut the score to 14–13. Rather than kick the extra point, Erasmus handed the ball to Samuel up the middle for the game-winning two-point conversion. College football recruiting rankings listed Samuel as one of the most prized running back prospects in the country. He received scholarship offers from Notre Dame, Florida, USC, Wisconsin, and many others. In August 2013, he chose Ohio State, and within a few years he would be drafted by the Carolina Panthers, convert to wide receiver, and climb his way into the starting lineup. So, the Tottenville game was not only a rematch, but a showcase for the best high school football player in New York City. Samuel, of course, had played for Mo Better.

Vick told Chris he wasn't going to the game. He was a security guard and he had a shift that afternoon. After Chris turned to head back off the field, Vick walked over to the dirt of the baseball diamond a few yards from where his Mitey Mites were practicing. He had deliberated for days on whether to skip work to watch his son, and he was already regretting his decision. He turned his back to the boys, squatted down, pulled his purple bucket hat over his face and cried.

Chris hitched a ride with a Mo Better parent, Antoine, whose oldest son was Fort Hamilton's starting fullback. Antoine's youngest son, a 9-year-old, sat in the back seat and stared out the window of the gold Ford Taurus as the men in the front talked. It was a 20-minute drive from Betsy Head to Brooklyn Tech High School, and as the car swept through central Brooklyn, the men in the front, two Brooklyn lifers, traded lines about how much their borough had changed. They drove north up Thomas Boyland Street, past the row houses built by church groups in the 1980s, past the shops on Pitkin, past Utica Avenue, then turned west on Eastern Parkway and into Crown Heights.

They remembered when Crown Heights, not too long ago, was one of the roughest neighborhoods in the city. Right in the middle of Brooklyn, halfway between Bed-Stuy and Brownsville, East New York and Red Hook, it was a hub for drug trafficking in the '80s and '90s. It was where gangs from all around the borough would meet and trade product and gunfire. They drove past Nostrand Avenue and Bedford Avenue, then turned north on Franklin Avenue, once notorious, a place you didn't go at night because the streetlights were always out and junkies lined the sidewalks and thieves hid between parked cars waiting to ambush the first fool who came their way. The Franklin they drove by now, though, was lined with new storefronts, home to one of the hippest bars in the city, with a Skee-Ball machine and a rotating selection of craft beers. Two blocks up, a shop sold artisanal chocolate, freshly baked bread, and locally made cheeses. A few of the longtime businesses, now getting pushed out by the rising rent prices, had put up signs on their windows that read "Moving to Flatbush."

This was a new Brooklyn, a new New York City, a new "inner-city" America. The violence, chaos, and ruthlessness that had once defined the city now seemed distant, driven away by many factors, economic, social, and political, the same ones that washed over inner-city neighborhoods all over the country. Younger brothers swore off the drug-ravaged paths they saw their older brothers take. More police officers patrolled the streets, aggressively enforcing low-level quality-of-life laws. The job market improved, the population aged, and city leaders initiated a new wave of business and cultural project in hopes of drawing more commerce to downtown areas.

It became a moment of reckoning with old problems left by the earlier era and recognizing new problems created by the transition forward. Newspapers in New York City and elsewhere were filled with stories about men freed from prison decades after being wrongfully convicted during the nation's push to get tough on crime. There were stories about inmates serving life sentences for nonviolent offenses, and stories about lawmakers rolling back policies created during the War on Drugs. And there were stories about young, middle-income white people moving into historically black and Latino neighborhoods. In Brooklyn, the march of gentrification began on its northwestern tip, just over the East River from Manhattan, in Williamsburg and Greenpoint, moving east along the L train into Bushwick and south along the subway lines that ran through central Brooklyn, from Fort Greene and Park Slope to Bed-Stuy, Crown Heights, and Flatbush. The black and Latino residents who had it hardest in that old era now carried suspicions about the changes they saw all around them. Longtime residents worried they wouldn't experience the benefits of their neighborhood's economic revival because the influx of wealthier people would push them out. They feared getting left behind in the wake of this supposed progress. This concern was so great and so widespread that, at the moment Chris and Antoine were driving through Brooklyn, the city seemed on the verge of electing as its new mayor the populist public advocate Bill de Blasio, who was campaigning on the idea that the transition from that old era to this new one had created "a tale of two cities."

This transition only underscored that America lacked the vocabulary to properly categorize the economically impoverished sections of a big city. In the most literal sense, "ghetto" denoted an economically weak neighborhood and the ethnic minorities trapped within its bounds, "inner city" denoted an area's geographic location, and "urban" denoted an area's social environment. But over time those terms had been weighed down by white people who used them to pin blame on black and Latino residents for poor economic and social outcomes. To reflect not a neighborhood's census data but an entire population's behaviors and motivations. To suggest that a neighborhood was poor and violent not because of long-term systematic oppression, but because of its people's apathy and incompetence. But what else to call low-income communities of color in postindustrial big cities like New York, Philadelphia, Chicago, DC, Baltimore, Newark, Saint Louis, Milwaukee, Memphis, Detroit, and Oakland? With no better option available, Chris favored "inner city." Obama, after all, used "inner city," he pointed out.

So-called inner cities were not the only places in America struggling through poverty, violence, and a lack of public services and private investment; some academics dubbed this wide swath, which includes rural and suburban communities, "disinvested neighborhoods." But the inner city was shaped by a particular set of intersecting factors and historical trends, not all of them accidental or well-intentioned. Black people followed the Great Migration north to escape Jim Crow and reach the oasis of industrial jobs and established black communities in big cities. Racist banking and housing policies by both private companies and state and federal policymakers suppressed wealth, shutting down lanes of geographic and economic mobility, creating dense pockets of poverty and blight. White people fled to the suburbs, shrinking the tax base in big cities facing fiscal crisis. Manufacturing jobs disappeared. Big city police departments, encouraged by desperate mayors, made more arrests, disproportionately targeting black and brown people, locking up breadwinners and youngsters. Lead particles in paint and drinking water damaged young brains. Guns became easier to access. Institutional neglect in every public sector, from education to health care to housing, continued on.

Now Chris's neighborhood, and really inner-city neighborhoods everywhere, had entered a new chapter. Brooklyn was no longer defined by poverty and violence. It was a place in the midst of dramatic change. The change began long before the private investment and the white people and the real estate section trend pieces. But now that the private investors and the white people had noticed the change, Chris Legree and his fellow Brooklyn lifers wondered how long they would get to enjoy the changes they'd helped create.

The men in the car followed Franklin north, into Bed-Stuy, Do or Die Bed-Stuy, of *Do the Right Thing* and Biggie Smalls fame. Everybody knew Bed-Stuy was real rough in the '80s and '90s, but it was still pretty rough just four or five years back, the men in the car remembered. One of the men told a story about a friend of a friend, a young Mexican-American 20-something who had grown up in a rough part of Sacramento and moved to New York City for a summer internship on Wall Street in 2010. The young man had signed a lease to an apartment in Bed-Stuy, on Nostrand and Fulton, sight unseen. He broke the lease and left after three nights because of the gunfire he'd heard on one of those nights and because of the young men who stood on the corner by the subway stop, clowning him every evening for wearing a suit. Just three years later, Bed-Stuy was perhaps the hottest rental market for young professionals priced out of the fully gentrified Williamsburg neighborhood on the borough's northwestern waterfront, or arriving from out of town looking for a place in Brooklyn. There were new condos to satisfy this demand, as well as all the expected signposts of New Brooklyn: an organic, fair-trade co-op; a spot that sold flatbread and artisanal grits and had a bowl of dog treats by the register; a coffee shop with a French press and baristas who drew foam art on lattes and a seating area packed with people in checkered shirts and knit beanies staring into MacBooks, rustic-looking backpacks on the floor beside their chairs.

The men drove past all these things then headed west on Lafayette Avenue, into Fort Greene, where the story was the same. Antoine parked and they stepped out of the car. When they looked to the north, they saw the shiny, sleek high-rises of Downtown Brooklyn gleaming in the sun—luxury condominiums and apartments, near the DeKalb Avenue subway stop, in buildings with names like "DKLB BKLN." They turned and walked south, toward the football field. The game had already started by the time they arrived. Chris went straight to the Fort Hamilton sideline. He shook hands with coaches and patted players on their shoulder pads. He found his brother Jeff, Sharif's dad, at the far end of the sideline, and the men slapped hands and hugged. Then their eyes were back on the field. You would've thought Jeff was a Fort Hamilton coach the way he paced along the edge of the field, calling out directions and encouragement. The Legrees were royalty around here. Sharif's older brother Jeff Jr. quarterbacked Fort Hamilton to back-to-back city championships in 2005 and 2006, both teams loaded with Mo Better alums. Their older brother David played at South Shore High School and went on to start at quarterback for Hampton University. David was now a coach at South Shore. Jeff Jr. was Fort Hamilton's offensive coordinator. There were great expectations for Sharif, given his last name.

In his debut, he looked sharp for his age, but he also made the errors sophomore quarterbacks tend to make, and Brooklyn Tech kept the game close deep into the second half, then took the lead. Yet Sharif didn't appear to panic, nor did he ever drop his head. He didn't pump his fist or raise his arms when he threw his first touchdown. He had played in big games before, championship games in the harsh cold of upstate New York and in Maryland against the best players in the Northeast. He had won big games and he had lost big games, and football was just football no matter the design of the uniform or the location of the field.

Sharif seemed unfazed about the prospect of losing his debut. Down 19–18 with fewer than two minutes left, he led the offense downfield and threw a touchdown pass to win the game. "He's gonna be a star!" Chris gushed. Two years later, after transferring to Grand Street Campus High School, Sharif would lead his team to a city championship. Another Mo Better prodigy in a long line of them.

∞∞∞

IT WAS THE same routine at the end of every Mo Better practice. "Everybody circle up," Coach Chris said. He called over the parents and coaches, and the adults gathered behind the circle of players, who had their helmets and shoulder pads in hands. "We got a special way of closing." A speech about the day's theme: perseverance, or responsibility, or accountability, or work ethic, or execution. Some words about keeping grades up. More words about maintaining the legacy of the program. Perhaps an anecdote about an old player he ran into the other day. Usually some rambling small talk peppered in. Then finally a closing prayer. He often spoke for 15 or 20 minutes or more, and it was a running joke among some parents and coaches that the former star quarterback took every opportunity to perform for a crowd. And Chris did love the spotlight. But he also aimed to stretch the final minutes he had with his boys before letting them back into the world outside Betsy Head, to throw as much knowledge at them as he could and hope it was enough to keep them coming back.

On this evening, cool and windy, Chris rattled off the names of star players who had passed through Mo Better: Jaiquawn Jarrett, now a safety with the New York Jets. Kevin Ogletree, now a wide receiver with the Tampa Bay Buccaneers. Jamal Schulters, who now played professionally in Poland. Lance Bennett, now a coach at Poly Prep Country Day School. Brian Flores, now a coach for the New England Patriots. Brandon Reddish and Wayne Morgan, now starting defensive backs at Syracuse University. Then the long list of standout players on some of the best high school football programs in the city.

"Who's next?" Chris said. A few small boys raised their hands. A few older boys, familiar with this call-and-response script, shouted, "I am!"

Many of the boys around him, he knew, would go on to the high schools of their choosing. He had built bridges to several high schools around the city, and the players of the past had stamped credibility onto the players who followed. High school coaches loved getting Mo Better players. "Very well-disciplined kids," said Dino Mangeiro, head coach at Poly Prep. "High-character kids, good students."

Chris and his coaches had rooted the team's philosophy in self-control, and former players often credited that philosophy for their success in life. "Even when you're in high school, the coaches continue to talk to you about being disciplined and doing what you have to do in the classroom," said Jarrett, the Jets safety. "They really developed us into some grown men. They always instilled toughness." There were laps for tardiness, more laps for bad grades. When Coach Vick and another coach were driving some players to a game one morning and the boys got rowdy in the back seat, the coaches pulled the car over on the side of the freeway and ordered the boys out to do push-ups. The kids dressed in suits before games and marched single-file and silent to the locker room. They hit harder than their opponents but seldom lost their cool after the whistle. "The kids that come out of the program, even though they may have all of these hardships and handicaps, they're pretty polished. Not only as football players, but as potentially outstanding young men," said Vince Laino, Fort Hamilton's head coach from 1990 to 2009.

Mo Better teams were known for their physicality, too. They ran the same power running offense every year, and every year they lined up, with no tricks or gimmicks, and pounded the ball through the center of the line. They were strong and fearless, and often the boys on the other team gave up after a quarter's worth of banging helmets. From the late '90s to the mid-2000s, Mo Better's most dominant stretch, many games ended with cartoonish scores of 42, 56, or 63 to 0. When coaches and former players thought back to those years, their memories always took them to Dajuan Mitchell. No player embodied Mo Better's mystique more than Dajuan. He was a big, strong, fast running back, and he was tough as hell. "You can't find kids like that no more," Chris said. When he was 12, Chris said, he had the body of a 15-year-old. He was a terror to linebackers who tried to get in front of him. One former teammate compared his running style to "a Mack truck going 90 on the highway." He led his teams to a string of league and regional titles. He seemed to play his best in big games, on fields long bus rides away, cold and rainy games against upstate white boys who probably didn't think they played much football in Brooklyn.

Dajuan's most memorable game, though, was at Betsy Head, in 2002 against the Mount Vernon Razorbacks, a rival regional powerhouse. Dajuan was a Midget that year and Brownsville locals had been hyping the matchup against Mount Vernon's Midgets all week. This was a battle between the two best teams in the region. The locals had also heard that the son of Sean Combs, then known as P. Diddy, played on Mount Vernon's Midgets, and word on the street was that the hip-hop mogul himself would make it into Brownsville for the game.

The game was early in the season and the morning was warm and clear. On days like this, when the field was dry and the slightest wind kicked up the dust, the fire department often came to hose down the field before the game, to try to spare the kids with asthma from wheezing in the dust. There was no sprinkler system at Betsy Head and the field had not been green since the 1980s. Some locals blamed the city for failing to keep up the park. Others blamed the influx of West Indian immigrants and the young men among them who tore up the field with soccer games every evening. But they all knew that the barren dirt expanse was a big part of Mo Better's great home-field advantage. Youth football programs, used to softer fields in richer neighborhoods with smoother roads, bused into Brownsville and struggled to adjust to the environment. "You'd go all the way down Flatbush Avenue, get lost, then GPS'll drop you off in the middle of the hood, and you'd be like, 'Where am I at?'" said a coach on the East Orange Jaguars.

Boys on the other teams would step onto the hard dirt field and see hundreds of taunting fans standing behind a rope around the edge of the field, because there were no bleachers at Betsy Head. Then the boys would fall on that hard dirt and it almost felt like falling on concrete, and they'd wish they didn't have to fall on it again. But they'd have to get back up and take more hits from the hard-hitting Mo Better boys, and the crowd fed off of the hits, took pride in how rough and tough their boys were, and the taunts would get louder, and young men in tall Ts and baggy jeans would say, "You soft, boy!" when an opponent got up too slow. The community rallied around Mo Better games, and more than one local would tell you that so many folks turned out at the field that "the crime rate would go down." "That's who Brownsville is," Chris's brother Jeff said. "When they respect something, everybody stops for that. They'd line the whole outside of the field. They'd crowd the hand-ball courts. People would get off the train to watch."

The park was packed as usual for the Mount Vernon game, and there was already a buzz humming through the crowd when the black SUV pulled up five or ten minutes before kickoff. It didn't draw much attention. "It's a big game, everybody anticipating," Chris recalled. "Everybody's looking at the field." Chris had expected Combs's arrival. The rapper's security team had called him nearly every day that week with questions and demands, worried that his presence would trigger a hectic, dangerous scene. As the players took the field, the SUV's doors still hadn't opened. It just sat there, engine running. Then, moments before kickoff, out popped P. Diddy. He strolled into the park and onto the field. "And nobody looks!" said Chris, chuckling at the memory. "He came into the crowd. He came by, says 'excuse me' so he could get to the front. They still weren't looking at him!" Their eyes were on the field.

The game lived up to the billing. It was a highly contested, smash-mouth affair. Dajuan was unstoppable that day. It took two, three, four defenders to bring him down on most runs, and by the second half Chris was giving him the ball on almost every play. With Mo Better down late in the fourth quarter, Dajuan pounded through the defense and broke away for the game-winning touchdown. Mo Better won 14–12. P. Diddy caught more eyes on his way out, but the majority of locals were busy celebrating. The big shot they wanted to meet was Dajuan. "Dajuan Mitchell, we thought he was gonna be a star," Chris said. "He was our top dog. A grown man on the field." The next year, he attended Sheepshead Bay High School. He played football for a couple of years, but "we just couldn't get him on track," said Chris.

He was killed a few years later. The locals who didn't hear through word of mouth might have seen the blurb in the September 11, 2006, edition of the *New York Times*:

> Two men were fatally shot about 2 p.m. yesterday in an East New York apartment building in what one witness said "looked like an ambush." One of the victims, Dajuan Mitchell, 19, was found on the sixth-floor landing of a building at 428 Sheffield Avenue, shot twice in the torso and once in the groin, the police and witnesses said.

He wasn't the only former player shot to death in his teenage years. There was Darrell, quarterback on the '98 regional championship team. There was the original Puerto Rico, who owned the nickname that Coach Vick would pass down to the new Puerto Rico. There was Pikachu, the best athlete Vick had ever seen. And there were others, another then another young man gunned down then laid to rest with a boyhood photo of him in his Mo Better uniform beside his casket. "With Mo Better, I've had some of the highest highs I've ever had, but I've also had some of the lowest lows I've ever had," said Erv, the program's cofounder. Football took up only so many hours in the week. And when they left the field, many Mo Better players stepped back into their other world, the one they'd been immersed in almost since birth. "One foot on the turf, one foot in the streets," Vick put it.

Some nights, hard-faced young men waited beside the field for practice to end. A coach would approach them, and they'd tell the coach they weren't looking to cause trouble with the team but just had a dispute to settle with one particular boy. The coach would tell them to take their beef outside the park, and they did. The OGs who controlled the streets respected the program and the respect trickled down to the younger generation. For many boys, Mo Better's purple and yellow offered protection. Players often walked home wearing their jersey and helmet, which served as a pass to get by without hassle. Many of those who ran the neighborhood had worn the colors themselves. Like Pup. Even while he was still on the team, Pup cut such an imposing figure on the streets that stick-up kids avoided targeting his teammates. "Leaving the park at night with their book bags, that's an easy target," Pup said. "But the rough guys were my guys."

One morning, when Pup was 14, the team was preparing for a bus trip to Syracuse for the regional championship game. The players, parents, and coaches met at the Brownsville Recreation Center, on the other side of the neighborhood from Betsy Head. As the bus idled, Pup and two teammates made a last-minute trip to the corner store to grab breakfast sandwiches. They ran into a group of Bloods inside the store. Pup lived in Crips territory, and he was out of bounds. The boys traded punches, and as Pup's crew broke for the bus, one of the Bloods reached out with a knife and slashed the back of his suit jacket nearly in half. Miraculously, Pup made it into the bus unscathed. The next day Mo Better won the regional title.

The stories of the street legends lived on in Mo Better lore right alongside the stories of the gridiron legends. The most infamous OG to pass through Mo Better was the Boogeyman. Vick remembered giving him that nickname when he was seven because he always had snot on his face. The Boogeyman was a skinny but strong linebacker and offensive lineman. Coaches recalled him knocking more than one ballcarrier out of the game with his ferocious hits. He grew up to become "one of the most notorious criminals in Brownsville," in the words of one local. "The sidewalks would clear when he walked past." Or as Vick put it: "He run the neighborhood. I mean he run the neighborhood. He say kill somebody, it'll happen." The Boogeyman was in prison now, though nobody was quite sure what charge they got him on or how long he'd be in. "Maybe murder," said a local. "Maybe armed robbery. Maybe something with drugs. Shit, maybe just gun possession."

Coaches estimated that at least 30 former players were in prison. And just as Chris asked his boys who would be next to get a college scholarship, he wondered who next would find a tragic end. The street life tradition pressed on at Mo Better. All the coaches could do was guide the boys while they had them and hope that their lessons were enough to keep them straight once they moved on from the program.

"You're only passing through us," Chris said to the circle of players around him, his post-practice speech winding down. "It's all about later."

He let the words hang for a few seconds. Some boys looked back at him with serious faces. Others toyed with their mouthpieces or helmet straps or Gatorade bottles.

"OK, everybody touch somebody," he said.

The players linked hands. The parents and coaches in the back put their palms on each other's shoulders.

"Lord God, we come to you to say thank you," Chris began.

"Thank you!" the players shouted back.

"Thank you," said Chris.

"Thank you!"

Heads bowed as he prayed and rose with the "Amen!" The players, parents, and coaches left the park and dispersed across Brownsville's dark streets. Chris walked a block to the Saratoga subway station and climbed the steps.

"Chris!" somebody behind him said.

He stopped, turned to see a familiar face from seasons past: a middle-aged mother in a red pantsuit. They embraced. She told him about how her son still talked about Mo Better and about how much he missed those days. He's still in love with football and watches every Sunday, she said. He had been teaching his nephews the game's nuances, encouraging them to play.

The train arrived.

"Anyway, it was really good to see you!" she said cheerfully, before hustling up the steps.

"Take care!" Chris replied, leaning back against the railing of the stairs.

When she was out of earshot, he exhaled. "That's tough for me," he said.

The woman in the pantsuit was the Boogeyman's mother.

– 4 –

THE FUNDAMENTALS OF LIFE
September–November 2013

Gio's Brownsville had come a long way from the Boogeyman's Brownsville. Its overall crime rate in 2013 was a third of what it had been in 1993, the number of murders down from 74 to 15. There were fewer blighted homes and vacant lots. The crack cocaine problem had diminished. The neighborhood had access to a growing number of well-run public schools. More than anything else, locals said, there seemed to be more hope these days.

For Gio, hope seemed highest on his first day of seventh grade. He strolled eagerly that morning, bouncing on the balls of his feet down the sidewalk, his face looking wide-awake even though he'd barely been able to sleep. A rush of adrenaline had hit the night before. Gio was looking forward to the start of classes, which he knew was unusual because he'd been hearing his teammates mourning the end of summer vacation for weeks. He had always liked school. His favorite subject was math. He enjoyed the challenge of quickly working through a problem, the feeling of his brain churning through the numbers, the satisfaction of rattling off one right answer after the next—cold, clean order in a chaotic world. But that chaotic world interested him too. As he walked to his new school on this balmy morning in early September, he was most excited about his social studies class. "I want to know more about how America became the way it is," he said.

He had inherited his interest in school from his mother, who instilled in him a reverence for education. On the Caribbean islands, she told Gio, they respected teachers more than perhaps any other profession—and certainly more than Americans did. In Brownsville and elsewhere in the States, teachers were paid poorly, dropped into unfamiliar neighborhoods, and often thrust into the role of social worker, tasked with helping kids navigate family troubles, medical problems, and the relentless challenges that weigh down a childhood in poverty. "A lot of us burn out quickly," said a fourth-grade teacher in Brownsville. "You have young teachers coming in, staying a year or two, and by the time they've become good, experienced teachers, they're on their way to another neighborhood where the job is not as hard. And then another batch of rookies comes in to replace them."

There were several very good schools in Brownsville. While administrators sometimes cited standardized test scores to prove a school's excellence, parents more often trusted word of mouth. Test scores could be deceptive, a result of teachers focusing their lessons on exam preparation at the expense of deeper learning. On the other hand, standardized tests—and a kid's ability to do well on them—partly determined which high schools he or she would get into. With so few objective metrics with which to grade a school, a parent's best bet was to go by what they'd heard from other parents and, if they had the time, to meet with the teachers and principals themselves.

For many parents in New York City, school choice was a complicated process. For those in Brownsville, where the pool of tax money and donations funding the local schools was smaller, this process brought especially high stakes: although the neighborhood's stronger schools were as good as any in the city, its weaker schools ranked far below the worst-case-scenario options for kids in wealthier places. The period leading up to enrollment was a stressful time for parents. They could request to send their kids to a better public school outside of their home "zone." Or, if their child did well enough on a certain test, they could send them to one of the city's gifted-and-talented schools, two of which shared a building in Brownsville: Public School 156, where Oomz was a fifth grader, and Intermediate School 392, where Isaiah was in sixth grade. Those schools carried strong reputations for capable teaching, orderly classrooms, and discussion-based lessons. Parents also had the option to apply to send their child to a charter school, which are publicly funded but operate independent of the district. At Brownsville Ascend, a majestic stone fortress on Pitkin Avenue where Puerto Rico was a third grader, students passed the 2013 standardized tests at a higher rate than the city and state average. Some of the best schools in Brooklyn were charter schools, but this fact came with a caveat: unlike traditional public schools, charters had the freedom to deny admission to kids and were usually quicker to expel problem students. So many parents were applying for the limited seats in these new charter schools that an annual lottery drawing determined which lucky few got in.

This whole dynamic created an increasingly stratified neighborhood school system, where the most promising young kids, with the most active parents, got filtered into the area's better schools while the young kids who struggled in their early academic years, or whose parents didn't understand or weren't aware of the local public-school landscape, got shunted into the same old subpar schools. The students most likely to struggle, including kids with mental health problems and learning disabilities, were concentrated in the schools that were already struggling—an education system analogous to the housing plan that pushed all those projects into Brownsville. "It's like we focus on one group of students and then kind of forget about all these other kids, who never really get the same chance to succeed," said the Brownsville teacher.

Gio went to one of those struggling schools, Middle School 588. It was the school closest to his home, just three blocks away, and it shared a building with one of the area's best charter schools, Kings Collegiate.

He had seen the building before, but the sight of the wide, four-story brick-and-stone structure still impressed him. "Everything is so big here," he said. "This whole building is just for three grades!" He arrived early on his first day of school and stood outside for a few minutes as kids around him greeted one another and caught up with friends. The loud, raucous symphony of middle-school joking filled the air. In front of a laundromat across the street, students gathered in tight circles, laughing, flirting, gesturing expressively with their hands. His stomach twisted with nervous energy, Gio entered the building. By his first day, the Thursday after Labor Day, the kids at Kings Collegiate had already been in classes for almost two weeks.

Gio and his classmates, who wore red and yellow polo shirt uniforms, had shorter school days and older textbooks than their counterparts on the other side of the building, who wore white collared shirts with navy pants. The student-to-teacher ratio at Gio's school was more than twice as high as in the charter next door. Only 4 percent of students at MS 588 passed the state math exams in 2013, worse than 85 percent of middle schools in the city. At Kings Collegiate, the 2013 class scored better than 75 percent of middle schools. The shared building embodied both Brownsville's progress and its limitations. New lanes of opportunity had opened, but they were narrow, and access seemed frustratingly arbitrary: names pulled from a basket was sometimes all that separated those who went to Kings Collegiate from those who went to MS 588.

Within days, Gio's excitement and optimism about school evaporated. The teachers seemed nice, and the principal seemed to care deeply and work hard, but Gio was struck by the lack of order in the classrooms and hallways. "A lot of kids there are troublemakers," he said. "They act like animals, messing around and causing distractions." He lost interest in his classes. His grades were poor, teetering on the precipice of failure in nearly every subject. But school had not been a total disappointment for Gio. He made new friends who lived nearby. He went to their houses after school, played video games, talked about girls, hung out with their older friends from around the neighborhood. When they asked him why he kept ditching them for football practice three times a week, he answered, simply, "Chasing my dream."

He'd developed professional football aspirations and was now taking the sport more seriously—a craft as opposed to just a hobby. He arrived at practice early to squeeze in extra drills. He was attentive when his coaches spoke. He discussed high school options with Coach Chris. On the morning of the second game of the season, he was awake by seven, rustling his mother out of bed earlier than he had to because he was worried about traffic—another thing he'd noticed that America had in abundance. When they stepped out of the apartment building, the neighborhood was quiet, relaxed in the Sunday stillness that held in the hours before the church folks paraded down the sidewalk in their fine, colorful dresses and suits. Gio's mother was tired as she silently turned on the ignition, her feet and back sore. She'd woken up with a headache and was in no mood for an extended drive.

Mo Better no longer played its home games at Betsy Head Park. A few years earlier, Pop Warner officials had deemed the field unfit for competition, and so every week the coaches had to scramble for a location, begging high schools throughout Brooklyn to accommodate their boys. Parents usually didn't know the time or place of a weekend game until Thursday. This Sunday morning's game was at Poly Prep, a half-hour drive from Brownsville and a world away. Gio and his mother had never been to Poly Prep before and were not quite sure how to get to the campus, which sat tucked away on the borough's southwestern corner. From the highway, Gio kept his eyes out for the school, unaware that a wall of trees shielded it from view.

They missed the exit. It was the last off-ramp before the highway crossed the Verrazano-Narrows Bridge, with nowhere to go but Staten Island. Gio and his mother bickered. They had been arguing more and more in recent weeks, and now even trivial disagreements were escalating into heated back-and-forths. After his mother paid the $16 toll and turned around to cross back into Brooklyn, she told Gio that they were going home. Her headache was getting worse. He told her to drop him off and give him money for a cab. She said no and they kept arguing all the way back to Brownsville.

∞∞∞∞∞

BEYOND THAT WALL of trees, the boys were trickling onto Poly Prep's campus, their eyes big with awe. As Oomz, Hart, and the rest of the Junior Pee Wees slipped on their shoulder pads and pulled up their football pants, they looked around at their home field for the day. Some boys reached down and picked at the rubber pebbles embedded in the artificial grass, scooping up a pinch, then sprinkling the stuff back down. The field was pristine, like most everything at Poly Prep. Next to the football field, on the other side of a black chain-link fence, stretched a grassy area alive with teens playing lacrosse and soccer in front of the school's main building, a colonial-style red-brick manor topped with a domed white clock tower. Beyond one end zone, a pond rippled with ducks. Past the other loomed the Verrazano-Narrows Bridge, gleaming in the late summer sun. Rows of houses with garages and neat lawns surrounded Poly Prep's Bay Ridge campus. Banners strung up on a fence by the bleachers boasted that three Mo Better age groups—Junior Peewee, Junior Midget, and Midget—won Pop Warner league championships in 2011, and that the Midgets won another in 2012.

"Yo, that field looks really nice," said one boy.

"It's a beautiful field," said Hart. "It's a shame we're gonna tear it up."

Oomz nodded, grinning. He appreciated Hart's confidence, which usually matched his own. The Junior Pee Wees had won their first game handily the week before, confirming Oomz's belief that the team was good enough to win every game this season, just as in years past. He looked over at the bleachers, where several fathers were standing, clapping and calling out to the Junior Pee Wees. He often thought about his own father in these moments. While there were just as many mothers and siblings in the stands, the fathers were loudest and most relentless with their shouts, and Oomz imagined his father standing among the men, complimenting their sons, complaining about the refs, critiquing the coaches. He sometimes felt cheated by the circumstances that led to his father's absence. Every game he played was one more his father would never see.

ooooo

BIG OOMZ HAD made his way into the drug game in his early teens. He got arrested for the first time when he was 15 and a grand jury indicted him on felony gun possession charges. He skipped out on court and evaded arrest over the next few years. In 2005, when he was 20, he and an associate drove down to Wilmington, North Carolina, to do business. While they were there, cops busted into their Sleep Inn motel room and found more than 900 packets of heroin worth $20,000 on the street, police told local reporters. He was convicted of felony drug trafficking and would spend eight years in prison. Oomz was 2 at the time.

Every month from then on, Big Oomz's mother, Monique, and her husband would drive down to North Carolina with Oomz and his older brother. The trip took 12 hours. They left on Friday, got two hours of visitation time on Saturday then two more hours on Sunday, before heading back up Interstate 95. Often, they returned early Monday morning, just a few hours before the kids had to be in school. Some of Oomz's earliest memories were of seeing his father on the other side of a thick glass partition. Oomz looked forward to the trips—the pit stops at quaint middle-of-nowhere diners, the thrilling indulgence of a freshly made hotel bed, the joy in his father's eyes when he stepped into the visiting room. Despite the circumstances, Oomz was close with his father. They spoke on the phone two or three times a week. His father was always lecturing him on the importance of education and being careful about who you spend time with.

Even without his father physically present, Oomz grew up surrounded by support. Both sets of grandparents lived in Brooklyn, as well as several aunts and uncles—plenty of loved ones around to babysit or pick him up from school or drive him to a football game. It was this familial infrastructure, his grandmother Monique believed, that ensured Oomz spent most of his free time inside, at somebody's home, rather than out and about in the neighborhood, where a boy is more vulnerable to the social pressures that sweep up so many others.

Oomz was well aware of these pressures. From an early age, he'd been exposed to the perils of the street. His father told vague, cautionary tales about his own experiences. His mother, Tasha, worked at a juvenile detention center and, with an endless supply of examples at her disposal, constantly reminded Oomz that even good kids face terrible consequences if they stray too far down the wrong path. Attuned to this world outside his doorstep, Oomz was aware that his neighbor, Poppa, was involved in the street life, though he didn't know the details. Poppa often spent the night at Monique's house down the block from the park, but while Oomz liked and looked up to the teenager, he knew better than to follow his trail. Oomz was never one to follow. He didn't like crowds and he crossed the street whenever he saw a group of people on the sidewalk. Once, when he got disciplined for disrupting class, Monique asked the teacher, "Was he just following other kids?" The teacher replied, "No, they were following him!" It was not the first or the last time Monique got such a call from PS 156.

Oomz had been getting in trouble at school more often in recent weeks. Though he went to a good school, Tasha worried that he'd "gotten too comfortable." He had many neighborhood friends there. He was one of the most popular kids in his grade. Now, early into his fifth-grade year, with Bs and Cs on his progress report, it was clear to his mother and grandmother that he wasn't taking school seriously. His coaches, too, noticed that Oomz seemed distracted. They couldn't blame him. The past year of his life had been an emotional drain.

Big Oomz was released from prison in 2012. His mother paid for his plane ticket to New York, and on his first day back in Brooklyn, all his family and friends were gathered at her home to welcome him. They feasted. Oomz smiled brightly all day, excited and euphoric about the new life he and his father would have together. Then, without warning, a few months later in February 2013, New York City police arrested Big Oomz. He still had a warrant out from the gun charge he picked up at 15. Oomz had hoped his father would be back out within a few weeks. But a few weeks turned into a few months, and now a full year was approaching. A conviction meant up to 15 years in state prison— maybe Green Haven Correctional Facility two hours away, or maybe Riverview Correctional Facility seven hours away, or maybe one of the other prisons in between. Oomz's mother and grandmother told him to keep his spirits up and that things would work out. He wanted to believe them, but he also understood that the situation—the laws, court dates, bail money, prosecutors—was too complicated for him to know what to believe. His confusion and anxiety fueled a simmering anger.

The Mo Better fathers in the Poly Prep bleachers saw the fruits of this frustration as they watched Oomz race down the field on the opening kickoff and bulldoze the poor blocker who tried to stop him.

"That boy Oomz play with some fire, huh," said one father.

"Like he wanna knock somebody's head off," said another.

ooooo

Oomz was a favorite among many of his teammates' fathers. Those men saw in Oomz a reflection of their own childhoods. Some of them, like Mr. Hart, had grown up in Brooklyn's roughest areas before escaping, somehow, to middle-class adulthood. These men often thought back on all the ways their lives might have gone off track—if a teacher didn't take interest, if a police officer didn't go easy, if a boss didn't make the hire, if a bullet didn't miss. The men considered what had gone differently for them, what had separated them from their unlucky peers, when they saw smart and ambitious boys like Oomz who seemed capable of going very far in life despite the headwinds.

It was different for boys like Hart, who were a generation removed from that struggle. While the fathers saw themselves in Oomz, they saw in Hart an example for their sons to follow. Hart didn't talk like most 10-year-olds. He carried himself like a much older boy, sometimes like a grown man. He enjoyed sharing his thoughts about events in the news and liked to ask questions that began with "What did you think about . . . ?" He extended a handshake when he greeted people. When asked a question, he paused to organize his thoughts before answering. He sometimes wore a bow tie and dress shirt to school—a public elementary school that didn't require a uniform. When his teammates clowned him with the type of jokes 10- and 11-year-old boys normally make, he pursed his lips and rolled his eyes. Before practices, Coach Chris quizzed the boys with math problems or trivia questions or asked them to give the definition of a big word, and damn near every time it was Hart who raised his hand first. One practice, after Hart meticulously explained why he had gotten a lower-than-usual grade in a class, Coach Chris chuckled, shook his head, and said admiringly, under his breath, "fuckin' attorney."

And indeed, Hart did think about becoming a lawyer when he grew up, but it was his plan B, if the NFL didn't work out. "If I do go to the NFL, I'ma get myself a nice house, pay it off so it's mine," he said. "I hope I do make the NFL. I'm worried if I don't. Then what am I gonna do?" He said this not with desperation but curiosity. He spoke about his future with the urgency of a high school senior waiting to hear back from colleges. And it troubled him that he was not yet sure about what exactly he wanted to do as an adult. "I gotta go get a master's," he said. "I'm definitely gonna get a bachelor's. But I still don't know what I'ma do. I got three years to high school, then four years of high school. Then four years of college. That's just 11 years!"

He was a polite and pleasant boy, but you wouldn't know it from the way he played football. He played as rough as Oomz. He wasn't fast or agile, but he was strong, knew how to use his size, and had remarkable instincts on the field. His goal on every snap was to hit somebody as hard as he could. This was easy enough from his spot in the center of the offensive line. He snapped the ball and had a boy right in front him to smash helmets with and drive into the ground. From the center of the defensive line, he was, in the words of one coach, "a wrecking ball." He blasted into the backfield and tackled runners barely a second after the quarterback handed them the ball. He studied the tendencies of his opponents and tried to predict when the center would snap the ball and which way the play would go, guessing correctly so often that teammates jokingly asked him to tell them the results of future sporting events. But on some plays, the running back received the ball closer to the sideline and ran to the outside, away from Hart. On those plays, Hart would seek out some poor offensive player trailing the play, like the gazelle at the back of the pack, and knock the boy over with a thudding shoulder bump. By the middle of the third quarter at Poly Prep, Hart was a big reason why Mo Better had kept the Montclair Bulldogs scoreless.

"Yeah Andrewwww!" his father boomed from the stands, after another tackle. "Way to go Andrewwww!"

But Mo Better had not scored either. Other than a few decent gains by Oomz, the offense had barely moved the ball. This was a disappointing development to the fathers and mothers in the stands. This Junior Pee Wee team was supposed to be a championship contender, and here they were struggling against the kind of program they used to steamroll. There was no doubt the team was talented. Quarterback Naz could zip the ball 40 yards downfield. Wide receiver Chaka could run past any defensive back who tried to cover him. Lineman Lamont had so much natural strength and athleticism that Coach Chris often reminded him that, if he paired his talent with a willingness to put in the work, colleges would be fighting over him one day. Linebacker Dorian was a sure tackler and, like Hart, smart enough to call out the other team's plays before the snap. Running back Time Out was quick and savvy and kept the team loose with his one-liners. And then there were Oomz and Hart—"The heart of this program," Coach Gary said. With the third quarter nearing an end, Montclair scored the game's first touchdown, putting them ahead 6–0.

ooooo

THE GAME WAS ticking away. Seven minutes left. Montclair had the ball and the offense took its time. The players lingered in the huddle and strolled to the line of scrimmage. Two-yard run up the middle. Three-yard run to the left. Six-yard run to the left. First down. Three more runs and another first down. Five minutes left.

"Andrewwww!" shouted Mr. Hart. "Get me that ball, son! We need that ball!"

Two more runs up the middle, and now a third down. Four minutes. The offense lined up and the center snapped the ball, but when the quarterback pivoted to deliver the handoff to the running back, the ball slipped from his hands and bounced on the turf. Everyone dove for the ball, and several bodies were piled up when the referees blew their whistles and approached. They pulled boys from the pile, and out of the mass popped Hart, holding the ball high over his head like a torch.

"Yeah Andrew!" said Mr. Hart. "Yeah Andrew! Andrew got it! Andrew got it!"

"Your boy got it?" said another father.

"Damn right he did! Yeah Andrew!"

"He's getting all the tackles too," said a third father.

"A ball hawk," said a fourth.

"Let's go Andrew!"

Mr. Hart was the loudest person in the stands every game. He was built low and sturdy, with thick arms and calves and a chest like an oil drum. He looked like a jail guard, which he was, and you could easily imagine his voice echoing through the long cement-and-steel halls at Rikers Island. One father joked that, when given the choice, Mo Better's coaches always picked the sideline opposite the bleachers because "they don't want Hart's mouth over here." Mr. Hart bellowed a constant stream of enthusiastic support, every game and every practice since the first day his son joined the program three years earlier. Yet his son sometimes questioned the depth of his enthusiasm, especially in the hours before a practice, whenever Hart was loaded with homework or had an essay or school project due. You better finish your work or you ain't going to football, Hart's father would tell him. Hart would put up a fight, but Mr. Hart would stand firm, and eventually Hart would give in and bust ass. He'd heard the "academics first" message from his dad long enough that he considered it fact. While he usually got his stuff done in time, every now and then, his dad would have to make the phone call Hart dreaded: "Wassup, Coach. This Mr. Hart. Andrew's not gonna be able to make it to practice today. Yeah, sorry 'bout that, just got too much work to do tonight."

But Mr. Hart understood the long-term value of football, too. It could be a ticket to a private high school. One Mo Better parent described the difference between private and public high schools in New York City as "lobster or crawfish." For middle-class folks like the Harts, the $38,000 yearly tuition at Poly Prep was imposing. Getting recruited onto the high school's football team meant a very good chance at a financial aid package large enough to cover the full cost. From there, a college scholarship opened the next path. And in the numbers game of college scholarships, football is king: a Division I college has 85 scholarships to allocate to football players, compared to 13 for basketball and 12 for baseball—much less for any nonathletic enterprise. Football talent could compensate for a family's money problems, though this particular avenue was open to sons and almost never to daughters—the latter path cleared only in April 2017 when Becca Longo became the first woman to get a college football scholarship, signing with Division II Adams State University.

While football scholarships could make the coming years easier, Mr. and Mrs. Hart were adamant that they would do what they had to do to get their children into good schools regardless. Generations of kin had worked hard and sacrificed much for Andrew Hart to have the opportunities he was born into. His grandparents had grown up poor, in the South on his mother's side and in Brooklyn on his father's. His parents had grown up less poor, working class, in rough areas of Brooklyn, and they had climbed into the middle class. They both worked steady jobs and built careers, and then in 2006 bought a modest three-bedroom house in South Ozone Park, Queens. Now their two children, Hart and his little sister Brianna, were growing up in a quiet, safe neighborhood with a good public grade school a few minutes away by car. Hart's teammates loved coming over to his house. They played basketball on a hoop set up in the small cement yard out back. They played video games in Hart's second-floor bedroom, which had a Spiderman poster on the wall, an Avengers blanket on the bed, and more than a dozen trophies on a shelf. They watched football or basketball on the big screen TV in the basement. They ate large portions of Mrs. Hart's food. "They cook up a storm," said Oomz. "They house mad big too. And as soon as you walk in the door you gotta do 25 push-ups. That's the rule."

For Hart, many afternoons were a mad scramble to grab a bite, finish homework, and get to practice. The drive from the house to the park took around 30 minutes, but it was closer to an hour if traffic was bad. Around a third of Hart's teammates lived outside Brownsville. Three times a week their fathers and mothers flocked in from middle-class enclaves like Bensonhurst, Kew Gardens, Westchester County, and Staten Island, rolling through tolls and traffic to get their sons to a dilapidated field in one of Brooklyn's roughest areas by 5:45 p.m. Some of these parents brought sandwiches for the other boys or donated their sons' old cleats. Some families helped pay the cost for families who could not afford the $350 annual fee, which covered equipment maintenance and Pop Warner registration.

These fathers and mothers, who had themselves grown up in rough Brooklyn neighborhoods, believed their childhood environment had given them the psychological tools they used to rise to the middle class. They worked harder than their peers because of their hunger to escape the environment. They managed their money well because the poverty they had seen as children taught them to appreciate the value of a dollar. One father, who worked in the corporate world, observed that the sharks in white-collar shirts were no less criminal and no more fierce than the sharks in tall white tees who operated drug rings in Brooklyn. To survive their neighborhoods, these parents had learned how to negotiate with sharks.

Now the parents worried a middle-class upbringing would spoil their sons. Mr. Hart knew his kids had everything they wanted. He had installed a merit-based system in his household. He would only get them things if they behaved and got good grades. And they always did, so they were always getting things, and he wondered if they had too much. His son had a PlayStation and an Xbox—"most kids don't even have one!" His son had "more sneakers than I do!" But in Brownsville, his son could see and experience another way of life. Line up next to kids in beat-up hand-me-down cleats who didn't take a single blessing for granted, hungry kids who didn't think twice about falling face-first into the hard dirt because they'd been playing tackle football without pads on this field since they were old enough to run. Kids like Oomz.

"Football-wise, it's harder here. It's tough," said Dorian's dad, Dwight, a Port Authority police officer who made the hour-long trek to Betsy Head Park from Bergenfield, New Jersey. "You play on this field, you can play anywhere. Here they get the fundamentals of life."

Seven miles west of that hard dirt field, a breeze swept across Poly Prep's artificial grass, fluttering the championship banners on the fence. Two minutes to go in the Junior Pee Wee game. Mo Better had the ball near midfield. Many of the fathers had left their seats in the bleachers to stand along the front railing. They watched the offense run the ball on first down for no gain. On second down, quarterback Naz dropped back to pass and the ball landed incomplete, far over receiver Chaka's head. Another incomplete pass on third down, not even close to the target.

"Why we passing?" a father shouted at Coach Mohammad Esau, Chris's deputy in charge of the Junior Pee Wees. "C'mon, Esau!"

It wasn't Mo Better's style to pass the ball. Not only that, passing the ball rarely worked at this level of football. Passing plays were sophisticated choreographies of joint parts, and every part needed to go right for a play to work. It took accurate throws from the quarterback, crisp routes from the receivers, sound footwork from the lineman, all skills that most kids this age had yet to develop. On top of all of that, it took precise timing that required more hours of practice than most youth football teams could spare. But Coach Esau had hoped to innovate his offense. He was young but a brilliant football strategist. He studied the game and had many ideas. Wide-open offenses that spread the field with deep passes and option runs. Aggressive defenses that blitzed from multiple angles. A standout player at Mo Better in his younger days, he'd joined the coaching staff and impressed Chris so much and so quickly that Chris decided to have him run Mo Better's most talented team. This was his first year as head coach and, because of his inexperience, parents were skeptical of the promotion. But Esau wasn't short on confidence. While Vick had three assistant coaches helping him with the Mitey Mites and Chris had two with him for the Junior Midgets, Esau's staff consisted of only his right-hand man, Coach Andrell, a former Mo Better player who was even younger than Esau; Andrell played wide receiver at a junior college, and wasn't always able to make it to Junior Pee Wee practice.

On fourth down, Mo Better had no choice but to pass. The defense was ready and the ball fell incomplete, ending the hopes of a comeback. The loss confirmed the parents' skepticism and shattered any presumptions that the Junior Pee Wees would dominate the season.

As the boys made their way to join their parents in the bleachers, the Junior Midgets took the field. Their faces glum, Oomz and Hart stood along the front railing, chewing on sunflower seeds, shouting encouragements to their Mo Better brothers lining up for the kickoff. Noticing that the eldest team was missing its best player, Oomz shot Hart a look of bewilderment, and said, "Where's Gio?"

ooooo

AGAIN, THE JUNIOR Midgets lost badly. Only six of their players showed up to the next practice that Tuesday. The turnout disappointed Gio, and he ran through the warm-ups and drills in a sour mood. A current of frustration was running through Betsy Head that evening.

"Why even show up if nobody else is?" said one Junior Midget father, who sat on the long green bench alongside other parents. "We can't practice with six guys!"

All three teams had lost on Sunday, and none of the parents at the park seemed happy with the direction of the Mo Better program.

"They got their butts kicked," said one father.

"For one thing, the other guys had more players, but we've got to improve our play," said another.

"The thing is, they scared."

"Boys gettin' soft."

"If that's the case, shouldn't be out there."

"Shouldn't be out there. Yup. Because that's a rough game, and if you don't look to hurt somebody—"

"They gon' hurt you."

"They gon' hurt you. That's right. That's the bottom line."

"You cannot let a boy be soft. Cannot. Can't let it happen."

A loud noise from the street interrupted them. It was mumbled and static-y, as if from an AM radio station just out of range. Heads turned, and they saw a black van with a speaker on the roof, slowly rolling down Saratoga.

Somethingsomethingsomething Vote for someone! Somethingsomething-something Vote for someone!

"It would help if we could understand it," said one of the mothers.

It was Election Day, and the Democratic Primary for mayor was said to be a close race.

"Have you heard anything about the results?" said a father.

"We'll know tomorrow morning," said another.

"What's his name's gonna take it. De Blasio, he's got it locked up."

"They keep saying de Blasio's winning, so it's almost like a sure shot—he's gonna be the Democrat running."

The parents had a mild and guarded interest in Bill de Blasio. He had given speeches about improving the lives of working-class and poor people. Ending stop-and-frisk policing, more money for public schools, slowing down the development pushing up prices across the city. But those speeches and promises felt far removed from this park, this neighborhood. While this de Blasio seemed to make better promises than the other candidates, and far better promises than Michael Bloomberg, the current billionaire mayor, they were still just promises from a rich man running for political office. The parents had sensed, more and more with each year, that their city was racing down a track that could no longer be changed. They looked back and saw a past of violence and struggle, but they looked forward and saw a future that had no room for them, and neither the starting point nor the end was particularly appealing. Brownsville locals took pride in the community they had built over the years, a community of unity and strength forged even despite the oppressive forces working against them. They had little faith that this candidate, or any other, was capable of preserving the character and virtues of their neighborhood when the borough's economic development—the restaurants, condos, boutiques—lured in a new, wealthier population.

"No, I'm not excited," said one mother. "I had enough of that."

"This year," said another, "I'm just a little jaded with the candidates. All of them."

"Just a bunch of thieves and liars," said a third.

"It's always blah blah blah blah blah, what we will do, what we will do," said a fourth.

"They pull the levers and control certain things," said a father. "But in my house, there's certain things that I control, you understand?"

Several heads nodded, and the parents shifted their eyes back to football practice. Chalky brown clouds floated above the park. The Junior Midgets jogged off the field and formed a line at the base of the red cement steps. Coach Chris blew his whistle. They sprinted up, then jogged down. Many took off their cleats for better traction. A few slowed down after five or six rounds to rub the soles of their feet. Others tiptoed to avoid stones and twigs. The only two boys who ran hard without pause were Gio and Isaiah.

"I don't care about no barefoot!" Chris boomed. "Our forefathers had to get up every morning to pick cotton! Your forefathers ain't have no shoes. Nobody feels sorry for us! Nobody feels sorry for us! They didn't have no Nike! Go back up! Not this crying and something's hurt! Let's go! Let's see who quits first!"

ooooo

Boys began quitting halfway through the season. Some of those who didn't quit simply stopped showing up to most practices. By mid-October, there were rarely more than six or seven Junior Midgets at practice, and only 13 or 14 were making it to games. It was embarrassing. In years past, the oldest team had been the program's flagship, the culmination of years of playing together and improving under Mo Better's vaunted system. This year, the oldest team was ending the season with a string of forfeits. Rather than waste the day, the coaches on both sides would agree to unofficial scrimmages. Gio was more dominant each week.

He didn't miss any more games, but he now occasionally skipped out on practice to hang with friends. With few teammates attending and the season in free fall, practice no longer felt urgent. Gio welcomed this new freedom. He'd begun to feel more comfortable around the neighborhood. He had a group of friends who'd taken him in, older boys looking out for him, girls he was crushing on, places to go when he wanted to get out of his apartment, which was quite often. His building, known locally as the Castle, had a notorious reputation. "That's a rough place, man, even for Brownsville," said Coach Vick. "Roughest of the rough come outta there. That's where the Boogeyman lived." Built in 1926, the apartment complex was now mostly used as temporary housing. The city paid the building's manager, a nonprofit called the Acacia Network, to take in people who had nowhere to live; the city's shelter system had been filled for years. In 2014, three city agencies tallied 48 total code violations in the Castle. "It's a hellhole," Chris said. "They live a little different over there. It's not a place you wanna be." Many rooms in the building housed homeless families, people with felony records who couldn't qualify for public housing, and people fresh from prison looking to get back on their feet. Gio stayed away whenever he could.

One night after an October practice, Coach Chris ran into Gio's mother at a takeout spot down the street from the park. A line of teens and Mo Better boys stretched from the counter, which was behind bulletproof glass, to the open doorway. A small boy at the front of the line playfully spun the revolving food slot, through which servers passed boxes of fried chicken wings, greasy pizza slices soaking through paper plates, and piping hot meat-and-cheese patties wrapped in napkins.

"What happened to Gio today?" Chris asked Gio's mother, a kind-eyed woman wearing a paisley blouse, black slacks, and kitten heels. "He wasn't at practice."

"He wasn't at practice?" she said, confusion on her face. "He told me he was going to practice. I don't know where he went to!"

She shook her head gravely and told Chris that this wasn't the first time Gio had misled her. He wasn't home as much, and when she asked where he was going or where he had been, he offered only vague replies, with a typically teenage don't-worry-about-it tone. She didn't know who he was spending his time with, but she noticed that her son's demeanor had turned a bit hard, a bit distant. Perhaps it was a natural development as a boy approached his teenage years and yearned for independence. He disobeyed her orders to finish his homework before football practice. Instead, he'd go straight to the park or meet up with friends after school. Some nights, he had to stay up past midnight to get his homework done. She was worried about him, she told Chris. Her son's transition into the neighborhood was even harder than she had expected, she added.

"I've been trying to talk to him," she said to Chris. "I need your help."

"We'll talk to him," Chris said.

"I just don't know what to do anymore. I don't know. I need to do something."

"He's a good kid."

She nodded. They stood there silently for a moment, both knowing full well that sometimes being a good kid wasn't enough.

ooooo

It was a bad season across the board. The Mitey Mites lost nearly every game, and alums wondered if Coach Vick had lost his touch, maybe even his drive. The Junior Pee Wees stood as the last hope to save the year. By mid-October they held onto an outside shot at making the playoffs if they finished strong. They did not. Against Newark's Brick City Lions, their biggest rival in the North Jersey Pop Warner League, they played tough and kept the game close through the first half, then fell apart in the second half and lost 35–0. They were out of the playoff race. It was the first time anybody could remember a season without at least one Mo Better team in the playoffs.

Rumors began to spread that the program would disband at the end of the season. Parents complained that the coaches were disorganized, unsure of practice schedules and game locations, and that Mo Better's time had passed. There were not enough kids coming out. There was not enough money to keep paying for fields and bus trips. And there was not enough success to justify further effort. Coaches from other programs contacted parents, trying to poach players for next season, circling the dying carcass.

Coach Chris assured everybody that Mo Better would be fine, but privately he considered the possibility of merging with another program. He began discussions with the coach of a well-respected team in Staten Island. He hadn't yet figured out where practices would be held, where games would be played, or how coaching responsibilities would be divvied up—it was too soon for all that. But Mo Better had drawn barely enough kids to fill three teams, and if participation continued to dip, Chris needed a fallback plan. Numbers were down at many, if not most, youth football programs, and Chris allowed for the possibility that the landscape had permanently shifted. He'd spoken with coaches at other programs who admitted that they too were nearing the point where their only options were to fold or merge. Yet none of those other programs had Mo Better's history. This had been a down year, but Chris believed the program's reputation had bought him the right to an occasional down year and, surely, widespread trust that he would turn things around. He had to turn things around. He couldn't afford two bad years in a row. It was a thought he pushed out of his mind. "We won't let that happen," he said.

It was not yet winter, and already Chris was eager for the next season to come. He was giddy at the year-end banquet in the Brownsville Recreation Center auditorium, where kids and parents feasted on a barbecue buffet and coaches gave out awards to standout players. He declared to kids, parents, and coaches that better times were coming. He had reason to be optimistic. In the unofficial scrimmages in the latter half of the year, 11-year-old Isaiah had emerged as one of the Junior Midgets' best players—even though he was often the smallest and youngest boy on the field. Chris had a grand plan for next season. Since Mo Better couldn't fill every age group, he'd channel his top talent onto a 9-to-12-year-old Pee Wee team, allowing Isaiah to join forces with Hart, Oomz, and the other Junior Pee Wees. "That team got a chance to go far, maybe even make it to Florida," Chris said in November, four months before the first practice and 10 months before the first game. "Next year's gon' be a big year for us."

Indeed, that next year got off to an eventful start. A few weeks into January 2014, Chris got word of some news from Oomz's family. Big Oomz was out of jail and Oomz was quitting the team.

– 5 –

CROSSROADS
January 2014

THERE WAS NEVER ANY QUESTION OOMZ WOULD PLAY football, never any question he'd play for Mo Better, and, once he was on the field, never any question he'd play running back. In his earliest memories, he was waddling around on his grandmother's hardwood floor with a toy football in his arms. "Just like his daddy," relatives and family friends might have said, or perhaps they would have kept the thought to themselves, because by then Big Oomz was freshly incarcerated—a sad and sore subject, the small boy who carried his name a constant reminder of the father's absence.

While Oomz played many sports, and was very good at basketball, football was always his favorite and best sport. As an 8-year-old on that Mitey Mite playoff team under Coach Vick, Oomz was named most valuable player. Everybody in the program assumed he'd go down as a Mo Better legend one day—one of those much-talked-about high school stars who often came back to the park to speak with the young-sters before practice about keeping your grades up and listening to your coaches.

Mentally and physically, he was suited for the tough game. He was a rough boy, but not recklessly so. He controlled his ferocity, channeled his anger, compartmentalized his internal turmoil about as well as can be expected of any 10-year-old. He was not particularly big like Hart, not especially fast like Isaiah, not athletically dominant like Gio. But he was, in every sense of the term, a *football player*, as Coach Chris would put it—the rare boy who understood the nuances, embraced the violence, and, as a result, excelled with an overall ability that was greater than the sum of his natural gifts.

Unlike other boys who careened across the field looking for the closest opponent to hit, Oomz operated within the confines of his as-signment. As a middle linebacker on defense, he kept his patience at the snap, processing the chaos in front of him, identifying the ballcarrier and anticipating his movements, before shooting forward and crashing bodies. On offense, his patience was even more impressive. Most boys, when they got the ball, impulsively ran forward at full speed and then, upon finding a wall of defenders, looped backward in search of some miraculous opening that exists only in video-game fantasies. Oomz ran the ball like a chess grand master. Three steps ahead of everybody else on the field, he waited for gaps that he knew would emerge, his pace steady, his mind running, calculating. Rather than try to force himself through the muck, he flowed with the wave of bodies like a surfer, shifting and turning, accelerating and slowing. He ran the ball artfully, played with a cerebral grace. In truth, his game was almost nothing like his father's.

Big Oomz was a tornado, whipping across the field with force and abandon, guided by instinct, it seemed, because he moved with such speed and intensity. Indeed, father and son were different in many ways. Unlike his father, Oomz liked school, was a strong student, and had tested into a gifted-and-talented middle school. While his father had spent much of his free time outside on the streets with friends, Oomz preferred to decompress with an evening of video games. Oomz was more sensitive than his father had been as a child. The Junior

Pee Wees' disappointing season had taken a toll on him. He often became frustrated during games, slouching his shoulders and shaking his head when the contest began to go the wrong way, going quiet and despondent at the moments when his team needed his leadership the most. His teammates looked up to him, took after him, and his body language was contagious. The coaches recognized that Oomz was more than partly responsible for the team's consistently sluggish fourth quarters.

It got worse as the season wore on, a vicious cycle of losing and frustration, frustration and losing. Oomz didn't hide his aggravation. He became increasingly bored. His favorite response to most questions was a sharp and harsh "So?" He missed more practices than usual and half-assed it when he was there. He seemed angrier than his coaches had ever seen him. He was angry at the losing. He was angry at the growing sense that the program his father helped build was now fading. He was angry that he couldn't turn it around.

The coaches tried to pull Oomz out of his gloom, sometimes with gentle encouragement, sometimes with harsh shouting, sometimes with stern and brief commands like "Step it up, Oomz" or "Take control of your team, Oomz." The breaking point came in October. During a late-season game, Coach Esau's assistant, Andrell, gave Oomz a good dressing down. It wasn't the loudest chiding Oomz had ever taken, nor the most unjust, but after it happened he began to think about quitting. He told a few teammates he wasn't coming back next year. He pouted at practice, and the evenings at Betsy Head turned darker as the season neared its end. That week, there was a gunshot at the park, like an omen. It was loud, close. Everybody inside the park looked to where the sound came from. A young man sprinted up the track. He tossed a gun to the ground and ran through the basketball courts out of sight. A police officer chased him. Oomz watched, barely fazed.

ooooo

THE NEWS CAME out of nowhere. Just as suddenly as his father had been taken away from him, he had been given back. Big Oomz said he was back for good this time. Prosecutors had dismissed the charges. Oomz was excited, of course, and over that winter he spent a lot of time with his father. They caught up, talked football. Big Oomz, eager to make up for lost time, unloaded a deluge of familiar lessons onto his son. When to run through a defender and when to run around him. How to properly hold a football when bulldozing through traffic. Which types of boys to avoid in the neighborhood.

Free and breathing easy for the first time in years, Big Oomz felt like a new man. He applied for jobs. He tracked down old friends. He decided, after some thought, to start his own youth football program. Oomz had not committed to quitting Mo Better at the end of the season. He hesitated to leave the friends he'd played with for years, and he wasn't convinced that he'd have a better chance to win and to play well at any other program in the city. But his father's new ambition swayed him. The team would be built around Oomz. His father would personally work on improving his skills. Oomz would learn the tricks of the position from the legendary running back.

Oomz's mother, Tasha, was not fully on board with this plan. She liked Chris, Esau, and Vick, and she still believed in them. But Oomz was now adamant. And anyway, nobody was quite sure that Mo Better would recover from its downslide—or that the program would even still exist by the fall. She called Esau to break the news. The coaches were heartbroken.

More than once that winter, Vick rode his bike over to PS 156 to check on how Oomz was doing. Oomz was shy and embarrassed. He'd give a small smile and shrug his shoulders. Vick was the last person he wanted to disappoint. The coach sensed the boy's concern. He knew Oomz was in the midst of a complicated time in his life, and he had no intention of pressuring him to come back. "You don't have to hide," Vick told him. "There's an open gate policy at Mo Better and you're welcome back anytime." But, he added, even if Oomz didn't return, Coach Vick still had his back.

ooooo

COACH VICK RODE his bike around the neighborhood to check on his boys and to clear his mind. His Mitey Mites had had their worst season in Vick's 17 years. Was he no longer the coach he used to be? He certainly wasn't shouting as much. He found that he wasn't as angry about losses as he used to be. Was his passion dimming? Those 17 years had worn him down, no doubt. Seventeen years of caring for others' struggles. Bad grades, court appearances, mom or dad on drugs, abuse in the home—you name it, Vick had seen it. He'd dealt with those struggles many times over as a coach. He understood his boys' problems. He knew the answers. He was good at this. It was his own problems that left him lost and confused.

Shortly after the 2013 season ended, he got laid off from his security job. His girlfriend, the mother of his 4-year-old son D-Lo, worked for the city's housing department and her salary was not enough to cover all the bills. The early months of 2014 were rough on Vick, and he wondered whether he'd ever be able to take care of his family. His mind kept returning to the one job that had made him good money. He knew the streets, and more than once he thought, "You know what, fuck it. Lemme go get a package. I can't pay my bills, I'm not working, whatever. And I start saying, 'Shit, I could go out here, make this money real quick.'" But one thing held him back from going down that path again. "How could I sell drugs, when if I was standing somewhere selling drugs, they'd see me out here, be like, 'Yo, what up Coach Vick'?" he said. "I'm identified as a coach. That right there saves me from the streets. So it's like, damn, I can't do that."

For the first time in his life, he decided to apply for welfare.

ooooo

FOOTBALL, IT SEEMED, had always kept Vick Davis from going too far down the wrong path. Back in his day, he was a savage on the field. He played for a youth team in the Bronx because there were no programs in his area, and he brought his neighborhood's reputation with him. He was never very big, but he was fierce. "Little but Deadly," one coach nicknamed him. He played cornerback, and when a ballcarrier came his way, he dove hard at his legs. "In any other sport, height and weight is really, really important," said Vick. "In football, it's the legs. I had a coach tell me the only uncovered part of a player's body is his shins." One year, when he was 11 or 12, he broke four kids' ankles, he said. Word spread around the league, and by the end of the season no coach dared send the ball to his side of the field.

To compensate for his size, he threw his body around recklessly. Opponents knew him to be a roughneck, a hard kid who hit like he had nothing to lose and played dirty when he had to. He threw quick punches into the guts of the bigger boys who tried to block him and struck them with shoulder bumps after the whistle so they knew not to fuck with him. But back in Brownsville, among his circle of friends, he had the opposite reputation. He was the good kid. He didn't spend much time on the streets. When his friends gathered to smoke weed and drink beer and bump Whodini on a boom box after school, he was on a two-hour train ride to the Bronx for practice. His coach was no-nonsense and didn't allow players to walk while they were in uniform, not even when they were off the field. After practice, the rest of his teammates, who all lived nearby, ran straight to their buildings. Vick, though, had to get to the train station a half-mile away. He'd run, in full pads, up the blocks, his coach slowly rolling in a car beside him. When they hit a red light, he'd stop and do up-downs, dropping chest-first to the ground and popping back up over and over until the light turned green. By the time he got back to his apartment high up in the Atlantic Towers, after the two-hour return trip and more stairs than he chose to count, all he wanted to do was fall into bed and sleep.

"I didn't get the chance to indulge in all they was doing, 'cause I was always involved in sports," Vick said. "If I wasn't playing football, I was playing basketball or baseball. I got friends that have been incarcerated twenty-five years, thirty years, and these are the same guys that I tried to hang out with but didn't get the opportunity to. I'm one of the success stories out there."

Even on days when he didn't have something to occupy him, his mom, Miss Elsie, "kept her foot on my ass." She was a single mother and he was her oldest son, and he learned the virtue of discipline from her. "I couldn't get away with little things that other kids could get away with. It wasn't happening," he said. "If my mom said be in the house at seven o'clock, if I was in the house at seven oh five, I got an ass whoopin. With an extension cord, a belt, a stick, a shoe, whatever was closest to her was what I got beat with. Not only did I get a behind whoopin, I was on punishment and my punishment was written assignments, as well as behind whoopins."

Miss Elsie worked as an assistant at a law firm and kept a stack of long yellow legal pads. One punishment was that Vick had to write "I will listen to my mother" over and over, filling a sheet front to back. Another punishment was that Vick had to take all the dishes out of the cabinet, wash and dry them, then stack them back in the cabinet. To make sure he didn't cheat, Elsie slid sheets of paper between some of the plates. If the papers were still there when Vick said he'd finished, it meant he didn't do all the dishes, and he had another week of punishment tacked on.

By the time he got to high school, he didn't have much interest in joining his friends around the neighborhood smoking weed and sipping beer. "I realized it was fuckin' boring," he said. "You stand there, drink, you get drunk, you stand on the corner, you end up fighting with your friends. To me it didn't make any sense. Once I got to that age there, I realized that girls like athletes. So to me, to hang out on the corner—it wasn't no girls at the corner. All the girls was at the games. So I didn't want hang out on the damn corner."

If teenage Vick did have a vice, it was girls. Girls were his focus from the time he got to school in the morning to the final bell in the afternoon. He put little effort into his studies, and his grades were bad. He was a smooth talker, charming as hell, and handsome. He had plenty of girls, but he didn't stop chasing. Being an athlete was one thing, he concluded when he was 17, but having money was where it was really at. This was the '80s. Crack was booming, and the dudes he knew with the most money were drug dealers, so he got into the drug game. "I thought having the money, I could get all the women," he said.

He was so scared of his coaches finding out about his business endeavor that he made a point to never slang in New York City. He'd travel upstate, as far as Rochester, to sell his product. It was risky, working so far from his turf and his people, but he made good money. He quit playing football before his senior year, and over the next few years he hustled. He had his first kid, then his second, and then another. Then he got arrested. His mom bailed him out of jail. He kept hustling. One day, in his early 20s, on a business trip to Rochester, somebody shot him. He took six bullets. On the hospital bed, he thought about what had become of his life. "I got caught up," he said. "Seeing my friends die. Ended up getting shot. Like, yo, I like the other life better, with the sports."

His oldest son played youth football for a program in northeast Brooklyn, and so he and Elsie volunteered as coaches. In 1997, two of the program's coaches, old friends of Chris Legree, jumped over to Mo Better, and Vick and Elsie joined them. Vick impressed Chris with the way he worked with the youngest kids, how he won their attention and instilled discipline, and within a few years, Chris put him in charge of the Mitey Mites.

The drug game behind him, Vick took a series of menial jobs but had trouble holding steady work. His role as coach helped, though. Parents hooked him up with jobs when they could. He worked construction for one father's company. He took shifts as a security guard for another's. He made enough to eat and help support his kids, but not enough to get his own place, so he stayed with girlfriends. He'd always dreamed of having his own place, and as he reached and passed 40, he still kept that dream. But things were getting tougher.

His mind cluttered and stressed, Vick rode his bike often in the mild fall and cold winter after the 2013 season. On too many of those bike rides, he spotted Gio outside with friends.

∞∞∞∞

GIO DID NOT wear any gang colors, did not flash any gang signs, did not appear to be dealing drugs or committing any crimes. The boy was simply out, in front of takeout joints and apartment buildings. But to Vick's eyes, simply being out was sometimes a bad sign. It was still cold,

NEVER RAN, NEVER WILL — 81

after all. Too cold for real trouble. The streets were calm and sparse, speckled with shivering people trying to get to and from subway stations and bus stops as fast as possible, a biting wind rustling their coats.

The sight of Gio on those street corners worried him. The way he stood huddled with other boys—some of them older looking, glaring all tough—reminded Vick of his childhood friends, the ones he'd lost to prisons and graveyards. It reminded Vick of what he'd seen in Pup and Dajuan and Big Oomz before they'd fully immersed themselves in the street life. Once the weather warmed, Vick knew, the streets would heat up.

He didn't stop and say anything to Gio. Just rolled past. Calling him out in front of his friends was a good way to win resentment. But he planned to talk to the boy soon. Spring practice was right around the corner.

Vick was looking forward to spring. On a frigid day in February, he finally made the trip to the welfare office. He'd been putting it off, but a job never came and he needed the money, so he swallowed his pride. Fate rewarded him. At the office, he met a man handing out fliers for a medical assistant training program. It was a seven-month course, the man told him, and steady jobs were nearly guaranteed for those who completed it. It was a career. Vick signed up. "Health care's where it's at," he said. Classes started in April.

— 6 —

PRESSURE CHAMBER
March–April 2014

A THICK, HARD LAYER OF ICE COVERED THE FIELD FOR three months. It was a cold winter, by far the coldest Gio had ever experienced. This was the 12-year-old's first winter outside the Caribbean, of course, but even his friends, Brooklyn born and bred, told him that this winter was harsher than normal. He was not as annoyed as they were about the cold and constant snow. He appreciated the novelty of bundling up in multiple layers, and he marveled at the snow. He would look back at footprints he had made, or bend down on his walk to school and crumble the powder through his fingers. He made his first snowman. This was the sort of winter he had seen in many movies. He was disappointed that it didn't snow on Christmas.

But while the cold and the snow did not wear on him, being stuck indoors did. He was an outdoor child. In his early months in the neighborhood, his hours at the park had stabilized him. At a time when most everything around him was strange and different, the field felt familiar. Soccer was the same, football was the same, footraces were the same. Sports had eased his transition into the neighborhood. Few traits can win friends, Gio realized, as effectively as the ability to throw a football.

With the field frozen over, though, Gio spent much of the winter inside his family's small two-bedroom apartment with his mother and 20-year-old brother. Antsy from being stuck inside, Gio was primed to butt heads with his mother. Their relationship had already begun to fray just weeks after his arrival. His mother was stricter than his father had been in Saint Lucia. She'd been worried about the influences of the neighborhood and vowed to protect him. She was cautious. She wanted him in before dark and she shouted at him when he missed curfew or when he went somewhere after school without first asking her permission. Gio, who craved independence, pushed back. He rebelled in small ways. He talked back. He ignored her calls. He stayed out at the park without telling her. The park was where he let off steam.

Over the winter, the pressure simply built up. The arguments between mother and son turned louder and nastier. One night, after his mother chided him for returning home too late, Gio punched the living room wall. He found other places to go after school and on weekends. This only made his mother angrier with him. By the time the field had thawed in late March, Gio's mother was ready to disown him. This was no empty threat. She'd contacted the family court, seeking to send Gio to foster care. The stress was more than she could handle. She'd begun the process and paused only when Coach Chris found out and convinced her to rethink the decision. Once he's in the system, Chris had told her, there's no going back.

So, though spring had come late, it had come at a much-needed time for Gio and his mother. He was eager to return to Betsy Head and the sanctuary of the field and the mind-numbing repetition of football drills. On the first Saturday in April, he arrived at the park at 11:15 a.m. for Mo Better's opening practice of 2014. He wore a black compression shirt and white basketball shorts and carried a small gym bag containing a water bottle and cleats. The coaches all shook his hand and told him how glad they were to see him. Chris pointed to the track. Gio knew the routine.

"How many?" Gio said.

"How many fingers on your hand?" Chris said.

Gio eased into a jog. He felt good running. It was sunny and the air was cool. He accelerated into a near sprint with long, effortless strides. He gazed toward the field, where a dozen or so kids played a carefree game of touch football and nobody seemed to be keeping score. They were all younger than him, nobody older than 11, but Gio had spent time with many of them at the park. It was usually younger kids who were playing ball when he dropped by after school.

He'd been coming to the park less often since the late fall. He'd been spending more of his free time with kids around the neighborhood his own age or older, at friends' apartments, on stoops, in housing project courtyards. They played video games and talked about girls and the NBA. Most of them were affiliated with a neighborhood clique that claimed an unofficial allegiance to the Crips. Some of them sold drugs. Gio didn't sell drugs, and he didn't consider himself a gang member. But he appreciated the other kids' company. They had the same day-to-day struggles he had. He concluded these were the ties he needed to survive in the neighborhood.

He saw himself as no different from most of them, except for his football abilities. He recognized his unique talents. His coaches often told him how good he was, and high school coaches had courted him after watching him play. He had manhandled nearly every opponent who lined up against him last season. He wanted to be a professional football player, truly believed he was good enough and dedicated enough to make it. That was why he was here, running around a track on a Saturday morning while most of his friends were asleep.

When practice ended, Gio headed to the long green bench. He swapped his cleats for sneakers, zipped up his gym bag, and turned toward the park's gate.

"Gio, come here," he heard behind him.

It was Coach James, standing on the edge of the field. They slapped hands.

"It's really good to see you here, Gio," said James, a big, goateed Puerto Rican man who worked with the Mitey Mites. "Stay out of trouble, OK?"

Gio nodded, and continued on. As he passed the benches, he saw Coach Vick headed straight for him.

"Giooo! Good work today," Vick said. They slapped hands and hugged.

"Thanks, coach."

"I don't know why I'm saying this." Vick paused and clasped his hands in front of him. "Stay off them corners. Stay off them corners. I don't know why I'm saying this. Stay off them corners. Where you live at?"

"Off Kings Highway."

"That's Crips, right?"

"Yeah," said Gio, eyes a bit wider with surprise, lips curled into a nervous grin.

"Crips. High Bridge. Wave Gang. Hood Starz. You running with any of them?"

Gio shrugged, stared at his shoes. He was taken aback.

"I don't know why I'm saying this . . . ," Vick repeated.

He did know why he was saying this. He knew this neighborhood, the pressures that pushed against a 12-year-old boy, especially one new to the country. He'd seen many of his players pass through the gangs. Hell, Mo Better players had founded the Hood Starz more than a decade earlier. Vick remembered when those kids started a beef with some kids from the Wave Gang, triggering a cycle of retaliatory beatings and murders and constant trash talk. During stretches when the beef was particularly heated, kids would take long, circuitous routes to get to a school or park a couple of blocks away. It was too risky to pass through enemy turf. A few years back, a group of Hood Starz boys shot a video on Betsy Head's red cement steps, lobbing vague threats at their Wave Gang rivals and boasting like teenagers do. One of them posted the video on Facebook and YouTube. Police saw it and rounded up the boys, charged them with making criminal threats. Two former Mo Better players spent eight months behind bars on Rikers Island. Prosecutors didn't pursue charges against a third because he was only 12, and that kid was now one of the best high school wide receivers in the city. That boy was lucky, and Vick had attended too many funerals to trust luck.

"I ride my bike out around here and I see you out here on them corners, you don't even wanna know what I'ma do," Vick continued. "You out on them corners, you gon' die. Do you wanna grow up? Don't be hanging around certain people. You know who I'm talking about."

Gio nodded.

"Them corners gon' bring you down or get you in jail. Can't get no coochie in jail."

Gio snickered. Vick pointed to Gio's bag.

"Focus on this right here and this'll take you to college for free. That's where the real coochie's at. You think you getting coochie now? Boy, they'll be all over you in college. Say you from Brooklyn, they'll be all over you. You seein' the same hood rat girls you grew up with. In college, you got girls from all fifty states. Name a state. And they'll be all over you. Stay off them corners. I don't know why I'm saying this. All right?"

Gio smiled and lifted his bag in recognition.

On his way out the front gate, Gio passed Coach Esau, who was standing with kids waiting for their rides.

"Stay safe, yo," Esau said. "Stay off them streets."

Gio nodded, slapped hands once more, then strolled up Livonia Avenue. He shook his head, chuckled, and said under his breath, "Like they planned it or something." His coaches were always looking out for him. He knew they worried about him. Coach Chris often spoke to his mom on the phone. Gio appreciated that his coaches cared. He respected them, and he really did want to be the kind of kid they wanted him to be. "He's a good kid. You won't need to worry about him," Chris would tell high school coaches about a kid like that. But the coming football season and getting into a good high school—those were distant concerns. Gio's immediate objective was making it to school and back home without getting jumped.

Gio was an obvious target during his first few months in Brooklyn, when he was new, with few friends and a thick West Indian accent. He was bigger than most kids his age, but older kids messed with him once in a while. It was nothing serious, just mildly threatening taunts: "Where you from?" "You live around here?" "Yo, we're talking to you." But Gio was no punk. He didn't walk by, head down and meek, absorbing the blows. He stepped to the older boys and told them to mind their business. Sometimes things would get a little heated, with smack talk back and forth, but in the end, everybody would cool and Gio would be on his way. Going solo was asking for trouble, Gio knew. He'd made a few friends who lived around his block, and he decided he should stick closer to them. They were cool kids, who wore Air Jordans and snapback hats, and they treated him warmly. He began walking to and from school with three, four, five others. The walks became easier. The friendships developed.

But Gio soon found that his decision to simply walk to school with a group brought its own complications, which Gio didn't like to talk about. A couple of his teammates had heard about the situation, and when they shared the story they made up pseudonyms because they didn't know the real names of those involved: Word on the street was, one of the kids in the group, DT, had gotten into an argument with a kid nicknamed Eazy over a girl. Eazy said he would fight DT. Out of solidarity, Eazy's friends declared each of DT's friends an enemy. DT's friends did the same. The two crews now had a beef. Like it or not, Gio was part of it. Eazy's crew had seen Gio out with DT and DT's friends. It didn't matter that he and DT weren't particularly close. They were associates, and that was enough. Lines had been drawn, ranks closed. Gio knew that he might get jumped if he was alone outside and ran into two or more boys from Eazy's crew. So, he tied himself even tighter to his neighborhood friends. It was these friends, not his coaches, who made sure he got back to his block every afternoon.

∞∞∞

THE STREETS HAD changed since Vick's days. Back when he was a teenager, kingpins ran the streets of New York City, ran streets across America: Freeway Rick Ross in Los Angeles, Willie Lloyd in Chicago, Frank "Black Caesar" Matthews in Brooklyn, "Boy George" Rivera in the South Bronx, Alpo Martinez in Harlem, and Howard "Pappy" Mason, Lorenzo "Fat Cat" Nichols, Kenneth "Supreme" McGriff, and Tony Feurtado in Queens. These kingpins and their armies ran sophisticated, interstate, multimillion-dollar operations, with strict hierarchies and rulebooks. "We ran it like a Fortune 500 company," said Lance Feurtado, who served as his older brother's right-hand man. "It was a bureaucracy, with managers and supervisors at each level, from the corners all the way to us."

Feurtado's Seven Crowns gang, based in South Jamaica, Queens, pulled in a million dollars a week, the *New York Times* reported at the time, and by the late '90s was sending packages to 23 states. Feurtado and the other kingpins provided Thanksgiving turkeys to their communities and jobs, with the chance for upward mobility, to scores of young men and women. "Back then, drug dealers were the rich role models who sponsored basketball teams and covered bill payments for families," said James Brodick, project director of the Brownsville Community Justice Center, a nonprofit that advises 16- to 24-year-old criminal offenders on how to avoid trouble in the future. "They served as a main economic driver in their neighborhoods, neighborhoods that lacked services and opportunities."

They also drove much of the violence in those communities. The streets were bloody in those days, with murder rates hitting new highs by the late 1980s. Some locals still remembered one early '90s gun battle, when drug gangs from the Brownsville Houses and the Tilden Houses traded more than 100 shots over a business dispute. For the kingpins, violence—and the threat of it—struck down up-and-coming competitors, kept their own soldiers in line, paralyzed the community into obedience, and shielded their turf from rival kingpins. Violence protected their power. Gang leaders frowned on violence that didn't help advance the bottom line, and those who went rogue were punished. "It was economics," Feurtado said. "On the whole murder is bad for business. Bodies can draw police attention or start some shit with another gang for no reason, and so you want to avoid violence as much as possible. But the drug game is what it is. And the unfortunate thing was that that's how disputes were settled."

In the late 1980s, authorities began to crack down on the kingpins and their soldiers. Congress passed laws creating mandatory minimum sentences for drug offenses, including especially harsh sentences for crack cocaine possession and sales, and expanded those laws so they applied to anybody tied to a "drug trafficking conspiracy," which meant decades in prison for even low-level dealers caught with a few crack rocks or heroin packets. The Department of Justice awarded federal grant money to local agencies focused on drug enforcement. Prosecutors used RICO (Racketeer Influenced and Corrupt Organizations) statutes— originally crafted to combat the Italian Mafia—to build conspiracy cases against inner-city criminal organizations. In 1992, US attorney general William Barr told the Senate Judiciary Committee that he had reassigned 300 FBI agents "from foreign counter-intelligence work to work on violent-gang squads and anti-gang task forces." This shift in focus toward drugs and gangs "represents one of the largest re-allocations of resources in FBI history," Barr said.

In New York City, longtime cops cite the murder of Officer Edward Byrne by Pappy Mason's gang in 1988 as the spark that ignited the city's strike against the kingpins. It became a rallying call to destroy the drug trade responsible for his death before it swallowed more officers. More than 10,000 cops from around the country showed up at Byrne's funeral. "Right after that murder happened, they went, like, crazy," said retired NYPD detective Steve Chmil. "They were locking up everybody. They were flooding areas that had a lot of narcotics. It was really a frontal assault. They really went after the drug dealers." The campaign brought thousands of arrests over the next few years and took down drug rings. Similar efforts were emerging across the country. Mason, Ross, Lloyd, Martinez, Nichols, McGriff, the Feurtado brothers, and many others ended up in prison. By the early 2000s, the age of the drug barons had come to an end, the old gang social structure significantly eroded.

Their absence left a vacuum. The socioeconomic factors that pushed young men into gangs remained, as did the anger, the fear of exclusion, and the yearning for belonging, purpose, and fraternity. Over the years, with a generation of street leaders gone, the younger generation formed new groups, smaller factions based around a housing project or a few square blocks. These crews were informal and loosely organized, made up mostly of teenagers and young men in their early 20s. Unlike the gangs before them, they weren't formed for the purpose of committing crimes. There was no initiation process or detailed hierarchy. They formed and dissolved and changed names. Some had scores of members. Others had several to a dozen. Their territories could be as small as a block or a single building in a housing project. Some crews had members who sold drugs. Others were simply a group of teens who grew up in the same area and hung out together and gave their clique a cool name. While some criminal organizations of the past lived on—the Crips, the Bloods, MS-13, the Latin Kings—the smaller crews became the dominant social dynamic of the streets, in New York City, Chicago, San Francisco, Saint Louis, and elsewhere.

This new social landscape brought new dangers. A higher number of groups meant a higher chance that two groups would come into conflict. Because territory was divided up into more slices, teens had to cross over another crew's turf more often, without even leaving their neighborhood. And when a conflict did arise, there were no shot callers or OGs to step in and mediate. "You don't even know who is the leader you go to," said Brodick. "In the past, if things were getting too hot, you could gather leaders and talk to them. They treated it like a business model, and at the end of the day it was driven by money. When things got too hot, there were leaders to call it off."

The drug trade no longer drove the violence. "Now that all the structure and leadership ain't here no more, everybody doing what the fuck they wanna do basically," said Cobe Williams, a former Chicago gang member who now trained anti-violence activists across the country for the Cure Violence organization. Now, many shootings were caused by personal beefs. Friends took sides with friends, perhaps showing their support on Facebook or Instagram, and personal beefs escalated into feuds between cliques. To many in Brownsville and other communities, the shootings seemed more arbitrary and senseless. "It used to be about money and territory: you slang weed there, I do it here, and that beef is over," Vick said. "Nowadays, it's not about money. It's about slights and stupid stuff. It's about girls a lotta the time. It's about pride and respect and revenge, and those are harder to cool down." Pride and respect could be valuable commodities for boys without the social status conferred by material wealth, and reputation was sometimes all that distinguished those who were fucked with from those who weren't.

The prevalence of guns on the streets made these disputes deadly. Though New York City had strict gun control laws, traffickers hauled in weapons from states with more relaxed policies, like Virginia, North Carolina, Georgia, and Florida, none of which required background checks in private sales. So many guns poured into the city from the South that police officials dubbed Interstate 95 "the iron pipeline." More than two-thirds of the guns used to commit crimes in the city in 2014 were purchased out of state—more than double the national average of out-of-state guns recovered in crimes, a pattern also present in Chicago and other big cities. The mix of guns, anger, disillusionment, and youthful recklessness created a climate of fear and panic. It was shoot first or be shot.

At a sentencing hearing in June 2013 for a young man convicted of murdering a member of a rival crew in Harlem, Judge Thomas Farber pointed out that the shooter and victim had lived in neighboring housing projects. "They were the same young men," Farber said. "They live in the same geographical area." Their differences, he continued, "don't exist except in the minds of the people who are fighting. So they are fighting over nothing, really nothing." But they had found a "feeling of purpose" in the feud. "Unless we are able to impart meaning into our children's lives, then this drama is going to keep playing again and again and again, and people are still going to die," he said.

Similar conflicts boiled all over the city. In Far Rockaway, Queens, two beefing crews lived within the same housing project: the Hassocc Boys at the front of the Redfern Houses and the 1270 Gangbangers at the back. During a seven-month stretch in 2007 and 2008 that one local called "the civil war," a 24-year-old, an 18-year-old, a 15-year-old, and a 16-year-old were shot dead. When tensions between rival crews were high, a neighborhood would become like a minefield for young locals, with violence popping off at the slightest disturbance. "It's like a game of telephone," said Brodick. "The story changes every time and by the end of the line the details are different and that is how the rumor spreads before the revenge happens." Young locals understood this. Kenneth, a 22-year-old Brownsville native, said that he carried a gun because he was scared. "Even if I didn't do nothing, maybe somebody I'm associated with did something, or maybe somebody just mistakes me for somebody else," he said. "Anytime, somebody could jump out at you, for reasons you might not even know, and so I gotta protect myself." Staying strapped didn't solve the problem, but Kenneth didn't see any other option. "Even though it really just makes things even worse," he said. "I know he got a gun and he know I got a gun, and now we both scared the other's gonna pull it first and so do I pull mine first because I know he's thinking the same thing? And that's why fights keep turning into shootings. I'm tryna look hard and so is he. It's like we just fuckin' in this spot where neither of us wanna die and neither of us probably wanna kill somebody but we trapped."

Back in the days of the drug barons, Lance Feurtado said, there was a clear distinction between "soldiers and civilians. Between who was in the game and who wasn't." That line was faint in the era of crews. Which meant that even weak associations could get a young person tangled in a beef—or a law enforcement sweep. While the street dynamic had changed, authorities still pursued the achievements that brought funding and praise in the previous generation. In June 2014, around 500 NYPD officers swarmed the Grant and Manhattanville houses in Harlem and arrested 103 people who ranged from 15 to 30 years old. Manhattan district attorney Cy Vance Jr. called it the largest "gang" sweep in the city's history. It targeted three crews who, Vance said, were responsible for two murders, 19 people wounded from gunfire, and 50 attempted shootings over the last four and a half years. Many of those indicted faced conspiracy to commit murder charges under RICO laws. Police pulled much of their evidence from Facebook, where young people made threats against rivals in posts or showed their association with a crew in photos. Some of those arrested were not charged with any crimes beyond their association with a crew. Prosecutors were using laws intended to take down kingpin-led criminal organizations against these casual neighborhood cliques. At a 2014 court hearing, when a lawyer asked a young man how he got linked up with the Wave Gang, he replied, "Just hanging out."

"It's damned if you do or don't," Kenneth said. "You grew up with these dudes and they been your homies. Y'all was kickin' it on the jungle gym, the slides and shit. Now that you're older, you still run with these guys and you can walk around the neighborhood feeling safe, as a pack. Look cool for the girls when you rolling up deep at a party. You got guys you know gon' have your back if somebody messes with you, and maybe they won't mess with you because they know these dudes got your back. But then when somebody you know gets caught up in some shit, that's you too. That's how the police see it."

According to street lore, the Hood Starz were formed in the late 2000s by a group of teens who lived in Marcus Garvey Village. By 2010, Poppa's cousin Hakeem Gravenhise was the crew's unofficial leader. He was 16 years old, charismatic, husky, great at drawing. He dreamed of becoming an architect. The Hood Starz spent a lot of time at the Betsy Head playground, and that's where younger kids usually joined up with them. Hood Starz turf was west of Rockaway Boulevard, and the Wave Gang, which was based in the Brownsville Houses, ran the area east. The Hood Starz greeted one another with "cho!" and the Wave Gang used "woo!" But even within these two crews there were smaller groups, circles of friends who affiliated with a crew only in name and territory. Addicted to Cash and 180 Crew were west of Rockaway, and Smoove Gang, Pretty Boy Gang, and Money Gang were on the east side. There were smaller, unaffiliated crews, too: Bully Boyz, Loot Gang, Young Guns, Keep Back Crew, Brownsville Fly Guys, 8 Block, and others. Yet even defining these crews granted them a formality that didn't exist on the streets. The only place where these groups existed as official units were in NYPD records. When a conflict arose, though, young locals had to draw lines in the pavement.

Nobody seemed to know for sure how the conflict between the Hood Starz and Wave Gang started.

"I heard it had something to do with clothes," Esau told a friend one day at Betsy Head.

"Like somebody spilled a drink on a white T?" the friend said. "Or somebody scuffed some Js?"

"Nah, like, 'Yo, you ain't flyer than me' bullshit," Esau said. "But I don't really know. And I bet these kids still beefing today don't even know how it started. They just inherited that shit."

At first, there were fistfights. Then gunplay. Over a two-day stretch in June 2010, Hood Starz affiliates shot and wounded two Wave Gang members. One of the victims died from his injuries in October. Two days later, a Wave Gang member shot and killed Hakeem Gravenhise on a street corner in front of his apartment building. His mother had been walking home from the grocery store when she heard the shots. She hid and waited until the gunfire stopped, and then when she stepped into her apartment, she found her son dying. The beef turned into a war. By January 2012, police had tied the crews to six murders and 38 people wounded. Police said that two of the dead and six of the wounded were bystanders caught in the crossfire.

The raid came on January 17, 2012. Officers arrested dozens of young people in Brownsville, none older than 21, and seized 35 guns. Prosecutors announced indictments against 43 people allegedly tied to the two crews. Authorities called it Operation Tidal Wave. Several Mo Better alumni were among those arrested and sent to Rikers Island's juvenile detention facility. None were convicted of a felony.

When they got out, less than a year later, they returned to a neighborhood that hadn't changed much, if at all. Even if their time behind bars had persuaded them to stay away from the streets, leaving the streets behind was not so simple. "Life doesn't stop for them," Vick said. "They might wanna change when they see where their road is going, but their history is always catching up with them. They've done stuff that ain't going away. These grudges don't go away." Some locals remembered that the shooting that killed one-year-old Antiq Hennis had stemmed from a dispute his father had gotten into two years earlier. Anthony Hennis had lain low for those two years because he knew his rivals were coming after him. He rarely strayed from his block at Garvey. "And they laid in wait for him until he least expected it," Brodick said.

Young locals felt the constant fear, hiding their vulnerabilities behind brash online personas, as peers lobbed threats and boasts in Facebook posts, in YouTube and WorldStar videos, and on Twitter. "That's how you expected to respond," Kenneth said. "You gotta show you strong, in hopes that it keeps other people from messing with you." Viviana Gordon, the director of operations at Brownsville Community Justice Center, recalled a photography class she hosted for local boys and girls on a recent afternoon. The plan was to walk a specific route and shoot the scenery. "But a lot of the kids said that they couldn't walk this street or that street," she said. "We had to adjust the route. We had to ask them in advance: Is everybody OK going down this street?" One afternoon last summer, the Brownsville Community Justice Center organized a mural painting outside Betsy Head Park. More than 100 people were there, including teachers, community leaders, parents, and dozens of local teens. In the middle of the event, a group of kids showed up and jumped one of the teens while he was painting. The teen's friends went after the group and chased them through the neighborhood.

ooooo

CHRIS WAS IN high spirits as the second practice of the year came to a close. It was the happiest he'd felt in months. More than 30 players had shown up, double last week's turnout. He had new purple Mo Better hats and new yellow Mo Better T-shirts to sell to parents for $10 each. Best of all, many of his blue chippers had impressed the high school coaches who'd come to Betsy Head to get a look at the latest crop of Mo Better prospects. Hart had wowed them with his demeanor and footwork. Chaka had displayed and his remarkable instincts for catching a football. Naz had rifled tight spirals across the field. And Isaiah, with his smarts and speed, had outshone everybody. Two weeks into spring and already Chris was sure his program was on its way back to the championship form of years past. "Been a while since I've been this excited for a season," he said to Coach Gary.

It had been a perfect Saturday but for one thing: Gio hadn't come to practice. This disappointed Chris. Gio had occasionally missed practice without good reason last season, so his absence wasn't a shock. But Chris had been eager to introduce Gio to the South Shore and Grand Street coaches at the park. With practice over, he asked the coaches to wait while he called Gio's mother. Gio lived a five-minute walk from the park, and Chris hoped the boy could hustle over before the coaches left.

Gio's mother was in a panic when she picked up the phone. Gio had been missing since Thursday, she told Chris. He didn't show up for school on Friday and he hadn't been home. He hadn't answered his cell phone, either. "I've already called the police," she said.

— 7 —

BETWEEN SAVIORS AND A DEAD END
April 2014

JUST A COUPLE OF HOURS EARLIER, CHRIS WAS THINKING this would be one of his easier days, with nothing on the agenda more nerve rattling than impressing a few high school coaches, most importantly the one from Poly Prep—a former Mo Better player who graduated from the prestigious high school and was now one of the few black coaches on the football team's staff. Chris was eager for the showcase. It was not often he had more than one middle schooler he could deem a "Poly Prep kid," but the 2014 Pee Wees had 10-year-old Hart and 11-year-old Isaiah.

Both boys knew they'd have to work even harder to make up for the vacuum left by Oomz. Hart was sad to hear about Oomz's departure from the team. Oomz was only a phone call away, and Hart hoped to maintain their friendship, but their relationship had been largely tied to football. The majority of their time together was at the park, and when Oomz came over, it was usually after practice.

Yet the news about Oomz was not even the worst news of the new year for Hart. His father had blown out both his knees during a basketball game at the jail where he worked. Mr. Hart was now stuck on his back, out indefinitely on medical leave. "You've gotta be the man of the house," his father told him. The injury had cast a pall over the family, but his mother helped Hart keep his thoughts positive. Football was back, she reminded him. And the field was a good place to get your mind off things.

Spring practice was light and loose. Footwork drills and agility work. Learning plays and building lungs. Catching up with old teammates and sizing up new ones. Hart eyed the fresh faces, wondering which boys would stay through the summer and which would drop out before the pads came on. It was too soon to know what his Pee Wee team would look like in the fall, but at least he'd have Isaiah by his side. Though Hart had more experience playing, he looked up to the elder Isaiah. They were like-minded boys, respectful, laser focused, and highly invested in the sport. One day, Chris prophesized, they could very well be teammates at Poly Prep—maybe they'd even end up at the same Ivy League university. Watching Isaiah, taking in his speed and smarts and discipline and commitment, Hart felt confident about his team's chances this year.

"Water break!" Coach James yelled midway through practice, as the high school coaches, all wearing ball caps and slacks, stood by the fence. The kids sprinted to the water fountain at the far end of the field. Isaiah was among the first there, but the fountain was broken. While most of his teammates jogged over to the bathroom to drink from the hose, Isaiah returned to the middle of the field. He stretched his legs and worked on his cuts.

This was an important season for Isaiah, and he took these months of preparation seriously. A year younger than Gio, he would be a seventh grader in the fall, and with the way things worked in New York City's school system, his performance that year would largely set his academic path going forward. This was the year he would take the admissions tests for the city's high schools, and this was the year he had to begin winning over the high school football coaches. It was a lot to think about, on top of all the other thoughts and pressures that flood a 12-year-old's mind. His body was changing, muscles tightening and voice cracking, and when he talked he tried to make his voice deeper so it didn't accidentally jump to a higher pitch. He often found himself distracted and preoccupied by the girls around him. He was developing a growing sense of self and a growing concern for his future.

He planned to play football in high school, but he wasn't sure where he'd play. He wanted to go to Lincoln High School because of its prestigious football tradition. His mother, Roxanne, wanted him to go to one of the city's eight specialized public high schools, renowned institutions that accepted only the select few students who scored highest on the Specialized High School Admissions Test. These schools were free, and city officials celebrated them as meritocratic bastions where all city kids had a fair shot at an elite education—"no matter what your ethnicity, no matter what your economic background is," Mayor Michael Bloomberg had once said. Yet the numbers didn't reflect that. In a city where 70 percent of public high school students were black or Latino, only 12 percent of the students accepted into specialized high schools in 2014 were. It was indeed a tale of two public school systems. At around a fourth of city public schools, more than 90 percent of students tested below their grade level in reading and math. Roxanne prayed that Isaiah wouldn't end up at one of these schools.

The ideal scenario, Isaiah and his mother agreed, was Poly Prep, which had a strong football program, excellent academics, and would get him ready for college. The institution's sterling brand had been tarnished after revelations that school officials had failed to act on reports that the head football coach from 1966 to 1991 sexually abused boys, leading to a lawsuit settlement in 2012. But to mother and son, the Brooklyn private school represented only a gateway to a bright future. Coach Chris told Isaiah, "When you go to a school like that, those are the people you get to socialize with and later on in life these are the people you'll know and it'll give you opportunities."

To get into Poly Prep he'd need good grades and high marks on the admission test. But even then, good grades and high marks meant little without what Chris called a "football scholarship." The yearly tuition nearly matched Isaiah's mom's yearly salary. Fortunately, Isaiah was a talented football player. By the end of the previous season, he'd shown the coaches that he might be the next great Mo Better running back. He'd also proven to himself that he had a future with the sport. Now that he had a taste of football success, he wanted more. Isaiah couldn't wait for the season to start, and though the first game was still months away, he was glad to at least be out on the field, juking past defenders with a ball in his arm.

"He's fast, ain't he?" Chris said to the five high school coaches who had stopped by to watch practice. "Real smart kid, too. And a good kid, never gets in trouble."

Isaiah and some of his other teammates couldn't help but peek at Chris huddled with the coaches. Isaiah had told Chris about his desire to go to Poly Prep, and Chris had assured him that he would get him there as long as he kept his grades up and played to his potential. Before practice, Chris had told Isaiah that a Poly Prep coach would be at the field. The boy felt an adrenaline rush.

"Isaiah!" Chris shouted, waving him over. Only a few on the team would be called over to meet coaches, and the call sounded almost the same each time: "Somebody here I want you to meet."

Isaiah jogged over and shook hands with the coach.

"Nice handshake," said the coach, who wore a blue hat with a silver P on the front. "Are you familiar with Poly Prep?"

Kids with Poly Prep potential like Isaiah and Hart—Chris knew he didn't have to worry about them. He just had to give them a platform and let them fly.

ooooo

GIO SAW THE missed calls, the texts. He knew the adults in his life were worried. He'd been spending more and more time out with his friends.

It was a beautiful time to be outside, warm, bright, and welcoming, and the streets seemed to sizzle with beautiful people. Young women floated up Pitkin Avenue, in tight jeans, pristine Jordan's, and low-cut

NEVER RAN, NEVER WILL – 103

V-necks, white earbuds dangling into purses, eyes looking past the staring preteens and the young men stepping out of the sneaker store carrying shoeboxes in big paper bags. These young men dressed with precision. Their snapbacks tilted to the side at just the right three-quarter angle. Their fitted jeans hung tightly below their hips with just the right sag, exposing a flash of boxer-briefs. Their T-shirts were crisp. Their watches popped with loud colors. And their sneakers, of course, looked fresh out the box.

Pitkin Avenue buzzed in early spring. Men and women lined up along the sidewalk by the Dominican food truck, and the smells of hot sauce, roasted chicken, and plantains hit anybody who walked past. Old women in long dresses rolled carts filled with grocery bags and old men in newsboy caps limped by on canes. Small children waited at the bus stop with their parents, arguing, say, about whether the tooth fairy gave money even if you couldn't find the tooth. A man standing in front of a tattoo parlor offered deals through a megaphone: "30 percent off! Tattoos, 30 percent off today!" Buses squealed to a halt then growled back to life. A car stopped at the light, windows down, bumping Drake.

People are funny, you don't even know 'bout the shit that I been through . . .

The scene was not much different from many avenues in many other neighborhoods across the city, many other neighborhoods across America. The main thing that made these streets different was that these were Gio's streets. He'd gotten to know them well, though he had lived in Brooklyn for only a few months.

Gio wasn't just out there to people watch. He needed to escape for a short while. He needed to be away from home. Some boys had been showing up at his building to wait for him. It had started as a small dispute—talking to the wrong girl, somebody feeling disrespected—but the conflict had heated up as the boys puffed out their chests, refused to back down. Gio lay low at a friend's place, spent a couple of nights there, kicked back. Then he returned home. His mother was angry and flustered. Two officers gave Gio a lecture about staying off the streets.

After they left, mother and son argued. Gio took off again. And again, his mother didn't know when he would come back. She called Chris.

"I'm just going to the family court," she said in a tired voice.

"They will take him then," Chris warned.

"They can take him. He's out of control, totally out of control. Nobody can get through to him. Cops spoke to him. I don't know what anybody can do anymore."

Chris stayed silent, and she went on.

"He says, 'Oh mommy, those guys looking for me. Those guys are outside ready to get me.' I say, 'You don't understand. You don't understand. You think this is a joke.' Every time I talk about Giovanni I get so upset. I just want to go to the court. I'm mentally stressed. I don't know what to do."

Chris and his coaches had seen all this before. For nearly two decades, they had watched kids age out of innocence. These years of early adolescence tested all boys. These were the years when boys began to forge their identities in relation to the world around them. When they stepped out of the fragile bubble their parents and coaches tried to keep them in. When they chased the cool. When they yearned to escape childhood and prove manhood. When the discipline and obedience they had valued in their younger days now threatened to make them look like suckers. To the coaches, a boy just needed to make it through these years alive and on track. If a boy could just get to high school, still thinking about grades and football aspirations, still dreaming about his future, still eager to make it out of the neighborhood, he'd already be steps ahead of many of his peers. Then he could go off to college someplace, away from the pressure, and he could return to Betsy Head during summer breaks and speak to the younger boys about how he made it through those years. But all that was far off.

In the meantime, there were mothers working two jobs who had trouble keeping their sons under control. There were abusive households. There were families without a home, who shuffled between shelters and relatives' living-room floors. There were arrests and court dates and prosecutors who threatened time in juvenile detention. When a kid had it really rough, Chris had him move into his mother's house, down the street from the park. Chris called his mother's place the "refugee house." His brother Jeff called it "the shelter." By their estimate, more than 50 Mo Better kids had lived with Lillian Legree.

The support helped save many boys. The 10-year-old who'd walk two miles from Canarsie to Betsy Head until Chris found out and paid for his MetroCard: he was now playing football at a four-year college. The 11-year-old whose probation officer brought him to Mo Better as an alternative to juvenile detention: he was now a starting running back for a top high school. One 14-year-old was convicted of armed robbery, but the coaches wrote the judge a letter that convinced him to send the boy back to Brownsville instead of to a detention facility. He was allowed back on the condition that he lived with the Legrees and remained on the football team. The boy was now a starting running back at a Division II college. Several times a year, some former player's parents would show up at Betsy Head out of nowhere to thank the coaches for keeping their son on track years ago and tell the coaches how well he's doing now. Studying to be a dentist. Going to college in California. Managing a restaurant. Starting his own business.

Yet there was no telling who would get saved. Getting saved meant getting lucky. It meant staying free and alive. Pup stayed on the streets late into his teens, through his high school football years. "Pup was one of the kids we worried would be six feet under in a matter of time," Coach Vick said. But he made it out. He went to college upstate. He got a job, a wife, and kids. The Boogeyman stayed on the streets, too. He'd lived with the Legrees for some months during his early teens, but dove deeper into the street life as he got older. He didn't get lucky.

Chris and his coaches knew that not every kid would be saved. A boy had to be lucky, but he also had to make an effort. He had to show at least some willingness to use the support the program offered. If Gio didn't choose to come to practice, Chris believed, there was little a coach could do. He had spent several days looking for Gio. "You know who he hang out with?" he'd asked one of Gio's teammates.

"I know he's out there on Kings Highway," the boy said. "Out by the Green-something Towers. Kingsbay or something. That's where he say he be."

But Gio wasn't at practice and he wasn't answering Chris's calls. With Gio again missing, Chris dialed his number once more, then twice more. Nothing.

∞∞∞

On Easter, after practice, Chris updated the coaches about Gio. They gathered under the shade of a tree near the front of the park.

"Man, I had just told him to stay out of trouble a couple weeks ago," Esau said.

"How's the family situation?" Gary asked.

"Mom's trying hard, but he's new here and he goes to 588," Chris said, referring to the troubled public school Gio attended.

"Never had a chance at 588," said Gary, shaking his head.

"Keep an eye out if you see him," Chris said.

Beyond the coaches, a joyous atmosphere enlivened the park. Several boys wandered over into the crowd that had gathered for the afternoon's festivities. Plastic eggs dotted Betsy Head's field. A marching band from a nearby high school performed, and when they finished a DJ played music that boomed through the neighborhood. A step team danced on the track. Small girls in sundresses and small boys in pastel button-downs shuffled across the field gathering plastic eggs. Spectators sat watching from the red cement steps behind the baseball diamond. Many in the crowd wore light green shirts that read "Happy Easter Antiq" on the front and "No child deserves to die" on the back. Smoke from a grill rose above the party.

Two of Mo Better's newest additions, brothers Donnie and Tarell, hustled through the crowd and found the line for the grill. They had lived in Brownsville when they were small, but their mother had moved the family around in the years since. There were five kids in all, and 10-year-old Donnie and 7-year-old Tarell were the youngest. They had resided in Far Rockaway, Queens, then East New York, then Virginia, where Donnie and Tarell stayed for about a year. Donnie liked Virginia. They lived with some relatives in a big house with a big backyard, a trampoline, and a small pool, and older cousins sometimes took him hunting. He didn't know why they had to move back to Brooklyn.

The brothers lived in the same building as Gio and sometimes played with him at the park. Their family had been at the Castle for more than two years. "It's violent," Donnie said. "A lot of fights. But it's cool, 'cause I know everybody there." While Gio was figuring out his place in the neighborhood, Donnie was already comfortable with his surroundings. He and his little brother ducked beneath turnstiles and rode the subways around Brooklyn. They charmed adults into buying them candy, sunflower seeds, Chinese food. They walked around the neighborhood as if they were rap stars home from a world tour. "'Sup pretties!" Donnie liked to say to older girls he saw on the sidewalk. One afternoon, walking home from practice, they passed an auto-shop garage, where several men leaned over open hoods and flipped burgers on a grill. Tarell declared, "I hope some of that food's for me! Better have it ready by the time I come back!"—which caused the men to break into roaring laughter.

During Donnie's first two years back in Brownsville, he didn't join Mo Better. He knew many of the boys on the team, but he preferred boxing. He was a very good boxer, his uncles had told him, with a right hook that could knock the snow off a roof. Recently, though, he had become bored by the sport. He had watched his older brother play high school football and decided that it was a better fit for him. "'Cause you could run around and hit and you have more space," he said. "In boxing, all you could do is just stand in one small box and punch." Donnie didn't know much about football, the rules and strategy of it. All he knew was that one person had the ball, and opponents tried to hit him, and teammates had to hit those opponents before they hit the person with the ball.

Donnie was a rough kid. He got into many fights at school. When he was 9, a boy kept teasing Donnie's girlfriend, so Donnie punched him in the nose. Blood was all over the cafeteria floor. "It just started pouring out," he said. "These clumps." When he moved back to Brooklyn in fourth grade, a classmate picked on him because he was the new kid. "Called me a pussy and a faggot," Donnie said. Donnie knocked the kid's front teeth out. He still had the marks on his right knuckles. "He thought I was an ordinary kid, but I don't play." A few months before Easter, Donnie began going to therapy sessions for his anger. It helped. He believed he was slowly learning how to control his rage, and he hoped to pass the lessons to Tarell. Tarell, Donnie said, was angrier than he was at 7 years old. The smallest frustration would send Tarell into a fury, throwing bottles against the wall or swinging open the door in a moving car.

On this afternoon, though, Donnie and Tarell were smiling and giddy as they reached the grill. Donnie looked up at the large man with the spatula. He smiled wide, showing the gap between his two front teeth, and raised his eyebrows—the face he always used on adults.

"Can I get a cheeseburger?" he said, his voice pitched higher than usual.

"You got two dollars?" the man said.

"No," Donnie said. He frowned and looked down. "But I'm really hungry. We just finished football. Please?"

"A'ight, lil' bruh," the man said after a second of thought.

"Can he get one too?" Donnie said, tilting his head toward Tarell.

"I want a hot dog!" Tarell jumped in.

The man chuckled. "Yeah, I got y'all. Don't worry."

They walked to the long green benches on the other side of the park as they ate. A few of their coaches stood by the front entrance trying to recruit kids. Donnie and Tarell sized the boys up. "He look like he can play." "I'd smash him." "That boy big, how old you think he is?" They finished their food. Tarell tossed his napkin to the ground. Donnie gave him a serious look and Tarell picked it up and dropped it into the trashcan a few feet away.

They were sitting on the bench, their legs dangling, when a woman ran into the park with a frantic look on her face. She went up to the coaches and said, "A girl jumped in front of the train!"

"When?" said Esau.

"Just now. Right in front of a mother with three kids. You could see her! She was all cut up."

The coaches walked to the Saratoga station a block down. Donnie and Tarell followed. They took in the scene. Dozens of people stood at the base of the stairs, looking up at the tracks. Police officers stood in front of the stairs. The station is closed, they told commuters, take the bus.

"I was sitting right there," a young man in a gray hoodie said to an older woman in a green parka. "I woulda done something if I knew."

"It was probably the same one that was crying," the woman said. "There were a bunch of people that saw it and didn't do nothing to console her."

"You see people crying all the time," the young man said. Then he added, "She was young."

"Nobody saw this woman crying and said nothing," the woman said, her voice turning angry. "They see her crying and say nothing. Everybody into their damn iPad and this and that and the other and see somebody crying and they don't say nothing."

A fire truck pulled up. The cherry picker lifted a firefighter to the tracks. Behind the crowd, a stream of people in bright dresses and button-downs strolled out of Betsy Head. A woman with two small boys approached. The boys each held a balloon animal from the Easter-egg-hunt party. "Somebody jumped?" she exclaimed. "Oh my God." The three of them stood there, beneath the tracks, for a few minutes, then walked away, toward the bus stop. When the cherry picker came down, the firefighter held a body wrapped in a white sheet.

"Yo, that's crazy," Donnie said, still looking up.

"Donnie," Tarell said.

"What?"

"You think it hurt?"

"I dunno," said Donnie. Then after a pause, "Probably for like a second."

"You think it hurt a lot?"

"Yeah."

They stared up at the tracks in silence.

"Can we get another hot dog?" Tarell asked.

"Yeah."

When they returned to the park, it was nearly empty. People were filing out. The music had stopped. The DJ said into the microphone that everybody had to leave "due to a situation." Several police officers waved people toward the exits. Police cars blocked the streets surrounding the park. More officers entered the park and marched around the edge of it. A woman at the side gate asked an officer what was going on. The officer said that somebody had reported shots fired at Betsy Head Park.

ooooo

SUMMER WAS COMING. Now Mo Better shared Betsy Head field with the Latinos who played baseball while blasting salsa music from speakers, and sometimes a well-hit ball would roll into a football drill and the boys would step back so the outfielder could run in and pick it up. Now the lady with the Italian ice wheeled her cart through the park, and the boys asked their parents and coaches for two dollars and crowded around her after practice. The days were hotter now, and at the end of one Saturday morning practice, a 9-year-old boy passed out, and Coach Vick had to carry him into his mother's car.

The nights were lively, filled with more people outside, gathered in courtyards and in front of fast-food joints and streaming out of house parties. Brownsville locals understood summer and what it meant and what it brought. "It's getting hot," Vick warned the boys one day. "I know you wanna hang out. Stay away from knuckleheads."

The previous summer, Brownsville's blocks were alive from the afternoon until long past sunset. People converged on stoops or set up chairs on the sidewalk. Laughter, chatter, and music often filled the air. But having so many people outside for so long brought dangers, too. In the summer, beefs that had gone dormant during the winter were back in play. "Now that everybody's out and about, you might see somebody you had a problem with and now y'all gotta deal with that," said Jay, a 15-year-old from Brownsville. "Gotta be on guard in the summer."

Locals feared that the coming summer would bring more shootouts. Some, like Coach James, were all the more worried because the police were now forbidden from using stop-and-frisk, which the NYPD cited as an important tactic for getting guns off the streets. For years, officers stopped anybody they deemed suspicious and patted them down. Cops used this tactic in Brownsville at a disproportionate rate. Though the neighborhood's population made up 0.2 percent of the city's, around 3 percent of NYPD stop-and-frisks happened here.

Police officials claimed the practice was partly responsible for the ongoing drop in crime citywide. Critics called it racist and pointed out that less than 10 percent of stops led to an arrest. Prosecutors found that police officers often lied in reports to justify some of those arrests—particularly arrests for trespassing in housing projects. These cops would report that a person didn't know anybody at the complex even when the person cited a resident's name and contact information. It happened so often that Bronx district attorney Robert Johnson announced his office would no longer prosecute housing project trespassing cases unless his staff had first interviewed the arresting officer. Prosecutors in Brooklyn said that they faced the same problem.

Bill de Blasio had campaigned on a promise to end stop-and-frisk, and, earlier in the year, a judge had ruled it unconstitutional, a violation of civil rights. "I know it's not the best thing and I'm sure they do target black and brown kids," James said. "But, I dunno, I'm for whatever they gotta do to get these guns outta the neighborhood."

New York City, Brownsville included, had become safer than it had been in decades. There had been a time, just a generation earlier, when nearly every resident had a constant fear of getting mugged, when public safety was a pivotal political issue. Back then, a politician needed to show he was tough on crime to get elected and stay in office. Mayor Ed Koch declared in 1988 that the pendulum had "swung too far," meaning that protections for people who broke the law were too great. "The pendulum has to swing back to protect society," he'd said.

By the mayoral election of 2013, though, the climate had shifted, and most residents weren't blinded by fear as before. These days, headlines showed stories about the injustices triggered by the policies of the tough-on-crime era: decades in prison for drug possession, innocent people spending years behind bars because of aggressive detectives and prosecutors, young black and brown men stopped and detained without probable cause. De Blasio's platform vowed to swing the pendulum back toward protecting civil rights. His Republican opponent, Joe Lhota, called this a "recklessly dangerous agenda on crime," and ran campaign ads showing subway cars covered in graffiti, scowling young black and brown men, fires, looting, and blight—a return to the bad old days of the '70s and '80s.

New York City's overall crime rate decreased during de Blasio's first five months in office, but not every neighborhood felt safer. The number of shootings climbed in the roughest neighborhoods: Jamaica, Queens, the northern tip of the Bronx, East New York, and Brownsville. Through the first five months of 2014, 35 people were shot in Brownsville, more than in all of Manhattan and a 75 percent jump from the previous year. Locals feared a violent summer. "It might get bad this year," Chris said. "At this point, everybody's just waiting and hoping, praying."

The police department had plans to counter this surge in shootings before the summer hit. New York City police commissioner Bill Bratton, who had been appointed by de Blasio, announced his policing strategy for Brownsville and several other neighborhoods. First, Bratton said that the department would end its decade-long practice of sending rookies to patrol the city's highest-crime beats. Since 2004, rookie cops started in places like Brownsville, to train and gain experience, before moving on to assignments they found easier and more comfortable in places with lower crime rates. Locals became accustomed to a constantly rotating cast of young, white, fresh-out-the-academy faces, sometimes scared shitless and thin-skinned, sometimes channeling that fear into aggression. These young cops barged through housing projects like soldiers in battle, screaming and shouting, guns drawn, stopping and detaining and searching every person in sight. "Some guys who aren't from the streets and are now policing the streets, they sometimes see the community in a certain kind of way," said Warren Bond, a Brownsville native who spent 22 years as an NYPD officer in Brooklyn. "They can be a little rougher on the residents. They can give 'em a little less slack. They marginalize folks. They see 'em as adversaries. While for me, I was arresting folks I knew when I was a kid. Anybody I arrested could have been people I grew up with or people my daughter knew or, hell, they could have been me if things had worked out differently." The rookie cops were strangers in the community and before they were around long enough to build strong ties to residents, they were gone, off to the next beat. One afternoon earlier that spring, Chris had watched two young white cops tip-toeing through Garvey, peeking their heads around corners, stern looks on their faces. He shook his head. "Look at these guys," Chris said. "Making no effort to get to know the community." Bratton sought to change that. In March, he said that new officers would train in their home districts and that more experienced officers would patrol the highest-crime neighborhoods.

The second prong of the department's Brownsville strategy focused on the neighborhood's crews. Operation Crew Cut, as the NYPD called it, aimed to track and gather intelligence on the loosely organized groups of young people who officers claimed were responsible for most of the city's violent crime. Law enforcement officials across the country had taken to calling these groups "crews" because they didn't qualify as gangs. Gangs were organized enterprises, with a structured hierarchy and an initiation process, devoted to criminal activity. Crews were groups of kids who lived near each other, hung out, and gave their collective a name, and some of them happened to commit crimes sometimes. NYPD officials claimed that more than 300 crews were active across the five boroughs and that they were behind 40 percent of shootings in the city. "It's like belonging to an evil fraternity," Inspector Kevin Catalina, commander of the NYPD gang division, told the Associated Press in May.

A beef between crews, police officials noted, led to a shocking shooting on a public bus earlier that spring. Angel Rojas had been working two jobs, and during his break between jobs in the afternoons, he often dropped by his home to spend time with his two kids. One of them, an 8-year-old girl, was Puerto Rico's classmate. On March 20, Rojas was on the B15 bus in Bed-Stuy when somebody stepped on and opened fire. A bullet hit him in the head. He was 39 years old. Police arrested 14-year-old Kahton Anderson. Authorities said that Anderson ran with a crew called the Stack Money Goons, who were beefing with a crew called the Twain Family. Kids from the Twain Family had shot at him and missed that morning, police said, and Anderson had gone out to get back at them that afternoon. Anderson saw them on the B15, police said, and followed them on. Prosecutors charged him as an adult with second-degree murder. They claimed that Anderson had acquired the gun when he was 12 years old. His first trial ended with a hung jury, then he was retried, convicted, and sentenced to a minimum of 12 years in prison.

The killing was front-page news in New York City: A working-man, father of young children, slain in the crossfire of street warfare. "Big Gun, Small Punk," blared the front page of the *Daily News*. "The stupidity of those gangs that basically, over nothing, are trying to kill each other," Police Commissioner Bill Bratton said in a press conference. "Unfortunately, in the process, they kill innocents." The incident brought back memories of the city's recent—but long gone—past.

To get ahead of the violence, the NYPD kept close watch over the social media accounts of suspected crew members. Officers created fake Facebook profiles, posed as pretty girls, and flirted with their targets. The department boasted, in press conferences and official statements, that the tactics had netted hundreds of arrests over the past two years. With summer approaching, Bratton said that he would increase the number of officers patrolling the areas where the most violent crews were most active. This effort mostly targeted housing projects: Though less than 5 percent of the city's population lived in housing projects, nearly 20 percent of shootings happened there. It was part of a wider policing strategy that emphasized a heavy presence and brought in lots of arrests. Crime was at an all-time low in the city in 2013, but the department still made nearly 400,000 arrests, around 60,000 more than in 2003.

For de Blasio and Bratton, there was much at stake in the coming summer. It was the first big test of whether the administration's new policies might push Brownsville and other neighborhoods back into the bad old days. By the end of May, the new police presence was noticeable. Officers strolled through Betsy Head Park two, three, four, or more times a day. Police cars rolled slowly down the blocks day and night. Two officers posted up outside the bodega on the corner of Saratoga and

Livonia, right in front of the subway station steps, a block away from the park. "It's gonna be a long summer," one officer said to another.

ooooo

FOR THE THIRD time in a day, Chris tried calling Gio. He hadn't seen him in weeks. After four rings, Gio picked up. Chris's voice was sharp but calm.

"Your mother put a bench warrant out on you. You know what that is? No? Well you better find out what that is. You spoke to your mother?"

"No," said Gio, in nearly a whisper.

"You gotta understand what I'm saying to you. You gotta call her. You gotta find out what she's gonna do. If they put out a bench warrant, that means they can pick you up on the streets at any time. I don't know what the issues are but she don't think she can handle you. She's gonna take that step. Now I don't want her to do that 'cause I don't wanna see you get into that system. Most guys think they can run from it but they really can't."

Gio stayed quiet.

"I don't know what's going on," said Chris. "You ain't telling me what's going on. Do you care? That's the first thing I wanna know. Do you care what happens to you?"

"Yeah."

"Yeah or yes?"

"Yes."

"Listen, I love you but this ain't no baby time. Now this is real. If you start messing with these courts that changes everything. It ain't gonna be your mother calling the shots. The other thing I got a problem with is you staying at your friend's house—he got parents there?"

"Yeah."

"What is it about your mother that you don't wanna be around her?"

"Nothing really."

"Why is it so hard for you to tell me the truth? It's gotta be something, man. Are you involved with any gang?"

Gio didn't answer.

"Which one?"

"Not anything like . . . not anything like that . . . or something like that."

"You selling anything?"

"No, no, no," Gio said quickly.

"But you're with a group, though? With a crew?

Silence.

"I just gotta know what's going on. Do you think that that's gonna lead to something good, whatever you're doing, honestly?"

"No."

"What do you want to do? Tell me. What you wanna do?"

"I dunno."

"Your mother's about to sic the courts on you. I think I can hold that off, but I can't do that if I don't know what's going on."

"She wanna act like she . . . I dunno," Gio said. "She, like, I dunno. She don't wanna listen to anything I say."

"She don't trust you no more. I'm keeping it real with you. You broke her trust. She only doing what a parent do. She can't do nothing with you. What could she do? Tie you to the bed? You ain't no baby."

For several seconds, neither spoke.

Then Chris said, "You ain't the first guy. I've been around guys like you a lot of years and I know the signs. I'm always worried about you getting hooked up with the wrong people. You could get out of it and get on the right track, but you gotta be honest with me and I got to know what you want. Some guys don't wanna be helped. The coaches, they were looking for you the other day. Because I think you got a future. You got a chance. But no one wants to deal with problems. Courts, cops, gangs, stealing, drugs. The fast money bullshit, nobody wants to deal with that."

"Yeah."

"What you wanna be doing three years from now? Do you have any idea?"

"No."

"No?"

"No."

"All right. If you keep doing what you're doing, what you think you'll be doing three years from now? Something good?"

"Nope."

"You want me to tell her to keep the courts out of this and figure something out?"

"Yeah."

"OK. But you can't make me look stupid. I need to know who you dealing with. Is there a leader or somebody?

"Mm-hmm."

"Can you talk now about it?"

"Nope," he said. Then, after a pause, "I'm about to go home soon."

"When can we talk about it?"

"I dunno."

"There's that answer again."

"Later in the day."

"Better call me. You say you're going home. Pretty soon you might not have a home to go home to. If you get shot, right, who gotta come to the hospital?"

"My moms."

"Yeah, I know. It ain't gonna be nobody that you hang out with. You gon' let me help you or not? If I'm wasting my time, tell me right now."

"No."

"Good. 'Cause I think you're worth saving. You're a good kid, man. We'll deal with one thing at a time."

"A'ight."

"What time you gon' call me?"

"Like about seven."

"A'ight, that's cool. Be careful, all right?"

"A'ight."

Gio didn't call that evening and he didn't show up for practice that Saturday.

WHAT'S BEST FOR ISAIAH
May 2014

CHRIS WISHED THE BEST FOR GIO, BUT HE HAD OTHER boys to spend his energy on. He would never admit that he had his favorites, but every coach has favorites. Gio had been at the top of Chris's list—the one he bragged about most, the one he considered the most likely future superstar under the right guidance, the one who got the lion's share of his attention. But he had a new favorite now, and you couldn't blame him: everybody had high hopes for Isaiah.

ooooo

ISAIAH OFTEN THOUGHT about his first Junior Midget game. It was his first time playing an official opponent in pads, and he was nervous before the opening kickoff. Skinny and long-limbed, he looked downfield at the 11 adversaries lined up in formation: the heavyset ones crouched in front, their fingers wiggling in anticipation; the lean ones standing tall in back, hands on their hips, waiting to catch the kickoff. Then he looked back at his own team, spread across the field in a straight line, and at the boy at the center of them, Gio, the biggest and strongest one. Gio raised his right arm then dropped it, jogged forward a few steps, and kicked the hell out of the football. Isaiah raced down the field. The ball bounced, and one of the boys in the back picked it out of the air and started upfield. Isaiah kept his eyes on him. He eased off the gas and veered to the right, angling for the boy, instinctively calculating where on the field their paths would intersect. He accelerated into a sprint. Bodies passed in and out of his periphery, movement swirling all around him, pads colliding, but his eyes were locked on the boy with the ball. The nerves were gone, replaced by a single-mindedness: he would make this tackle. The chaos seemed to part, leaving an alley, and there was the ballcarrier with nothing but 10 or so yards of open grass between the boy and Isaiah. Isaiah slowed and squared his body, feet chopping, hips balanced, shoulders back, arms cocked and ready to pounce, and he—

Crack!

Isaiah was on his back looking at the sky. He had caught a block he didn't see coming. His ears were ringing, and the noises all around, the *oohs* from the crowd and the whistle from above and the shouts from the sideline, were muffled. He let himself lie there for a second or two. He didn't feel any pain, but he felt embarrassed. Perhaps he didn't belong on that field. Perhaps this was a mistake, he recalled thinking. At 11 years old and barely 100 pounds, Isaiah was playing against boys as old as 13 and as heavy as 159. Despite that, he was committed to playing out the season. Isaiah had loved football for as long as he could remember. His older brother got him into it when he was little and taught him the game. Isaiah appreciated its strategic complexities, the matchups and adjustments, the idea that you had to outthink your opponent before you outran him, the chess match behind the brutality. He'd watched his older brother play in high school and wanted to play himself. One day in the summer before Isaiah's first game, his brother was on the subway when he saw a large man in a purple windbreaker that said "Mo Better Football" across the chest. He asked the man—Coach Chris—about it, then brought Isaiah out to Betsy Head, just a few blocks from their home, the following Saturday.

After a few seconds on the ground, Isaiah popped up to his feet and took his spot on defense. He'd taken a hard hit but he was not sure how hard it really was. He had nothing to compare it to. Had he been laid out by a weak hit? Were there bigger hits to come? He braced himself for the next play.

ooooo

AT THE START of the season, Coach Chris rarely gave him the ball. He worried about Isaiah's size and inexperience. But Isaiah proved to be tough and resilient. Fast as a motherfucker, too. By the middle of the season, Isaiah was getting more carries with each game—mostly unofficial scrimmages at this point, thanks to the forfeits. In the second half of the last game, Isaiah got the ball on a pitch. He jogged a few steps and saw an opening between the linebackers and the sideline. He accelerated to the outside, turned the corner, and hit full speed. The defenders had no chance. In the final game of his first season playing tackle football, Isaiah scored an 85-yard touchdown. It was the first touchdown he'd ever scored. When he got back to the sidelines, Chris said to him, "Bet you can't wait to do that again."

ooooo

HIGHLIGHTS FROM THE season flashed in his head as he sat in the back row of the classroom. The school year was nearly up, and Isaiah was daydreaming about football. It was still morning, but Isaiah was ready to get to the park for practice that evening. The stretch of warm, bright, dry days had brought many kids out to the park, and Isaiah hoped that meant his team wouldn't have to forfeit this year.

On the other side of the classroom, his teacher explained the equations she had drawn on a whiteboard. The twenty or so students, all in maroon polo shirts and khaki pants, were quiet as they watched the teacher. In most of his other classes, he could pass the time with his good friend Javon. They discussed NBA games, flicked crumpled scraps of paper at each other, and whispered about girls. They were in sixth grade now, and the girls had become more forward than in years past. They talked about the girls they FaceTimed on their phones over the weekend, the girls who had texted them that morning, the girls who liked the photos they posted on Facebook. But Javon was in a different math class, and so Isaiah had to get through the hour on his own.

School was easy for Isaiah. He pulled passing grades without much effort and never had trouble organizing his time between homework and sports. Most days, he finished his homework before the end of the school day. He'd half pay attention in second period while burning through the homework assignment he'd gotten in first period. And this school was no joke. Intermediate School 392 was a gifted-and-talented school, which meant that a fifth grader had to score high enough on the standardized test to get in. Isaiah had qualified for both of the gifted-and-talented middle schools his mother had applied to. The other school was in Coney Island, two buses or three subway lines away, an hour commute. IS 392 was in Brownsville, a 10-minute walk from home. The choice would have been easy except IS 392 didn't have a basketball team. Isaiah resisted at first, but his mother held firm and he gave in. Many of his friends from the neighborhood went to a middle school on Eastern Parkway, and they played together on the same basketball team. Sometimes Isaiah joked with his mother that he would fail out of his school on purpose so that she'd have to send him to his friends' school. His mother gave him a sharp look whenever he said this, and Isaiah would keep the joke going long enough for her to catch the sarcasm in his tone.

He liked his school. He heard from friends about their rowdy classrooms and indifferent teachers, about fights in the hallway and condescendingly simple homework assignments. When he looked around his own classroom, he saw his kind of people. He saw kids who thought about high school and college, kids who were eager to raise their hands and show off their knowledge, kids who went straight home after school. Most of his classmates lived in Brownsville, 96 percent of them were black or Latino, and 80 percent came from households that lived below the poverty line. And nearly all of them—9 out of 10 sixth, seventh, and eighth graders—passed the state and city reading and math exams, which nearly half of New York City students failed. The school's hallway floor was polished to a shine and the walls were bright blue. The hallway was a showcase for achievement. Several book reports, on *To Kill a Mockingbird* and *Of Mice and Men*, hung from pushpins on corkboards. Photos of Nelson Mandela and essays about him lay on a shelf. A display case presented more than a dozen Ivy League diplomas from former students. During class time, the hallway was mostly empty and silent, and between classes the movement was brisk and orderly.

Isaiah checked the clock behind him. Class was more than halfway over. He looked back down at his notebook then heard the door click open. The principal walked in, and Coach Chris walked in behind her. Isaiah's eyes went wide. The principal introduced Chris. He gave the students the same speech Isaiah had heard from him dozens of times at Betsy Head. A rambling lecture about perseverance and work ethic and focusing on getting good grades because you shouldn't dream of being an athlete or a rapper but should dream of becoming a businessman or a doctor or a lawyer. You all heard of LeBron James? Don't be LeBron, he said. Be the guy who manages LeBron's money. And then he went on about colleges and high schools and how he's got connections to top high schools and if you're interested in playing football, and even if you're not but just need some guidance, you should come to Betsy Head Park at 10 a.m. on Saturday. Then he locked his eyes on Isaiah, whom he had spotted seconds after walking in.

"I'm lookin' at one of my guys," Chris said with a smile. He called Isaiah to come up. Isaiah stood up slowly, eyes on the ground, and walked slowly to the front.

"This is one of your guys?" the teacher said. "I need to talk to you."

Chris nodded. Then he told the class about how much potential he saw in Isaiah, how hard he saw him working on the field, how smart he was, how bright his future could be. Isaiah stood there, hands at his side, eyes shifting between the ground and his coach, face halfway between bashful and embarrassed.

Chris turned to Isaiah and said, "I'ma stay on you because I love you, but I need you to love you back."

Somebody in the class giggled. Isaiah let out a smirk. Chris turned back to the class and said, "If you think it's corny to be loved, I can take you to a courtroom and show you guys getting taken away from their parents."

Minutes later, Chris, Isaiah, and his teacher were out in the hallway.

"He's smart but lazy," she said to Chris. "Always messing around with his friend. Always goofing off. I gotta drag him in from lunch."

Isaiah stood beside Chris. His head was bowed and his eyes were on his sneakers.

"How's his homework?" Chris asked.

"Good when he does it."

"So it's inconsistent. How would you rate how he's doing in school, one to five?"

"Potential is five."

"Everybody got potential. How is he doing?"

"Three."

"So he's not ready for Poly Prep."

"He can get there."

"I'm not gonna embarrass myself recommending a kid to Poly Prep who can't handle it," Chris said, this time looking at Isaiah. "Listen, I ain't tryna put you on the spot, but you gotta step it up."

Isaiah nodded and let out a quiet, "Yes, sir." Then Chris left and Isaiah walked back into the classroom. He looked straight ahead and walked quickly to his seat in the back, and it felt like every eye in the room was watching him.

∞∞∞

THE PLAYERS GATHERED around Coach Chris at the start of practice, and he asked them questions. He asked them about current events first. What Dr. Dre just do? Anybody know? Got three billion dollars for his headphones, Chris said. He ain't get that money from rapping. He got that money from business. What New York City just do? What law they just ended? Anybody?

"Stop-and-frisk!" Hart said.

"That's right," Chris said. "Police can't stop you unless they got a good reason."

Then he lined the boys up into an offensive formation and asked football questions. If the safety come up right here, how many guys they got in the box?

"Eight guys," said Isaiah.

If the defensive tackle lines up here, what's he playing?

"One technique," Isaiah said.

What about if he's right here, head-up with the center? What do we call that?

"Bear," Isaiah said.

"Yup," Chris said, then turned to Esau. "He could be a hell of a coach one day, huh?"

At the end of practice, the players raced. They formed two lines on the track and ran two at a time, side by side. They began on their stomachs, palms on the ground, and at the whistle they shot up and sprinted to the finish line 25 yards away. Coaches called out matchups. Boys challenged each other. They had spent nearly two hours jogging through plays and cycling through blocking and footwork drills, and they were eager for the competition.

"Let's go!" Chris shouted. "Come on! Who want it more?"

"He ain't faster than you, right?" Esau said to a boy. "You better beat him then."

"Don't let him beat you!"

"Catch him!"

The boys ran hard. Winners taunted and losers demanded rematches. For Isaiah, though, it wasn't much of a competition. No boy on the team could keep up with him. Even the faster boys, like Chaka and Time Out, could barely match him through 10 yards. The only drama in Isaiah's races was how badly he would beat his opponent. To give Isaiah a test, Coach Andrell raced him. These races were always close. Andrell won most but not all of them. Yet even when Isaiah raced his teammates, he ran as fast as he could. He tried to finish each sprint faster than the last one. Isaiah took spring practice very seriously. When he thought back to last season, he realized that he'd been hesitant on the field. He'd often not run full speed because he couldn't clear his mind. He had thought too much about his movements before he made them and second-guessed his decisions. He had worried about getting hit and tried to avoid contact whenever possible. He hadn't learned to rely on his instincts until late in the season. It was a revelation. And this year, he'd get to unleash this new comfort on kids his own age.

He was the oldest player on the Pee Wees. He was also, it was becoming increasingly clear, the best player on the team. Coaches expected him to be the team's leader, and Isaiah embraced the role. He was normally a quiet boy, an introvert, but at practice he cheered on teammates who worked hard and called out teammates who messed around. His talent earned him automatic respect and deference from the other boys, but his focus and dedication earned him more. He arrived early for practice and knew every player's assignment on every play. It was like having an extra coach out there, Chris said.

So, Isaiah was disappointed that he had to miss so many practices that spring. His mother had signed him up for a high school entrance exam preparation class. He didn't mind the extra work or spending Saturday mornings in a classroom, except that practice was on Saturday morning and every lost practice was a missed chance to get better. Isaiah's seriousness both amused and impressed Chris. He had encouraged Isaiah's mother to take him to the test prep classes. That's where Isaiah needed to lock in his energies, Chris said. He'd be fine on the football field. Chris had seen hundreds of kids pass through his program, and maybe less than a dozen had as much natural ability as Isaiah. Fewer also had his intelligence, and fewer still his drive to improve. Chris was confident that Isaiah would be a football star beyond Mo Better, probably beyond high school, and maybe even beyond college. This, Chris thought, was what that gym teacher at IS 392 couldn't understand.

Chris had met with that gym teacher, a pony-tailed Romanian immigrant named Ovidiu Grozav, after passing by Isaiah's classroom, on his way out of the building. Ovidiu had stopped Chris, as he walked through the gym, to shake hands and chat. He was also the school's rugby coach, and he told Chris that Isaiah was a phenomenal rugby player, with the potential to be world-class. Isaiah, the gym teacher said, was perhaps the most talented rugby player to come through his program. Ovidiu had started IS 392's rugby team in 2007. Ten kids made it to the first practice, but over the following weeks more came, until the team had around 40 players. They won the city's Rugby Cup championship that first year, then won it again the next two.

Ovidiu told Chris that he hoped to send Isaiah to some rugby camps this summer. Chris countered that Isaiah was a special football player and was more than good enough to get high school and college scholarships. But, the gym teacher shot back, wouldn't he have a better chance at scholarships in rugby, which had a smaller pool of boys competing for spots?

With football, Chris said, he's got a good chance of going to Poly Prep.

He'd also be able to get a rugby scholarship to Xavier High School in Manhattan, Ovidiu said, and didn't Xavier have better academics than Poly?

"Isaiah reminds me a bit of Issa," Ovidiu said.

Chris nodded but said nothing back. They both remembered Issa Sylla very well. He had starred on Ovidiu's early championship rugby teams, while also shining on Chris's championship Mo Better teams. Chris considered Issa one of the toughest players he had ever coached. Issa, a practicing Muslim, fasted for Ramadan—a 12-year-old kid running around the dirt field in late-summer heat, hitting and blocking, without having had food or water until the sun set close to 9 p.m. Issa was valedictorian of his eighth-grade class, and he went on to play football and rugby at Xavier, which granted him full financial aid. Then he got an academic scholarship to Dartmouth College, where he'd just finished his freshman year. He played rugby there.

"Issa was a hell of a kid, man," Chris said. "Real special kid."

The men went back and forth for 10 minutes. It's all about what's best for Isaiah, they agreed. I'm glad he has you looking out for him, they told each other and shook hands.

Chris didn't know it, but Isaiah had already decided which sport to focus on. He enjoyed rugby and planned to play whenever he could, but he loved football. He preferred its stop-and-go rhythms, its structure, and the armor that allowed for more satisfying collisions. He watched it on TV and played football video games, and his friends in the neighborhood played football in the park and talked about NFL players. Isaiah's mother preferred rugby. She didn't know much about either sport, just that they were both rough and they could both help get her son a free high school and college education. She knew enough to know that many more boys in America played football than played rugby, which meant less competition for athletic scholarships. "It's not quite as rough as football and there's more opportunity there if he starts now," she said. But with how much Americans cared about football, there were undoubtedly many more athletic scholarships offered for football skills than for rugby. The math wasn't simple, and the best path wasn't clear.

The deciding factor was that football made Isaiah happy in a way rugby didn't. She rarely heard her son talk about rugby, but he talked about football all the time, at the dinner table and on weekend afternoons in the living room and on weekday evenings when he arrived home from Betsy Head. All the better that this game, which made him so happy, might also open doors to his future. Chris had told her many times that Isaiah was just the sort of kid Poly Prep and other high schools wanted. "Thank God for football," she said.

ooooo

ISAIAH'S MOTHER, ROXANNE, had grown up in Guyana, a tiny country east of Venezuela, and left for America in her early 20s. She'd heard much about the United States over the years. Many of her relatives had already moved to the States. "Everybody want to come to America," she said. "In my mind it was a such a nice, clean, beautiful place." She had seen pictures of tall, shiny buildings and stylish people in New York City and heard stories about how even the poorest Americans drove cars, ate hamburgers, and wore leather shoes.

She arrived in 1986. A cousin met her at the airport and accompanied her on the subway, which they took to Flatbush, Brooklyn. When she climbed the station steps and emerged above ground, the first thing she noticed was all the garbage on the sidewalk and streets. The smell of rot was strong on some blocks. She saw graffiti on nearly every building and dead-eyed men and women in tattered clothes staggering around. She found a job as a nanny for a family who lived on 44th Street and 9th Avenue in Manhattan, and on her way to the Times Square subway station every evening she passed prostitutes, sex shops, and porn theaters. The apartment she rented with two other women was much smaller than the home she'd left in Guyana, yet it ate up most of her salary. Many of the streetlights outside her front door were broken, and at night you could walk several blocks on Church Avenue in nearly pitch dark. Some nights, she heard groups of young people stampeding through the streets, chasing somebody or running from something. She heard gunshots several times a week. Practically everybody she knew in Brooklyn had been mugged, usually more than once. Some people she knew had overdosed or been shot or stabbed to death.

At first, she'd been stunned and confused by what the country was offering her. Nobody had told her about this side of America. She felt she'd been cheated, tricked. This new country seemed to have no less suffering than her old one. But after some months, she moved past her old image of America, realizing that it was a silly thought. She went to house parties and made friends, and they'd eat jerk chicken on their way home while watching the sunrise. Then she had her first child, Shaquille. She worked two jobs and found a one-bedroom apartment she could afford in Brownsville, three miles east of Flatbush. Shaq gave her some trouble when he was young. He was an energetic child and acted up at times. She believed it was because he had nothing, no siblings or activities, to take up his attention. Then, when Shaq was eight, Isaiah was born. Shaq took his role as an older brother seriously. He disciplined Isaiah when he misbehaved, picked him up from school when their mother was at work, and made sure Isaiah only saw him acting right, getting good grades and doing chores and coming home on time. Isaiah was at the top of his class from kindergarten on. Teachers complimented his mother on how obedient and quiet he was. Even as he neared his teens, Isaiah rarely gave his mother trouble. Sometimes she'd have to tell him to take the trash out more than once. Sometimes he'd ask her where the cereal was even though she had just told him the morning before. But that was about it.

His mother and older brother built a protective household around him. "We're indoor people," she said. "We go about our business and come back. We don't mix." Isaiah looked up to his brother, and his brother was a homebody. Shaq never hung out on the streets, and Isaiah did the same. Shaq watched sports on TV and played video games, and Isaiah did the same. Shaq played football at Lincoln High School, and Isaiah watched every game. Of course Isaiah was soon telling his brother and mom that he wanted to play.

ooooo

COACH CHRIS FINISHED the prayer and the circle around him broke. Several boys ran back onto the field to throw a ball around. Several others raced to the chicken joint down the block to a buy slice of pizza or a box of wings. A few others found seats on the steps at the front of the park to wait for their parents to pick them up. Isaiah walked straight toward the tall, thick cement light post at the edge of the field, where the Pee Wees usually piled their bags before practice. It was past 8 p.m., and Isaiah wanted to get home. From yards away, though, he could see that his red backpack was not where he had left it.

He circled the post, his eyes searching the grass. His bag was not there. He looked up and around, his head jittery as it turned, his eyes wide and brow raised. He looked toward the light post on the other side of the field, where the Junior Pee Wees and Mitey Mites stashed their bags. He walked over quickly, as quickly as he could walk without breaking into a jog, and when he got there he saw many bags in a pile, but none was his. He tried not to panic, but it was getting harder now. His books, his homework, his Kevin Durant sneakers, his wallet, his keys, his cell phone were in that bag. His mind wandered forward. How would he tell his mother? What would he tell his teachers? How long until his mom could afford to get him a new phone? Could he get a new school ID? What else was in that bag? Why didn't he carry it with him into the prayer circle like other boys did?

Isaiah ground his teeth and tightened his jaw, squeezing his lips together. He looked straight ahead and walked back toward where the coaches were gathered, near the front of the park. He'd tell Coach Esau. Esau was smart and practical and seemed to always know the next move. He'd shoot Isaiah that *areyouforreal?* look of disappointment and hiss out a short lecture at first, of course, but then he'd tell Isaiah how to handle this.

Isaiah walked past the boys tossing the ball around and laughing. He weaved around the parents still standing on the track. He kept his face straight, almost hard. Esau was leaning against the fence and talking to a parent, so Isaiah stood off to the side and waited. He clenched and released his fists, which hung at his sides, tapping them against his waist. He cast his eyes downward. Then, there by Esau's feet, he spotted his red backpack, and he felt his whole body relax. He stepped forward and picked it up.

"Isaiah. Don't leave your shit out there when we come over here next time," Esau said sternly, and Isaiah nodded and said, "Yes, coach." Then he slung his bag over his shoulders and left the park.

He lived a 10-minute walk from the park, on the western edge of Brownsville, and when people asked him where he lived, he usually said Crown Heights. His daily routine was a tight circle, from home to school to park to home. He rarely strayed from that circle. Perhaps on a Friday night in the fall he'd head to Poly Prep or Lincoln to watch a high school football game with a few coaches and teammates. Perhaps on a Saturday afternoon he'd catch a movie with three or four friends at the big theater in East New York. Every now and then he might spend a few hours at a friend's place playing *Madden* on PlayStation or at a park in Crown Heights shooting hoops. But these were special excursions. And while his mother believed that it was important for boys to develop independence out in the world among themselves, she felt relief each time Isaiah got back home, the one space in her control.

To many in Brownsville, staying indoors was valued almost to the point of being a virtue. Staying indoors meant avoiding the risk of trouble, the older boys on the corner and the stray gunfire. Isaiah took this to heart, and he walked fast down the sidewalk, eyes straight ahead, leaning forward, hands high on his backpack straps, minding his business as he passed the young men leaning against a fence, smoking cigarettes, talking about whatever—their conversation nearly drowned out by the music bumping from speakers on a windowsill down the street, the youthful, intense voice of East Flatbush native Bobby Shmurda ringing through the block.

> *Runnin' through these checks 'til I pass out*
> *And shorty give me neck 'til I pass out*
> *I swear to God, all I do is cash out*
> *And if you ain't a ho, get up out my trap hooooouuuse*
> *I been sellin' crack since like the fifth grade*
> *Really never made no difference what the shit made*

The night was warm and comfortable, and people were out and about on Livonia Avenue, in and out of the corner store, the barbershop, the shoe store, and all the food spots that lined the sidewalks below the elevated train tracks. Light from inside stores poured out the windows, brightening the pavement. Isaiah walked past the panhandlers in front of a pizza place, past the dozen or so sleepy-eyed working folks standing at the bus stop. The train rumbled above, and soon a stream of people flowed down the subway station steps. Isaiah crossed the street and turned down the block on the next corner. A few streetlights were broken, and the sidewalk was darker and emptier. Other pedestrians looked straight ahead with hard faces, and so did Isaiah. He passed brick row houses with the blinds down. He passed an empty lot filled with overgrown grass. He crossed the street, not a car in sight, and reached the front gate to his building, a three-story brick walk-up. The gate clinked when he shut it behind him. He fished his key from the front pocket of his backpack, opened the door, and stepped inside.

GOODBYES
June 2014

Summer practice on Mondays and Wednesdays began at 5:45 p.m., which was tough for Coach Vick. He had to hustle from class to the subway in lower Manhattan and was lucky to arrive less than an hour late. He sometimes showed up still in blue scrubs. April, May, and June were difficult months. Classes were three days a week, from 8:30 a.m. to 5:30 p.m. He'd never been a good student and found that he had to push himself very hard to keep up. He was normally a late sleeper and a late riser, and the new schedule drained him. He sometimes dozed off in class. When he caught his eyelids getting heavy, he'd tell the teacher he had to go to the bathroom. But really, he'd step into the hallway and pump out some push-ups to get his energy back up. "I need a Coach Vick to get on me," he joked.

To pass the medical assistant course, he would need to type at least 30 words per minute. He tested at 17 his first week. He struggled to focus on the lessons and retain the information. When he got home in the evenings, he studied for three hours. "I found I have trouble remembering stuff," he said. "That muscle in my mind hasn't been worked out in a while." The young women he was surrounded by didn't help either. Vick was the oldest in the class, older even than his teacher, and he was the only man. His classmates flirted with him. He loved to flirt, and it was so tempting to engage, but he resisted.

His own children had inspired him to zone in. Two of his sons were graduating high school that spring and had been accepted into four-year colleges. Vick locked himself into a discipline he hadn't known since his football days more than two decades earlier. He began waking up at 6 a.m. to squeeze in extra study time. By his second month, he'd gotten into a rhythm. He was proud of himself. But the dedication had come with sacrifices. He had midterms approaching in a few weeks, so he spent nearly all of his free time in the books. He missed Mitey Mite practice for more than a month straight, leaving his assistant coaches—Elsie, James, and Oscar—in charge. The kids didn't respond to them the way they did to Vick, and practices became sloppy.

Brownsville pulled at Vick even when his mind was on his own challenges. One Monday in early June, he got some terrible news. By chance, classes had been canceled that day, so Vick got to Betsy Head Park before many of his players. He walked quickly across the field, which was nearly empty. The air was warm and breezy beneath a clear blue sky. A nice evening that belied his despair. Vick made his way to Chris, who was leaning against the fence. Vick's face was serious. He smelled as if he had rushed a few Newports on the way to the park.

"Yo, is it true about Kameron?" he said to Chris.

Chris looked at Vick and sighed. He pursed his lips and nodded.

"Yup."

"Damn."

Chris had heard the news at church yesterday. Kameron McKay, 21 years old, a Mo Better football player for eight years, shot in the head at the Brownsville Houses on Friday night. They remembered Kameron fairly well. He played center. He wasn't a kid who hung out on the streets. He wasn't one of the kids they worried about. He had graduated high school, then went to work. He held maintenance jobs at an apartment complex and a packaging plant. Just weeks earlier, he had taken a test to get a commercial driver's license and passed.

"His mom was real strict," Vick said. "I can't understand how he ended up in that shit. It's the neighborhood, man. You can be a good kid."

Vick and Chris were at the funeral three days later, at a big church in East New York. They stood in a long line that snaked down a hallway, around a corner, into a small viewing room, and to the casket, gray and shiny, with white roses on top. Kameron wore a blue denim button-down over a white crew-neck shirt. His hair was freshly cut into a mini Afro. He had a cherubic face. When Kameron's mother had first looked into the casket earlier that morning, her knees had buckled and she had stumbled backward into the wall, sobbing and shaking as two relatives consoled her. But now, as the mourners filed into the church and lined up, she stood beside the casket, composed and graceful, greeting each visitor with a smile, a hug, and a thank you.

From there, the mourners walked slowly into the sanctuary of the church and slid into the pews. Gospel music played on the speakers. Gray light from the overcast morning streamed through the windows in the steeple. Screens above the altar showed photos of Kameron: leaning against a pool table, sitting beside a birthday cake, swimming in a pool, dancing in a white T-shirt, holding baby nieces and nephews, wearing a tuxedo at a wedding, standing beneath the Borough Hall subway station sign with his arms spread wide, kneeling with a football in his arm wearing his purple and gold Mo Better Jaguars uniform. Dozens of young men sat in the pews watching the images flash across the screen. Some wore dress shirts and leather shoes. Others wore jeans, sneakers, and track jackets. After a few minutes, one of the young men, a lean 20-something in a long pinstriped shirt, stomped his foot on the ground—a loud echo through the quiet sanctuary—and buried his face in his hands. Then he stood up, turned, and marched down the aisle, his face flexed and hard as if trying to keep from crying. When he stepped out the front doors of the church, he released and burst into tears. He leaned forward against the brick wall and cried. On the sidewalk a few feet behind him, six police officers stood watch.

∞∞∞

WITH SCHOOL OUT for the summer, Gio's mother feared what would happen to her son. He had already stopped coming to practice. His absences from home were becoming longer and more frequent. Now, he had two months of free time ahead.

When she reflected on it, she was stunned by how fast things had gotten bad. She and her son could barely hold a conversation anymore— at least one that didn't turn into an upsetting argument. She got stricter, held the line on the rules she'd set, made threats to send him away. He resisted her efforts. She was at a loss. All the more troubling were the vague anecdotes he told her about the boys who were trying to jump him. She came to the heartbreaking realization that she was no longer capable of taking care of her son. For the sake of his future, and her own mental health, she believed her son needed to live elsewhere. She believed it would only get worse if he stayed. Foster care was an appealing answer. There'd be guardians with experience handling problem kids and family court judges setting and enforcing boundaries. Perhaps it would be the shock Gio needed to get himself back on track.

She wondered how different their situation would be if she'd landed in another neighborhood. It was a common thought. Many parents believed Brownsville was holding their children back. At least several others with kids on Mo Better were trying to move out of the neighborhood. Coach James saved money from his job as a late-night pizza deliveryman in hopes of getting his family a place in Crown Heights, Flatbush, or somewhere in Queens. Puerto Rico's mother, Alicia, aimed to take her family to Miami, where her brother lived and affordable housing was easier to find. Many more wanted to leave one day, but had no immediate plans because they didn't have the means to live anywhere else.

∞∞∞∞∞

Gio, like every kid in America, was excited for summer. He envisioned long, lazy days with friends in apartments free from adults, who were away at work. He'd had a hectic few months. Though he'd been skipping school on occasion, he had also recommitted himself to passing his classes. Coach Chris had convinced him that football talent couldn't get him very far if he was a failing student. So, Gio made sure to do his homework, even if it kept him up late. He always showed up on exam days. He didn't sacrifice his social life, but he worked hard, and by the end he had a decent report card to show his mother. She was pleased at the progress but believed he'd underachieved. He was smart enough for better-than-decent scores.

Even without homework and daily responsibilities, Gio didn't expect a summer without stress. His conflict with the rival boys had not cooled. He walked around the neighborhood with his head on a swivel and avoided being outside alone. It was possible the rival boys were just trying to intimidate him and had no taste for violence. But Gio had no desire to call their bluff. There were times, quite often actually, when he felt like he was drowning, swept up in a current, drifting into the deep middle of the river without first learning how to swim. He mostly kept these thoughts to himself, hiding them behind a mask of courage, toughness, and self-sufficiency. The mask had become such an essential tool that it was fair to ask if he still knew how to remove it.

His mother had seen too much. Early in the summer, she decided on a plan for Gio's future. He was unhappy with the plan but didn't put up a big fight. His brother convinced him it was the right thing to do. Gio packed his clothes into a duffel bag, loaded it into his mother's car, and they drove off, onto the highway and into Queens. When it was time to leave, he hugged his mother and brother, and they said their goodbyes. Gio made his way through the airport, boarded the plane, and, after a few hours, was back in Saint Lucia. He didn't know when he'd see his old Mo Better teammates again.

PART II

FOOTBALL

– 10 –

THE DAYS AND NIGHTS OF SUMMER
June–July 2014

BOYS LEFT THE TEAM, BOYS JOINED THE TEAM. THE COMing season was on the horizon, the first game less than 10 weeks away. If Hart had learned anything from the past year, it was that success was never assured, a memorable lesson for an 11-year-old whose life experiences had otherwise provided much evidence that hard work and talent necessarily led to the achievement of goals. Circumstances, it turned out, could make all the difference—especially in a game where even the best player relied on the competence of his 10 teammates on the field. After the disappointment of the previous season, Hart entered the summer of 2014 feeling grateful for the circumstances around him. Though he missed Oomz, he believed that his Pee Wee team was good enough to win a championship even without his talented friend. Skilled players, some with years of experience, occupied nearly every position in the starting lineup. It was an opportunity Hart was determined not to squander.

He arrived at practice with high hopes on this Wednesday in late June. School was out and the day was warm and clear. Cheerful and chatty, the Pee Wees stood and sat around the cement light post by the fence, pulling on their cleats, zipping up their bags, and arguing about basketball, a passionate debate triggered when Hart told his teammates that he didn't like LeBron James.

"What you think Coach Esau?" said Time Out, the shortest boy on the team.

"LeBron played football," said Esau. "Iverson too. That's why they so tough."

"Michael Jordan didn't play football," countered Hart.

"That's why he soft," said Esau.

"Michael Jordan soft?" said Hart, his voice high pitched and skeptical, his eyebrows raised. "He got a lotta money, though."

"So what?" said Esau. "Bill Gates got a lotta money."

Hart nodded, taking in the information, crafting a response in his head. He'd spent the previous week out of town with his family. They went to Alabama, where his mother's parents lived in a big house on several acres of land. Hart loved the space and lying in the grass. His dad was back on his feet, on crutches, and well enough to play catch. For Hart, the summer was relaxing, refreshing, filled with the uninhibited joy of knowing the good times of today were guaranteed to continue tomorrow. He was a happy child, and he felt right in his element, preparing to play football on a dusty field, engaged in a battle of wits with his football coach. But before Hart could fire back a response, Esau shouted, "All right, on the track! Two laps!" The boys jogged off the field, formed two lines on the track, and began the run.

The Pee Wees were halfway around the track when Oomz strolled into the park. He passed the benches, went through the gate, and stepped onto the field. His chest was puffed, his back straight, his head tilted slightly back and to the side, and his legs and hips waddled forward. Oomz had a walk like no other boy on the team. It was a confident, flat-footed walk, a walk in no hurry, and Oomz capped it with off the amused smirk he often wore. Miss Elsie spotted him first.

"Oooooommzzzzz!" she shouted.

She shuffled over to him and hugged him tightly, rocking side to side in excitement.

"Hey, Miss Elsie," Oomz said, grinning wide.

"It's been so long!" said Elsie, releasing him from the embrace, then straightening the purple pantsuit she'd worn to work that day. "Why we don't see you no more? Why you don't come say hi?"

Oomz shrugged.

"You here to pick up your birth certificate?"

The coaches still had Oomz's birth certificate, required to confirm a player's age, in their files. Elsie and the others had figured he'd be back at some point to pick it up. He couldn't play on his new team without it.

"Nah, Miss Elsie," Oomz said. "I'm coming back."

Elsie let out a cheer and shot her arms into the air in excitement, then hugged him even tighter. The Pee Wees were all looking over there now as they rounded the track. Hart figured out what was happening, and behind his facemask a smile widened. Later, after practice, he said to anybody who'd listen, "Nobody beating us this year."

∞∞∞

BIG OOMZ'S PLAN to form a team hadn't worked out. Not enough kids had joined, and the logistics of organizing a staff, ordering uniforms, and scheduling opponents required more time than he was able to find. Instead, he sent Oomz to another program, the Brooklyn Saints. Some of Big Oomz's favorite coaches from his Mo Better days were on the Saints. They'd left Mo Better to start their own program a few years back, and Big Oomz felt closer to these men than to the current Mo Better staff. Oomz's new team began practicing late in the spring. Progress was slow. Their numbers remained low when summer hit, and the talent was limited. Many of the boys had never played before. The result was that Oomz had to play quarterback. No other boy was capable enough to handle the position's responsibilities. Oomz didn't like playing quarterback. He didn't like having to take the snap from between the center's legs every play. He didn't like throwing the ball and didn't have an accurate arm anyway. And he damn sure didn't like handing the ball off to someone else, someone weaker and more hesitant, only to see the boy get dragged down by hits he could've handled. Oomz wanted that action. Oomz was a running back. So, Oomz became unhappy. "The kids just wasn't good like they were at Mo Better," he said. "I didn't want to be there no more."

He tried to hide this unhappiness when he ran into his old Mo Better coaches around the neighborhood. He'd see Vick or Esau in the hallways of his school, and they'd say what's up, ask him how he was doing. Some days, Oomz would run into Coach James on the streets. They lived a few blocks from each other. "We want you back Oomz," James would say to him. "When you coming back?" And he'd give Oomz a handshake and a big hug. The coaches all showed him a lot of love, even when he said he wasn't coming back. He appreciated that. He missed them and missed practices at Betsy Head. He told his father he wanted to go back to Mo Better. "I was thinking about how I been playing here for so long, and then I bailed out on them," he said. At first, his father resisted. But his father was no fool and understood where Oomz was coming from. Soon, he gave in, and there was Oomz strolling into Betsy Head.

The Pee Wees gathered around him. He slapped hands with nearly all of them. He grinned, and the attention seemed to fuel his confidence further.

"Yeah, yeah, I'm back, I'm back," he said, nodding his head.

He arrived early at the next practice, joked with his teammates by the light post, ran the two laps with them, and lined up shoulder to shoulder facing Esau, who assigned them one by one to their position on the offense.

"Oomz," said Esau, looking away from the team and toward some invisible formation he was imagining, piecing together, on the empty and dry grass. "Go to—"

"It's Javuan," Oomz cut in.

"Huh?" said Esau, turning his head back to the team.

"My name's Javuan."

"OK. Javuan," Esau said, smiling now. "Why don't you like the name Oomz?"

"It's a gang name."

And just then a teammate next to Oomz turned to him and shouted, "Oooomz!"

Oomz shoved his forearm into the boy's neck and pushed him backward.

"What's Oomz, my father or me?" he said forcefully, anger in his voice.

"All right, all right," the boy said.

"Oom—I mean, Javuan!" Esau said, and Oomz backed off the boy. "Go to running back."

With his father back home, Oomz had felt a stronger sense of how much his nickname did not belong to him. People on the street or coming over to their house were not calling his father "Big Oomz" or "Oomz Sr." but simply "Oomz." Oomz wondered if perhaps he should earn his own name, though his distaste for his long-held moniker didn't last more than a couple of weeks. While he was glad to have his father around, it was an adjustment. "They butted heads not long after his father got back," Oomz's grandmother, Monique, said. Big Oomz, who now lived with his girlfriend in Marcus Garvey Village and was still looking for a job several months after his return, was strict with his son, banning him from video games and TV if he scored poorly on a test or talked disrespectfully to adults. "Oomz was used to his grandmother spoiling him," Monique said. The son had inherited his father's strong personality and stubborn tendencies, and so the two clashed—nothing major, but an ongoing state of frustrating disputes.

His father wanted to play an active role in his life and resisted anything that might get in the way of that. Specifically, he wanted Oomz to continue his education in Brownsville, at the gifted-and-talented school where he had been an honor student, where he was a short walk from his grandmother's house and his father's apartment. Oomz's mother, Tasha, was making moves to get Oomz into a new charter school opening up in Fort Greene, where she now lived, a gentrified but racially diverse upper-middle-class neighborhood near downtown Brooklyn. Monique supported the decision. She believed that a boy growing up in Brownsville didn't get enough exposure to society and its different cultures, and that that could set him back as he got older. Crucially, she believed, he wasn't exposed to enough white people. She believed that understanding how to deal with white people was key to success.

"Our children need to see a little diversity," she said. "As they grow up in the world, they need to be able to relate to different types of people. When you don't understand other people, that's when ignorance starts to creep in."

Monique's great-grandfather had arrived in New York City from Jamaica in the 1920s. He raised his family in the nearby neighborhood of Bed-Stuy through the Great Depression. In the postwar boom, he got a good factory job, and his kids grew up and found decent work. By the time Monique was born in 1969, the neighborhoods had begun to change. Heroin had emerged on the streets, crime was rising, and New York City's darkest time was dawning. Her family moved to Brownsville, and she watched the crack epidemic begin its destruction. When she was 15, as the city's murder rate reached new highs and the country ramped up its War on Drugs, she had a son. She got him through the worst of the years, when murder numbers were at their highest, and by the time he reached high school, the city's crime rate had begun to drop. The social and economic conditions in Brownsville, however, hadn't changed much otherwise.

The circumstances pulled down her son, and she worried the same would happen to her grandson. "The pressures are even greater for my grandson than they were for my son," she said. "With the Internet and social media and all that. People putting their lives up for everybody to see, all these influences coming at them that you don't know about. Those social influences are so important."

She'd heard about boys repping their crews online, starting trouble, talking trash, and sometimes turning to violence. She believed that those boys and their influence were not much different from the boys in nice sneakers and gold chains out on the streets a generation earlier—only now their jeans fit a little tighter and they favored dreadlocks over cornrows.

"You gotta keep them away from that pressure as best you can," she said. "If not, the streets will get them, the system will get them, and then there's nothing you can do about it."

This was why she had supported Tasha's efforts to pull Oomz out of Brownsville, away from its pressures. Big Oomz, though, didn't like this plan. He had pride in his longtime neighborhood and believed Brownsville taught lessons Fort Greene couldn't, especially with him there to guide his son away from wrong paths he knew well. Over the months since he had come back from jail, Big Oomz had given his son many lectures about "staying off the streets," Oomz said, "and telling me what's going on out there." Big Oomz pleaded his case about keeping his son in Brownsville, but Tasha had the final say on the matter. If the new charter school in Fort Greene accepted Oomz, he'd attend in the fall.

Oomz wanted to go to Fort Greene. Before one summer practice, as Oomz and his teammates put on their cleats by the light post, they overheard a parent tell another parent about a nice restaurant he and his wife had gone to in Fort Greene over the weekend.

"Fort Greene," Oomz said to his teammates. "That's where I live."

ooooo

Monique watched the boys line up shoulder to shoulder. She leaned her elbows on the fence around the field, just as she had two decades before, when her own son ran across this field. "He's not as good as his dad yet," Monique said, eyes on her grandson. "Not yet. I think he will be. He got to get a little more aggressive. When his dad was growing up, those boys were so much more aggressive." The fathers and mothers alongside Monique had not seen those Mo Better days, only heard about them. They were younger than Monique and their sons had come to the program in more recent years. They didn't expect the 60–0 dominance of a past generation. But they did expect a league championship and maybe a regional championship and, if they were truly blessed, a trip to Florida for a chance at the national championship. They had been very disappointed by last year's struggles, but they believed that the losing had made their boys stronger, had made them hate and fear the feeling of losing so much that they would dedicate themselves to avoiding it. They would run harder during workouts and stay focused throughout practice. The parents were optimistic. They saw much talent out on the field.

Some of the parents sat in lawn chairs and others leaned back against the chain-link fence that separated the field area from the basketball and handball blacktops. It was Saturday morning in the summer. The handball courts were alive with middle-aged women in sneakers, tights, and T-shirts, dancing to the R&B music blaring from a boom box as a woman with a megaphone led them through exercise movements. On the basketball courts, a group of teenagers played two-on-two, the sound of their dribbling drowned out by the music. On the field, Coach Esau's voice pierced through the noise.

"Run the play!" he said to the boys lined up on offense. Naz, the quarterback, took the snap and turned to hand the ball to Isaiah, who took a smooth hop step to the side, like a cheetah recoiling before a chase, then snatched the handoff and ran up the field.

"Ohhhhkaaayyy, you got that bounce to it!" Esau said to Isaiah. "He been watching ESPN. Got that bounce to it. Ohhhhkaaayyy!"

Esau smiled. He scanned the field and nodded his head. This was maybe the most talented team he'd ever coached, he thought. There was Isaiah, of course. But there was also Chaka, the tall and fast wide receiver from Marcus Garvey Village, who Coach Chris predicted would be the most prized college football prospect out of this bunch. There was Naz, from Bed-Stuy, who, at 11 years old, could throw a football farther than some high school quarterbacks. There was Hart, from Queens, the smart and solid core of the team's offensive and defensive lines. There was Dorian, the sturdy linebacker from New Jersey, and Lamont, the big and quiet lineman, and Time Out, the tiny but quick Swiss Army knife, who over his several years at Mo Better had played quarterback, running back, tight end, defensive end, cornerback, safety, and linebacker.

The Pee Wees had gained new talent, as well—two players in particular. Donnie had impressed coaches throughout the spring with his strength and instincts, and though Donnie was small for his age and didn't know much about the rules of the game, Esau believed he'd make a good defensive tackle with a couple more months of practice. He was raw, with no finesse in his moves. Many of the Pee Wees already knew this from the pickup tackle football games they'd played with Donnie at the park in recent weeks. When he had the ball, he bulled forward in slow, choppy steps until enough defenders piled on to bring him down. When he didn't have the ball, he collided with the nearest opponent, thrusting his shoulder like he was trying to bust open a door.

The other player was a boy named Marquis, who joined them at the start of the summer. He had drawn stares from his teammates at his first practice. While the rest of the boys wore just T-shirts and basketball shorts, Marquis fitted his look with the full range of accessories: Nike gloves, a white Nike towel hanging from his shorts, a camo-patterned sleeve on his right arm, knee-high yellow-and-white striped socks, and black leg bands just above his shins. One boy joked that he looked like a customized create-a-player from the *Madden* football video game. But at that first practice, Marquis backed up his loud look with loud skills and quickly won the respect of his new teammates. Marquis lived in South Jamaica, Queens, and had played running back for a program in a Nassau County youth football league on Long Island. His coach had named him the team's MVP three straight years. He'd been much better than the boys around him and had become bored at practice. "That's when you gotta throw 'em to the wolves," his father, Ramsey, said. Ramsey and Marquis decided he needed to play with and against better players in order to keep improving his skills, in order to become good enough to earn a scholarship to a private high school. "I can't afford private school, but I'm definitely not sending him to a public school," said Ramsey, a bus driver at the Rikers Island jail facility. He heard about Mo Better and decided to make the 40-minute commute to Betsy Head.

Ramsey was impressed by what he saw: the speed, the focus, the discipline, the toughness. He sat on a lawn chair, among the other fathers and mothers, as Coach Esau excused the boys for a water break. Oomz and Chaka raced to the water fountain, then raced back, snickering as they joined the rest of their teammates sipping water bottles and Gatorade around the light post, where several fathers had walked over to talk to their sons.

"Oomz!" said Dorian's father, Dwight, with a smile.

Oomz smiled back bashfully. Dwight extended a hand and they slapped palms.

"You a leader on this team," Dwight said. "You gotta lead this year. You got too much talent to throw it away. You got a lot of talent. Lead by example. Go hard in practice. You see somebody slacking, give 'em a tap. You a leader out here."

Oomz nodded, a proud and serious nod, and they slapped hands again. Oomz was starting to embrace his role as a leader. He was a different sort of leader from Isaiah, who was older but quieter. Isaiah led by his actions, with work ethic and discipline that others strove to meet. Oomz was loud. Oomz called people out. He pointed out when he saw boys jump offside and told them to do push-ups. He yelled at boys who were whispering to each other while Coach Esau was talking. He yelled at boys who were walking off the field when they were supposed to be running. When a boy slowed down before the finish line during end-of-practice sprints, Oomz said to him, "You didn't listen! He said run all the way and you slowed down!" He made sure he was at the front of the line during warm-ups and again when the boys lined up in two columns to walk off the field at the end of practice. "Stay in two lines!" he ordered, before leading the march one afternoon, and when he saw that the columns were crooked, he said, "Stop, stop, stop!" and told Isaiah to go down the line and straighten everybody up.

His teammates respected him, in part, because he didn't set such a high standard of work ethic and discipline. While the Pee Wees looked up to Isaiah, they saw Oomz more as one of them. He was occasionally late to practice. He sometimes walked off the field when he should have been running. He goofed around. Yet his teammates didn't consider his leadership hypocritical. Instead, his faults gave him more credibility. When he got serious, his teammates followed.

Oomz was the team's center of gravity, the one who loosened the mood, the one the others looked to for judgment on style. He offered tips on how to talk to girls and decided what game they all played after practice. Isaiah was the team's wise statesman. Oomz was the homecoming king. Together, the coaches believed, they could lift the Pee Wees to become one of the program's best teams in recent years. Oomz had always been charming and popular, but in the past his anger and gloom had overshadowed the rest of personality. The Oomz they were seeing this summer was different. He smiled more. He seemed to take practice more seriously and enjoy it more. The coaches observed Oomz hold court with his teammates one early summer afternoon. They stood too far away to hear, but they watched Oomz crack a joke and saw the other boys break into laughter, their young faces carefree, their hands making lively gestures.

"He was arrogant last year," Chris said. "He was lazy too, and he didn't follow directions."

"He thought he could do all that 'cause he was the star running back," Esau said.

"He had a lot of anger in him," Chris said.

"He's a lot different now, ain't he?" Elsie said. "He looks so much more happy."

"Mm-hmm," hummed Chris. "It's probably 'cause his father's back."

The coaches had seen many times the way anger could overwhelm a boy, could hang over him endlessly like thickening smog and poison every piece of his essence. They had seen it cause indifference and apathy. They had seen it drive boys to violence. They had seen it turn sweet and warm boys into hard and cold young men. The coaches saw the anger take root at its earliest stages, before boys were able to recognize it themselves and perhaps learn to control it. The coaches felt helpless in the face of that anger. They could try to give a boy space to get his mind off of it. They could show him a love to compete with it. They could help a boy channel it into the controlled violence of football. But they could do little to strip him of it. The sources of the anger—the turmoil in the household, the bloodshed on the streets, the unrequited wants of poverty, the vague sense of being trapped in a world of struggle, or the convergence of all of these forces and more—floated through Betsy Head like the dust kicked up from the dry dirt.

The anger simmered beneath the laughs and smiles on this overcast Thursday afternoon. The Pee Wees, in T-shirts and shorts, formed two parallel lines, facing each other, for a blocking drill. On the stage, between the lines, two boys went on offense and two on defense. One of the boys on offense carried the ball and the other, his blocker, had to clear the way for him. The boys on defense held large foam shields, with which they tried to hit the boy carrying the ball. It was a physical drill even though the boys weren't wearing pads. On the first run-through, Isaiah hit Donnie so hard with the shield that he knocked him over. The coaches and the other boys cheered, and Donnie laughed as he pushed himself back onto his feet. Isaiah's shield landed with a loud *smack!* each time he went, and Coach Chris made sure to harden all of the team's best players with a round against Isaiah.

"Now that's a tough guy!" Chris shouted, after Isaiah bumped another boy off his feet.

Then it was Chaka's turn. On Chaka's first attempt holding the shield, the blocker easily drove him backward, clearing a wide path for the ballcarrier. "Again, Chaka, again!" Chris ordered. And on the next go, Chaka again was driven backward. To Chris, it looked like he'd barely put up a fight. "You gotta get tougher!" Chris shouted. "Do it again!" The third go was worse than the second, and this time, after getting driven back three or four yards, Chaka dropped the shield and walked off the drill. "Yo! Stay on the bag!" Chris shouted. But Chaka kept walking toward the line of teammates at the edge of the drill. "Back on the bag!" Chaka kept walking, past the line of teammates, past the coaches standing behind them, and it became clear that Chaka could hear the orders and was ignoring them.

The Pee Wees watched in silence. They watched Chaka walk slowly toward the gate on the far side of the park. They watched Coach Chris follow, march right up next to him, lean into his ear and say, loud enough for all the boys to hear, "You gon' quit?" They watched Chaka keep his eyes straight ahead and say nothing. Then they watched him pull off his purple mesh jersey and throw it on the ground. "So you quitting?" Chris said. "This ain't babysitting camp!" Chris turned from Chaka and marched back to the drill, hands on his hips, shaking his head.

Isaiah, his mouth open and his eyebrows raised in shock, turned to Marquis and whispered, "What happened?"

Still watching Chaka with wide and worried eyes, Marquis shrugged.

ooooo

THE ANGER BOILS and cools. At the next practice, two days later, Chaka was in good spirits, as if nothing had happened. The other boys didn't bring it up. The coaches didn't bring it up. They all understood. "Chaka must have had something going on in his life," Coach James said. "It got to him, and he just needed to vent it out." They didn't know the details, and they didn't ask. Chaka tried to keep a hard front, but he was a sensitive boy. When he saw old friends drop by Betsy Head, he leaped over the fence to greet them on the track. When somebody extended a left hand for a high five, he called him out with, "Other hand, man. Supposed to be the right hand. It's rude to use your left."

His father was in prison, he lived in the housing projects where a 1-year-old had been killed months before, and he was a 12-year-old boy, on the verge of puberty and in the midst of middle school's social pressures. To his coaches and teammates, the precise source of his anger at that particular moment on Thursday afternoon was his business, and the important thing was that he was back on Saturday.

He remained in good spirits when practice ended and a dozen boys gathered for a pickup football game.

"Yo, is it tackle or touch?" Chaka asked.

"It's tackle," said Oomz.

"Nah, watch when somebody get hurt!"

"We playin' tackle!"

As the game began, four preteen girls, passing through Betsy Head, parked themselves along the fence to watch. They shared a bag of chips and a bag of sunflower seeds. They watched several boys dive after a football bouncing on the ground, and they gasped at how the boys jumped on top of each other, forming a pile of bodies.

"It's so crazy the way they go for that ball!" one girl said.

She pointed at Chaka, who had stayed out of the pile.

"See that boy in the black shirt?"

"Yeah."

"He good."

"Oh yeah?"

"He like a basketball star, right?"

"He hot."

"I like that other boy, with the long hair," said another girl, pointing at a 10-year-old named Masiah.

"Oh, Masiah?"

"Yeah. He's 10. And it's weird 'cause usually I like older guys."

"He's 10?"

"Yeah. I'm 12."

And the girls giggled.

The boys knew the girls were watching, of course, but they didn't stare. Instead, they trash-talked louder among one another. "Go, ugly!" Chaka shouted at Donnie. "You slow!" Oomz shouted at Chaka. The boys tried to play it cool. When Chaka caught the ball, he held it in the palm of his hand—like a loaf of bread, a coach would have grumbled—and jogged up the field nonchalantly, smiling wistfully as if the sport were just so easy, and then, when a defender got near, he sprinted past him for a touchdown. Then he peeked over at the girls, just a quick glance, before strutting back for the next play.

Only Oomz had the nerve to acknowledge the girls, and as they watched the boys line up for the next play, he turned to them and shouted, "Brittany! You playin'?"

The four girls smiled.

"No!" she shouted back.

"Brittany don't wanna lose!" Oomz teased, grinning at the girls.

The girls left the park long before the boys finished playing. When the boys tired out, more than an hour after practice had ended, they slapped hands and dispersed. Oomz took a puff from his inhaler, changed out of his cleats, and headed toward his grandmother's house. He went inside and lay down on the living room couch. Soon his grandma and father arrived. They watched ESPN. There was a report on about retired NFL players demanding more information from the league about long-term brain damage. Oomz asked his grandma and his father what was going on. "Players are getting concussions," his grandma said, "and when they retire, they don't do so well." She told him that there had been cases of depression, that some players had killed themselves, and that scientists had linked the suicides to the brain damage. To Oomz, though, those concerns seemed distant. These men had played for many years and had played until they neared middle age, he assumed. He didn't think these reports had much to do with him. The thought of not playing football didn't enter his mind. He had always played football. His father had always played football. Most of the adults he had looked up to all his life had always played football. He remembered when he was young, and his uncle's friends came over to the house. One of his uncle's closest friends was their neighbor, Poppa, who had been Mo Better's star quarterback. He remembered how cool he thought Poppa was, this well-dressed, big-shot young man who took the time to play with him. And Oomz remembered how he wanted to be a football star one day, just like his dad, just like his neighbor Poppa.

ooooo

NATHANIEL "POPPA" GRAVENHISE was killed on July 3. He was shot walking down the street in Crown Heights at around 7:45 p.m. Coach Chris got word early the next morning. He went to Poppa's mother's house and gave his condolences. He knew the family well. Poppa was Coach Gary's nephew. Five of Poppa's brothers and cousins had passed through Mo Better. Poppa had played on Mo Better for nearly a decade, just about half his life. He had listened to hundreds of Chris's speeches.

On July 5, Chris arrived at practice dispirited. The summer morning was cooler than normal, with clouds blocking the sun and a breeze blowing in. Chris leaned back against the fence and watched the boys warm up on the dry grass. He made efforts to know what went on in the boys' lives beyond the field. He asked questions, about school, about who they'd been hanging out with, about what seemed to be bothering them. The older a boy got, the less he opened up. The older boys, the 11- and 12- and 13-year-olds, preferred one-word answers and shrugs, or scripted lines that fit their perception of what Chris wanted to hear. This was a constant frustration for Chris. He wondered what lay beneath the hard shells of these boys. He knew the statistics: a black boy born in 2001 had a one-in-three chance of going to prison, while a white boy born that year had just a 6 percent chance; that murder was the top cause of death for black boys and men from age 15 to 34. His best efforts had failed many times before, and he wondered whether maybe it was all just fate and chance, whether maybe his own pull could not compete with those forces.

The boys gathered under the tree when practice was done. Chris told them the news about Poppa.

"How old was he?" one boy asked.

"He was 19."

He told them Poppa had helped lead the program to league championships. He nearly led the team to Florida for a shot at the national championship in his Junior Midget season. With 40 seconds left in the regional championship game, his teammate returned a kickoff for what appeared to be the game-winning touchdown, but a referee called a holding penalty, negating the score, and the team lost. "Everybody still talks about it," Chris said. He told the boys that Poppa was generous and popular. He told them that Coach Gary would be taking some time off to grieve and spend time with his family, and that if they saw him around the neighborhood they should show him some love. Chris spoke softly and slowly at first, but then his voice grew louder and turned forceful. He had lost kids before and it hurt more and more each time, he said to the boys. He didn't want to lose any more.

"When you go to high school, you can pick the path that goes to Harvard, or what?" he said.

The boys looked on silently. Oomz wore a look of indifference, fiddling with the bottom of his T-shirt, but he felt badly hurt by Poppa's death. *It's not right that that could happen*, he'd thought the day before, after his grandmother told him the news. To memorialize his friend, Oomz changed his Facebook profile picture to a photo of Poppa. He was vaguely aware of Poppa's ties to the streets, and after his grandmother explained how Poppa died, his father gave him a fresh lecture about staying off the streets, about veering away from the paths he and Poppa had taken. Big Oomz knew well how swiftly and completely a boy could be swept up by the neighborhood's crews and beefs. His son understood it too. During Oomz's first practice back with Mo Better that summer, four boys on bikes had rolled up to the field. They were Oomz's age and they knew him and a few other Pee Wees from around the neighborhood. A couple of them had been on the team in years past. The boys parked their bikes beside where the players were standing. They greeted Oomz, Time Out, and Chaka. Oomz had been holding a football; one of the boys called for the ball, and the two of them played catch. Oomz engaged the boys, but coldly. He kept an eye on the field, trying to pay attention to practice, but they didn't seem to get the hint. The coaches, with their strict open-gate policy, didn't ask the boys to leave or get mad at the players who spoke with them.

Chris watched the interactions warily. Eventually, after a few minutes, he turned to Oomz, Time Out, and Chaka and said, "Ay, come over here," as if he had some new play or strategy to show them, though his only aim was to pull them away from the boys with the bikes. The three players slapped hands with the visiting boys, then jogged over to Chris. One of the boys said condescendingly, "Oh, they got you like that?"

Oomz knew the boy was calling him a sucker. In some communities, boys face a social pressure to play football: The sport is a ticket to popularity and validation. It makes life easier—maybe some teachers give you a passing grade because you're good at football, maybe other boys look up to you because you play. For Oomz and his peers, the pressure was reversed. "The easy path is the one where you stop playing sports and go out with your friends after school. Sleep in on weekends. Too cool to be taking something so seriously," Vick said. Or as Chris put it, "This neighborhood, it can suck you up like a vacuum." Like in any community, the pressure picked up as a boy approached his teens, developed a self-consciousness, and started thinking about the clothes he wore and who was cool and who wasn't cool and who the girls were hanging out with. "It's a turning-point age," said Justin Cotton, who coached at Mo Better for 15 years.

The neighborhood pressures affected every boy. TJ, an 11-year-old who'd played on the Junior Pee Wees the previous year, came from a stable family in Brownsville that spent many hours every Saturday at a

Seventh-day Adventist church. He was enrolled in a big brother program. He joined an African dance group. He attended a top-notch charter school in East New York, where he pulled As and Bs. He'd already made a list of his top three college choices. When an adult asked him one day if he was going to stay off the streets, he said, "Yes." Then, after a beat, he added, "Probably." He paused. "I'll try." Another pause. "I don't know. Just probably. Because, I just . . . I might, like . . . I'm trying to see a way to put it." He contemplated for a few seconds. "I might, like, one day get in trouble," he said. "I know people that get in trouble. Like I got into a situation when my cousin, he got in trouble, and the people he got in trouble with were looking for me. My cousin told me, 'Watch your back.' I tried to tell him, like, stop being in a gang and stuff. I dunno. He said probably, probably not."

The pressure derailed the football careers of Big Oomz, Dajuan Mitchell, Vick Davis, and many others. "Stay off them streets," boys like Oomz and Gio and Isaiah heard all the time. But staying off the streets required skill and finesse; navigating the gauntlet meant understanding it. "Knowing where to walk and where not to walk," said Ellis, a 19-year-old Brownsville native. "Knowing how to act and how not to act." The boys internalized the necessary survival tactics. Which is why Isaiah walked home quickly and with his eyes straight ahead, and why Oomz shoved a forearm into the chest of a boy who disrespected him. It took a hardness to stay ahead.

That hardness didn't always play well outside the neighborhood. Erica Mateo, a 25-year-old from Brownsville, remembered her first day in the cafeteria at Bard College, a liberal-arts school in upstate New York. A girl next to her reached across to grab the saltshaker, accidentally brushing her elbow on Erica's arm. Erica blew up at the girl, got in her face and shouted her down. The whole cafeteria went quiet. "And everybody was just judging me, and they were all probably thinking I wasn't smart," she said. "It's a tough adjustment. Because you've been thinking one way for so long, and then suddenly you're out in the world and it takes a minute to realize that the rest of the world doesn't work like that." Some boys, like Isaiah and Oomz, learned to operate successfully in both worlds, to code switch. Some, like Donnie, wore their hardness at all times.

When everyone and everything is hard, there is no room for mistakes. Poppa's death was a reminder of that. It saddened the community and injected fear. Brownsville locals remembered what happened after Poppa's brother had been gunned down a few years before. "It was a war going on outside," Erica said. Locals worried the cycle of retaliation would begin again. As Chris left Betsy Head after practice, his mind was already on Poppa's memorial service in a few days. "Gonna be like Al Capone's funeral," he said. "All those cops."

ooooo

THE TRAGEDY PUT Oomz into a reflective state. He left practice that night thinking about his future. His younger cousin, Tymeke, walked with him toward their grandmother's house up the block from the park, dribbling a basketball while he reassured Oomz that his future was bright.

"You good at football like your dad," Tymeke said.

"I wanna be like him, but I could do better. I wanna play like him, but I wanna go farther than him."

"He teach you anything?"

"He told me keep my head up, get low, make a move, but don't make too much moves. One cut and go."

"You think you'll play in the pros?"

"I wanna be a football or basketball player, but if that don't work out, I wanna be a scientist I guess."

"Why?"

"Everybody got a point in life when they got death," Oomz said. "I wanna make people live as long as they want to."

They crossed the street outside the park and turned onto Strauss Street. Oomz slapped the ball out of Tymeke's hand and took over the dribbling responsibilities, keeping it away from the bumps and potholes in the sidewalk. Some of the houses he passed had neat lawns and potted flowers on patios that were caged in by iron bars. Other houses had weedy yards and patios cluttered with rusty furniture. A few looked vacant, with boarded-up windows and broken doors. Oomz had lived in Brownsville his whole life, and he didn't like it.

"I wanna move outta this neighborhood," he said. "Because there's too much violence. I don't know where I wanna move to, but outta here."

ooooo

POPPA'S MEMORIAL SERVICE was on July 10 at Grace Funeral Chapels in East New York. An NYPD van parked on a grassy field across the street, lights flashing, two cops watching from the front seat. Threats of revenge had popped up within hours of Poppa's murder. That night, one former Mo Better player, who was now a star wide receiver for his high school team, posted on Facebook: "hahaha ya took pop fuck y'all think imma do now lols #ripmyrealbropop." Another teen commented on the post: "Owe BigTime." Another: "Dead ass." Another: "Facts I got da perfect plan."

Anger filled the funeral home. In the second row of the chapel, three teenagers, all in white T-shirts and jeans, cried behind sunglasses. One boy stood over the casket, a pack of Newports in his hand, looking down at Poppa, who was dressed in a blue shirt. Silver balloons floated above the casket. The boy then turned around, his face anguished and holding back tears, and stormed down the aisle. Three more boys followed him, their fists balled, their faces hard. Two adults quickly stood up. "I'll go that way, you go that way," one woman said to the other, and they hustled out of the chapel and into the hallway and corralled the boys around a set of couches. One boy collapsed on the couch and began sobbing. A woman put her arm around him and whispered into his ear, slowly rocking him back and forth. Another boy leaned back and looked up at the ceiling, tears dripping from his eyes. Two others leaned forward, their faces in their hands, their bodies shaking.

The line of mourners marched past the boys on the couches and into the chapel. Poppa's girlfriend sat in the front row, the mourners hugging her on their way to the casket. She was seven months pregnant. The last thing Poppa had posted on Facebook, a month before his death, was a photo of him kissing her belly.

∞∞∞

THREE DAYS LATER, Poppa's 19-year-old brother Clayton Graven-hise shot and killed 17-year-old Beverly Turner in Bed-Stuy. He later told police that she was a cousin of the man he believed had killed his brother. A month after that, on August 29, Clayton opened fire inside a liquor store in Brownsville. A 20-year-old woman was wounded. Jahzeph Crooks, a 19-year-old student at Saint John's University, was killed. Clayton later told police that he was aiming at another young man inside the store, the young man he believed had killed his brother.

Clayton was arrested in November, when officers caught him fleeing the scene of a shooting a few blocks east of Rockaway Avenue. Police said he confessed to the two murders.

∞∞∞

SUDDENLY, THE SEASON felt monumental to Chris. He'd already considered that the fate of the program might be on the line, but now the stakes felt even higher. The summer's tragedies had heightened Chris's desire to see his boys win their games. He wanted them to believe that good things happened to those who worked hard and acted right.

"It never gets easier," Chris said. He'd been coaching for nearly 20 years and he was seeing the same struggles he'd seen when he got started. Like always, he found temporary peace at the park, where there were too many duties to think about to dwell on the sadness. The first game was six weeks away and the Pee Wee team was coming together.

Chris wanted them to show their opponents that Brownsville had more to offer than a string of sad stories for the evening news. He wanted to draw attention to his neighborhood for something positive, and maybe if enough people paid enough attention, their collective interest would help bring progress to Brownsville—though not even Chris was certain what this progress was supposed to look like.

Oomz during halftime of the first game of the season in September 2014.

Oomz in September 2014 practicing on the same field his father once practiced on during Mo Better's glory years.

Isaiah reaching for a water bottle during halftime of the first game of the 2014 season.

Isaiah (jacket) and Oomz lead their team off the bus
before a game in East Orange, NJ, in September 2014.

Coach Chris Legree speaking to the Junior Pee Wees
before a game in East Orange, NJ, in September 2014.

The Mo Better boys kicking up dust doing up-downs
during a September 2014 practice as Coach Gary looks on.

Chaka putting on his gloves as Dorian looks on before
practice at Betsy Head in late September 2014.

Marquis and his father hoped that football
could pave a road to private high school,
which was too expensive for their family
without a sizable financial aid package.

Hart listening to instruction from Coach Esau
during halftime of the first game of the 2014 season.

Hart (center) and his Pee Wee teammates were nervous before
their big game against East Orange in September 2014.

The Pee Wees and Junior Pee Wees board a school bus bound for East Orange, NJ, early on a Sunday morning in September 2014.

Donnie (black shirt) and other boys gathered around Oomz (with phone) after a victory in East Orange, NJ, in September 2014.

Coaches Esau (white shirt) and Andrell (NY hat) address the Pee Wees
at the end of a Friday evening practice in late September 2014.

Esau and Andrell going over strategy before the Pee Wees'
big game against Brick City in late September 2014.

Isaiah (2) and the Pee Wee offense seek a game-winning score in the fourth quarter of a tie game against Brick City in late September 2014.

When the coin was tossed for the first game of the season at Franklin K. Lane High School in September 2014, the Pee Wees had 16 players on the team, the minimum required by league rules.

– 11 –

ON THE HORIZON
July–August 2014

Football gave Chris Legree purpose and power, but it didn't pay the bills. For that, he worked at Consolidated Edison, his employer for three decades. He'd started as a general utility worker, digging holes, climbing poles, and checking meters, then worked his way up to supervisor. These days, he oversaw a team of emergency workers, who were dispatched across the city, day or night, to fix gas leaks and downed power lines. The crew arrived at the scene in a boxy red van. They dropped their orange cones, jackhammered into the street, and entered the earth. Sometimes they had to dispose of hazardous waste.

Chris didn't talk about his job much. Sometimes he showed up to Betsy Head still in his gray Con Ed jumpsuit, and parents joked that they'd forgotten that Chris was a workingman. It often seemed to them that the football program was all he did. Chris liked it that way. He believed that his legacy would be rooted in Brownsville through Mo Better. He modeled himself after Greg "Jocko" Jackson, the longtime manager of the Brownsville Recreation Center. Jackson died in 2012 and was a neighborhood legend. At his funeral, the line to pay respects at his casket went around the block. "It was all day," Chris said. "Like a dignitary died." During the memorial service, Chris remembered, he stood next to then mayor Michael Bloomberg, who turned to him and whispered, "Chris, I'm not going to have this many people at my funeral." And Chris replied, "Around here, we don't forget where we came from." The *New York Times* wrote Jackson's obituary, proclaiming him "unofficially, the mayor of Brownsville" and quoting him from an old interview: "If you can grow up and survive in Brownsville, you can do it anywhere in the world." Local leaders named a new community center after him. The city renamed a street in his honor. Chris often mentioned Jackson in his speeches and often noted that Jackson had been his good friend and mentor. He told people that he hoped to fill the hole Jackson had left.

The Con Ed job subsidized the community work that made Chris one of the most well-known figures in Brownsville. When Chris first got the job, he saw it as a symbol of his shortcomings. It was the job he needed because he'd returned to the neighborhood without an NFL contract, and playing semipro football on dirt fields for $50 a week wasn't going to pay the bills. "Everywhere I walked, everybody wanted to know what was going on," Chris said. He was ashamed. "Brownsville often feels like a village," his brother Jeff said. "When you do something good, people know about it, and when you do something bad, people hear about it. Word spreads fast. When you was from Brownsville, you was expected to blow up. You was expected to be great." Chris figured the whole neighborhood saw him as another has-been, the latest in a long line of local stars who failed to earn a spot in the pantheon of Brownsville greats. He missed the head nods and hand slaps when he walked down the street. He missed being somebody important and the pride that came with it. "It was a transitional period of realizing your dream won't happen," Chris said. "That's a big deal."

He began to believe that he was forever stuck with the feeling that he'd let Brownsville down. But then came the Million Man March, the inspirational words he needed, and the idea that would change his life. He found peace through Mo Better. "It stabilized me," he said. "For not fulfilling the promise, the potential, or whatever you wanna call it, I put myself on a guilt trip for a very long time. This helps me a lot. This gives me a way to give back to this place."

Now here he was, one of the most respected and admired figures in Brownsville: a man who slapped hands in barbershops and corner stores, who personally knew the NYPD precinct commander, the city council representative, the state legislature representatives, and the borough's district attorney; a man who put on a suit and glad-handed at political fundraisers and civic functions, who touted his program to rooms full of rich liberals and received donation checks in return; a man who wielded enough political influence to draw candidates to Betsy Head Park seeking his support, just as Lori Boozer did one day in late July. Boozer was running for state assembly, and she seemed to win Chris over. He knew he needed more allies in elected office. Brownsville's city council representative, Darlene Mealy, had stopped giving Mo Better a slice of her discretionary funding two years ago. She used to give them around $5,000 yearly. Now she didn't even meet with Chris in person. He had to make his pitch to one of her staffers.

He considered running for office himself, a dream he'd held for a few years now. Perhaps he'd run for Mealy's city council seat. He'd already drawn up the plan in his head. He'd retire from coaching football, hand the program to Esau, and campaign on the name he'd built up over two decades of community service. Not yet, he said, but one day. He wasn't ready to leave Mo Better, he said. For now, he was happy to work behind the scenes. He had Boozer give a short speech to the parents and players, then offered to escort her a few days later through Brownsville's Old-Timer's Day, an annual neighborhood reunion that drew former residents from across the country.

It was an overcast and breezy morning, and the Brownsville Recreation Center was already lively when Chris and Boozer got there. Police officers had shut down the surrounding streets so they could be used as parking lots and pedestrian walkways. Long lines snaked out from beneath tents selling fried fish, oxtail stew, jerk chicken, lemonade, and chicken wings. A large man in a white T-shirt and camo shorts pulled a rolling cooler, from which he sold potent cocktails called nutcrackers that left customers stumbling after two or three five-dollar bottles. Teens played basketball on three blacktops surrounded by families sitting on benches along the chain-link fence. Grown men in full baseball uniforms played slow-pitch softball on a turf field. Spectators filled the indoor gym to watch a basketball tournament. A DJ on a stage outside played soul music that reached every corner of the place.

Chris, in a purple Mo Better jacket and purple Mo Better sweatpants, brought a small entourage: a cousin, two nephews, and two brothers. One of those brothers, Ricky Legree, was in town from San Diego, where he'd lived since college. He and Chris only got to see each other once or twice a year, and Chris was eager to catch his older brother up on the neighborhood happenings. "I'ma get her elected," he whispered to Ricky, as Boozer stood at the center of a small crowd. "I think we got a winner here."

He'd been introducing her to every face he recognized. "Oh, there's somebody I want you to meet," he'd say when the opening small talk reached a natural pause, giving Boozer the floor to make her pitch. She'd lived in Brownsville's Langston Hughes Houses all her life—still lived there, in fact—and had gone to Boys and Girls High School in Bed-Stuy. She had attended Vassar College after that, then returned to Brownsville to do community work.

"You're from the projects, and that gives us comfort," an older man said. "Says a lot about the person that you are. That determination."

"It seems like every person we elect into office lets us down, though," a woman in the crowd said. "They turning corrupt and going to prison while we're left here with their mess. What will it take for things to get better?"

"We've been burned too many times," Boozer replied, before giving an answer about how she hoped to restore their faith in government. The seat she was running for was currently vacant: the last state assembly representative for District 55, William Boyland, had been convicted of bribery, extortion, and fraud.

"We don't get nothing," said a middle-aged man in the crowd. "Reason why, nobody ever comes through here. They don't send resources here. But they know how to send the cops here."

He said that police harassed his teenage sons nearly every day. Then he brought up Eric Garner, the 43-year-old man who had been killed by a police officer in Staten Island earlier that month. The officer had confronted Garner for selling cigarettes on the street, which was illegal. After a short argument, the officer jumped on Garner's back and pulled him to the ground in a chokehold. Other officers joined in, pinning Garner down on the sidewalk. "I can't breathe," Garner said over and over, but the officer kept the grip around Garner's neck even as his body went limp. A bystander captured the entire thing on video, and the incident sparked outrage nationwide. "What can be done about that?" the man said, his voice dripping with exasperation as he correctly predicted that the cop who choked Garner wouldn't be convicted.

Chris listened with a stern face. He thought about his Mo Better boys. It made him uneasy to think about the frustrating reality that he was but a small cog in the machinery driving the world. He preferred to focus his thoughts on the operations within his domain. Brownsville, his neighborhood—the old star quarterback had no doubt he had a hand in shaping its future, even as its present seemed to be changing faster than he could keep up.

What he loved most about Old-Timer's Day was all the reminiscing. As Chris, Boozer, and the entourage walked through the crowd, strangers and old acquaintances stopped him, hugged him, asked him how he'd been. He was warm and leaned toward them as they talked—about lost friends, about high school football championship runs, about stickball games in housing project courtyards. He wore a broad smile on his face and slapped them on the back, and a distant observer might have thought that he was the political candidate in the bunch.

ooooo

CHRIS REMEMBERED THE pigeon keepers who housed their flocks in rickety rooftop coops and raced their birds against one another, taking bets. The kids who snuck up to those roofs and stole the birds to sell to pet stores. The adults who played cards on Friday nights while the children listened to their banter from another room. On nice days, somebody threw a fish fry and neighbors and relatives passed through the house until the food was gone, and then the people still awake gathered with beers on the stoop. When somebody expected to be short on next month's rent, they threw a "waistline party": cooking a feast and opening their door to guests who paid one cent for every inch in their waistline. The public housing experiment was young then, and the elevators and front doors worked fine.

Sports ruled the neighborhood in those days. They played stoopball—throwing a rubber ball against the steps outside the project building and running around a set of makeshift bases until somebody picked it up. They watched the high-dive shows at the Betsy Head pool, and some nights kids would sneak over the fence to swim. They played two-hand touch football in a cement yard filled with obstacles that they strategically ran around to avoid defenders—drainage pipes big enough to drive a car through and waist-high stone posts sticking up from the ground. When they got older, they organized football games against boys from other housing projects. The way Chris remembered it, "two or three thousand people" showed up at Betsy Head to watch the teens from the Brownsville towers play against the teens from Tilden. "We had more people at that game than the high schools do now," he said.

Hours later, after Boozer had left and the clouds began to darken, Chris and Ricky ran into a friend from childhood, Don Blackman. In 1970, Blackman became the first black player to receive a basketball scholarship from Duke University. In the years prior, he played pickup games with Ricky. The men spoke about those games, how much talent was on those blacktops and how much talent never made it out.

"Don, I gotta question for you."

"What's that?"

"Why does Brownsville produce so many great athletes?"

Blackman contemplated for a few seconds, eyes locked on the horizon. Then he pointed at the skyline of red brick towers.

"See them tall buildings?" he said. "You take this many people, you put 'em in this small space and give 'em one ball, what kind of competitors you think you're gonna get? Simple mathematics."

Ricky nodded and grinned. He wondered if the neighborhood still produced the caliber of greatness he saw in his youth. And if it did, he wondered how much longer it would continue. In recent years, the neighborhood looked different each time he visited. He didn't see the same tight-knit community where he'd grown up. He didn't see as many kids in the parks and playgrounds. He didn't see the fish fries on nice days. He believed that something special was being squeezed out of Brownsville. "I see a transition to yuppie-ville," he said. "The white flight, like seasonal animals, they migrated. Now they migrating back. It's cyclical."

ooooo

THE LOCALS SAW signs. A Subway and a Dunkin' Donuts popped up next to a cash-checking joint. New murals sprouted on Pitkin. White people were creeping south through Bushwick and east across Crown Heights, pushing up against the Brownsville border. The city proposed a redevelopment zone in East New York to allow for construction of new residential buildings, right along Brownsville's northeastern edge. Speculators scooped up the cheap land of east Brooklyn. In Ocean Hill, the small neighborhood to Brownsville's north, 1 in 10 houses had been flipped within the previous two years, and some had sold for nearly one million dollars. In East New York, a property that had sold for $140,000 in November 2013 resold for $600,000 six months later. There was talk in the real-estate business that the wave of development and gentrification would soon reach Brownsville—Brooklyn's "final frontier," some called it. Affordable space was available just off the 3 train, only a few blocks deeper than Crown Heights.

The locals saw their property values rising. Speculators who had bought houses in Brownsville within the past year or two were, on average, reselling them for more than twice the purchase price. From 2000 to 2014, the neighborhood's median rent jumped from $714 to $951, even as the median household income dropped from around $31,000 to $25,000. Over that stretch, the price of a monthly public transit pass in the city nearly doubled, from $63 to $112.

The locals knew what always followed the rising property values. They'd seen it in other Brooklyn neighborhoods over the past decade. Their friends and relatives experienced it firsthand. Longtime New Yorkers from around the city were familiar with this pattern. They'd seen it in the 1980s, as the migration to the suburbs reversed, when boutiques and chain stores wiped out the bohemian culture in Greenwich Village, SoHo, and Tribeca; when affluent families replaced the working-class communities in Park Slope and Brooklyn Heights. "Those special landlords dedicated to rapacity are still throwing poor and elderly and disoriented people out of buildings because of the enormous profits to be wrung out of converting the structures into co-ops and other luxury housing," a 1982 *New York Times* op-ed stated.

This wasn't limited to New York, of course. People who once moved to the suburbs to settle down were now moving into big cities. In San Francisco; Washington, DC; Nashville; Saint Louis; Los Angeles; Atlanta; Philadelphia; Seattle; Chicago; and elsewhere, neighborhoods once rough and blighted were filling with people who had avoided them. Working-class and low-income people were now moving to the suburbs, not by choice but because that was where they could afford to live.

In Brooklyn, as elsewhere, landlords had much incentive to drive out longtime residents—offering cash buyouts in exchange for their departure, hiking rents after minimal structural improvements, making homes uncomfortable with early morning construction work, and failing to fix deteriorating facilities. Once the rent-controlled old-timers were flushed out, the money flowed in. In Fort Greene and Brooklyn Heights, the median rent price rose by 58 percent from 2000 to 2012. In Williamsburg and Greenpoint, rents rose by 76 percent over that stretch, and the number of households making more than $100,000 a year more than doubled. In central Harlem, median rent increased by 90 percent. The consequence was a cascade of displacement. People who used to live in Park Slope or Williamsburg were moving to Bed-Stuy or Crown Heights or Flatbush, and people who lived in Bed-Stuy or Crown Heights or Flatbush were moving to Brownsville or East New York or the Bronx or leaving the city—over the past decade, the black population had dropped by 2 percent across New York City, including in Harlem, Bed-Stuy, and Brooklyn as a whole.

By 2014, Brooklyn had become, by at least one measure, the most unaffordable place to live in America: a household making the borough's median income would need to spend 98 percent of its monthly earnings to pay the median monthly mortgage. In 2000, residents who made between $20,000 and $40,000 in salary spent 33 percent of their income on rent; by 2012, that figure had reached 41 percent. Brooklyn, as many longtime locals saw it, had less and less space for poor and working-class families. Brooklyn had become a brand. "The Coolest City on the Planet," *GQ* magazine declared in 2011. There was a place called the Brooklyn Diner in Dubai and a snack booth called Williamsburg in a park in Moscow. Brooklyn, once perhaps the epicenter of the crack epidemic in America, had grown so distant from those years that local establishments had taken to commercializing the drug that once ravaged the borough's communities. A Mexican restaurant, with locations in Williamsburg and Park Slope, made a special house dressing called "crack sauce"; a popular bakery, with locations in Williamsburg and Carroll Gardens, served a sweet gooey dish called "crack pie."

New Brooklyn ate away at Old Brooklyn, and the gulf between the two worlds continued to grow. The median income in the borough's richest neighborhood, Dumbo, was $140,000 higher than in Brownsville. The average life span of Borough Park residents was 83 years; for Brownsville residents, it was 74, the lowest in the city. In Brownsville, 61 out of every 10,000 children had been hospitalized for asthma; in Greenpoint and Williamsburg, 18. In Brownsville, 180 of every 100,000 residents were victims of nonfatal violence; in Park Slope and Carroll Gardens, 32. In Brownsville, eight of every 1,000 infants died before their first birthday; in Sunset Park, less than two. In Brownsville's school district, just 61 percent of students graduated on time, the second-lowest rate of the city's 55 districts.

All of which led to the fundamental question many Brownsville locals asked: Was it possible for a neighborhood to experience the benefits of development without longtime residents getting displaced? "I don't think any neighborhood anywhere has shown how that can be done," said Darren Johnston, a 32-year-old community activist.

Brownsville locals wanted a better neighborhood—nicer grocery stores, fancy bars, and outdoor cafes. Of the 25 restaurants along the neighborhood's most-commercial avenues—Pitkin, Belmont, Mother Gaston, and Rockaway—not a single one offered sit-down service. "I'm ready for the change," said Clyde, a Brownsville native whose son played on the Pee Wees. "I like to eat organic. I wanna be able to eat organic without having to go to Manhattan." The neighborhood was headed in the right direction, he said. Twenty years earlier, he wouldn't have felt safe at Betsy Head Park once the sun went down. "The lights would be busted and it would be dark and dangerous," he said. "It's so much safer now." But progress in Brownsville was relative. As one local, paraphrasing Malcolm X, put it: "If you stick a knife nine inches in my back and then pull it back to six inches, can you call that progress?"

Brownsville's housing projects meant that the neighborhood would remain a welcome place for tens of thousands of low-income residents. It also meant that the neighborhood would retain the problems that emerge when tens of thousands of people are crammed into poorly maintained and socially isolating facilities. In Chicago, New Orleans, Philadelphia, Memphis, Saint Louis, and Newark, city officials were tearing down housing projects and promoting mixed-income communities instead. Those cities had decided it was time to end the housing-project experiment of the twentieth century. Brownsville locals wondered how their ubiquitous brick towers would shape the neighborhood's future. Would developers build restaurants and condominiums alongside the projects? Would the placement of expensive apartments alongside housing projects emerge as the new model of the seemingly mythical mixed-income community? Was this how development occurred with limited displacement? Or would the city sell the facilities to private developers to turn them into mixed-income apartments, as it had done in parts of Manhattan? Would working class families be driven out by rising rents and replaced by the young creative-class types who often mark the first stage of gentrification? Or would Brownsville just always remain a pocket of poverty and blight, skipped over for more shimmering land in Queens and the Bronx? "Brownsville has always been a place of experimentation," said Johnston, the community activist. "If there's a community that figures it out, maybe this is the one."

ooooo

THE FOLLOWING SATURDAY was cloudy, and Isaiah showed up to Betsy Head early. He had no other plans that weekend. A few years ago, he'd spent many weekends with his two closest friends, who lived several blocks from his apartment, just over the Brownsville border in Crown Heights. But one of the boys moved to Queens and the other to the Bronx. Their families could no longer afford Crown Heights.

Hart was second to arrive. The two boys sat on the long green bench and talked about basketball. A rotund 50-something man who went by Boonie overheard them as he walked by. He had seen Lance Stephenson play high school ball years ago, he told them, back when he was a prodigy from the Coney Island projects, an eighth grader hooping with Lincoln High's varsity squad. Best player he'd seen come out of Brooklyn since Lenny Cooke, he said.

"Lenny Cooke was number one, but he wasn't humble and didn't work hard. Y'all remember that," he imparted. "That was a different time, though. Brooklyn ain't what it was then no more."

The boys nodded absentmindedly.

"Do y'all know Lenny Cooke?"

The boys shook their heads.

"How old are you? Fifteen?" he said to Isaiah.

"Nah. Twelve."

"Twelve! When you twice that age, this ain't gonna be the hood," Boonie said, sweeping an arm across the landscape. "No. It'll just be vanilla walking all around."

− 12 −

HELL WEEK
August 2014

THE HITTING HAD BEEN WEAK BEFORE ISAIAH AND OOMZ got a turn. Isaiah picked up the football and dug his cleats into the dirt. It was a warm and clear August afternoon and the dust kicked up and drifted into Oomz, who stood facing Isaiah several yards away. Both boys wore helmets and shoulder pads, but while Isaiah wore padded football pants, Oomz wore basketball shorts. He'd forgotten to buy football pants. Today was the first day in pads and the rest of his teammates, who were lined up on either side of the tackling stage, had the foam cushions on their knees, thighs, and hips. At the start of practice, Hart had said to Oomz, "How you gon' practice with no pads on your legs?" and Oomz had replied, "Don't worry about it." Oomz leaned forward, pulled the bottom of his shorts above his knees, and crouched down. He wore a relaxed, indifferent expression. Isaiah's face was stoic, as if he were angry but trying to hide it. The park was quiet and their teammates could hear their shoulder pads rustling against the mesh jerseys as they rocked side to side in anticipation.

"Been waiting for this all summer!" Esau shouted, clapping his hands and nodding his head vigorously. "Set! Go!"

Isaiah jogged forward, the ball in his right arm, and Oomz chopped his feet, his hands at his sides like a gunslinger. Isaiah accelerated, faked to the left then cut to the right. Oomz didn't buy the fake. He shuffled sideways to meet Isaiah and Isaiah lowered his shoulder and braced for impact. Oomz crouched down lower and thrust forward, and when the two boys hit, their bodies made a loud smack. Oomz wrapped his arms around Isaiah and drove him to the ground, his back hitting with a thump, and a thick cloud of dust puffed into the air and engulfed the two boys.

"Ooooohh!" their teammates roared, jumping up and down.

"There you go!" Esau said.

"That's the sound I've been waiting to hear!" Andrell said.

Oomz was smiling when he stood up. He helped Isaiah off the ground and Isaiah tapped him on the helmet and said, "Good hit, boy!" Oomz giggled and tapped Isaiah back on the helmet.

"You gon' let him do you like that, Isaiah?" Andrell said. "Good shit, Oomz!"

"Y'all want some more?" Esau said to the two boys. "Run it back."

They lined up and barreled toward each other again. Oomz's helmet hit Isaiah's chest with a smack louder than the first, but this time the collision rocked Oomz backward and Isaiah surged forward, falling onto his stomach as Oomz dragged him down.

"There you go Isaiah! That's what I'm talkin'bout!"

Oomz hopped to his feet, shook his head, and slapped his hands together.

"One more time!"

The third time, their hit was louder than the first two—"Oooohhhhh!"—and it knocked dust from their jerseys. On impact, their crouching bodies straightened up, chest to chest, legs churning, in a stalemate. Oomz couldn't knock Isaiah off his feet and Isaiah couldn't shake Oomz's grasp. After a few seconds, Isaiah slapped Oomz on the helmet, "Yeah, boy!"

"'Bout time I see some damn hitting out here!" said Esau.

"Glad they both on our team," said Hart.

"How you feel, Oomz?" said Andrell.

Oomz smiled wide, then said softly, "Good."

The back of his purple jersey and all of his silver shorts were brown with dirt. He pulled his helmet off, took a knee, and dusted the dirt from his sleeves and shorts. Isaiah walked over to him and wiped the dirt from his back, and then Isaiah turned around and Oomz wiped the dirt from Isaiah's back.

The fathers standing along the fence clapped for the performance.

"Good hit, kids!" Marquis's father, Ramsey, bellowed. "That's how you supposed to hit!"

"Both ways good hit!" shouted Dorian's father, Dwight. "Makin' some noise now."

Isaiah and Oomz had sparked an excitement that now hovered over the field with the dust. It was an excitement familiar on fields across the county: the hitting had finally begun, which meant the season wasn't far off. At every level of football, the first day in pads marked the start of Hell Week, a late summer ritual of rigorous hitting and running, enough hitting to get the body used to contact again and enough running to chisel the body into condition for the season—enough to pare a team down to its toughest parts. Heads would ache and bodies would bruise. Legs and lungs would burn. Boys would pray that the eighth or ninth 50-yard sprint would be the last, and then their hearts would drop when their coach said, "Set!" and blew the whistle again. Coaches would blow the whistle over and over, so many times that every last kid would think about quitting, would question his love for the game and wonder how much he was truly willing to sacrifice for this punishing sport. The boys would fall to the grass, sucking air, chests heaving, splashing water on their faces, groaning, too tired to talk but silently thinking *Fuck this shit.* And then their coach would tell them to get their asses up and get back on the line because water break was over and it was time for 100-yard gassers, and if everybody doesn't make it across in 18 seconds, the whole team's gotta run it again. And when practice was finally, mercifully over, they would pray that the next day would be easier, fully knowing that it would, in fact, be harder. But when the week was finished, they would know that those who made it through were now forged together through this fire.

On fields across the country, there was hope that the efforts through the long spring and hot summer months would yield wins in the fall. And on this hard, dusty field in Brownsville, Brooklyn, that hope mostly rested on the two boys wiping dirt from each other's jerseys.

"Y'all two thunder and lightning!" shouted one father. "Bruise and cruise!"

"They don't know what they in for when they step on the field with y'all," another father shouted. "But soon they gon' see what we seeing right now! They gon' learn what we knowin' right now!"

"This a big day," said a third father. "First time Oomz and Isaiah went heads. And they did not disappoint! I'm gon' remember this day!"

It was a big day and everybody at Betsy Head that Saturday afternoon would remember it, but for other reasons. That very hour, 1,000 miles west at an apartment complex in Ferguson, Missouri, a police officer shot and killed 18-year-old Michael Brown.

ooooo

To Coach Chris, the first day in pads was the most important practice of the year, and he woke up that morning feeling a rush of adrenaline. This was the practice when he would learn the most about "what kinda heart some of these kids got." The moment a football player lined up for his first hitting drill was unique to the sport. "You see somebody hit a baseball: OK this kid can do this. You see somebody shoot a basketball: OK this guy can do it. In football, you can't tell until you see people play. We're gonna find out who responds to getting knocked down. Some guys quit." Unlike in basketball, which required exceptional height, and in baseball, which required exceptional eyes or an exceptional arm, in football, a boy could advance through high school and college primarily through toughness and technique. The way Chris saw it, anybody could play football if they wanted it enough, but anyone who didn't would wash out.

He'd seen tall, athletic boys who ran fast and acted tough all summer turn soft on the first day of hitting. He'd seen slow, clumsy, skinny boys who'd been afterthoughts all summer emerge as hard-nosed *football players* on the first day of hitting. There was no higher compliment from a coach than, "He's a *football player.*" It denoted toughness, will, discipline, work ethic, desire, leadership—the most revered values in the sport. "Today is when we find out who's a *football player,*" Chris said to Coach Gary before practice, as the Pee Wees lined up for shoulder pads, helmets, pants padding, mouth guards, and jerseys. The boys picked out their numbers: 2 for Isaiah, 7 for Oomz, 32 for Hart, 44 for Donnie, 4 for Chaka, 5 for Naz, 1 for Time Out, 21 for Marquis. As the boys put on their gear, they showed off the accessories they'd added. Hart had a neck roll. Isaiah wore a clear visor on his facemask. Time Out attached a back flap below his shoulder pads. Marquis had his nylon sleeves and colorful knee-high socks. One player joked that you could spot the best players on another team by their jersey numbers (single digits) and their accessories (the more the better). "'Cause if you can't play you look like a fool wearing all that," Esau explained. Oomz, though, kept a minimalist look. He wore a ratty T-shirt under his shoulder pads and old white tube socks that he folded down so that they wrapped the heels of his cleats.

"How you gon' practice with no pads on your legs?" Hart said.

"Don't worry about it."

Chris called the boys over.

"It's a good day!" he said, as they circled around him. "What a day! We gon' learn a lot today. Now we gon' really be playin' football. Who's excited? I'm real excited. We gon' be hitting today. Y'all ready?"

"Yeah!" the boys replied in unison.

He paused and nodded his head, hands on his hips.

"Now—what's the big national issue in football right now?"

"Concussions!" Hart and a few other boys shouted.

"President of the United States said if he had a son he might not let him play football," Chris said. "How can you help prevent getting a concussion in football?"

No boy spoke up.

"First off, you gotta make sure you got on the proper equipment," Chris continued. "Gotta make sure your helmet fits properly and it's strapped up. And this is important: you gotta keep your head up when tackling. See your man"—Chris bent down and mimed a slow motion tackle—"and bam! Your facemask right on his chest, or right on the ball, might even pop that ball loose. Always keep your head up. That's very important. Very important. Football is a very serious game. Make sure you get a mouthpiece from Coach Gary 'cause we gonna be bangin' today."

The adults lined the fence to watch their boys hit. They weren't worried much, though they had seen the stories in the news. Scientists were saying that the risk of long-term brain damage was heightened for kids who played football before their teenage years. Studies showed that the primary cause was not concussions, but rather the accumulation of smaller, sub-concussive hits, which were unavoidable in the sport. Perhaps football's days as America's pastime were coming to a close. Perhaps one day soon basketball would surpass football the way football had surpassed baseball. Perhaps football would fall from public consciousness the way boxing had. The growing fear about football's impact on the brain had convinced many parents to pull their kids from the sport. From 2010 to 2012, participation in Pop Warner dropped by 10 percent—the first decline in the organization's more than 80-year history. In a 2013 Robert Morris University poll, 40 percent of respondents supported a ban on kids playing tackle football before high school. That year, a state assemblyman from the Bronx, Michael Benedetto, became the first legislator in America to introduce a bill banning youth football statewide.

"He never played football, I guess," said one father.

The adults lined up along the fence believed the recent public outcry about football was overblown. And indeed, there was no doubt they were part of a very broad stronghold. "I received an awful lot of criticism about this bill," Benedetto said at a press conference. "I have certainly received dozens of emails for and against—mostly against—this proposal, I'll be honest." Only six other assembly members, from a body of 150, signed on to back the bill, and not a single state senator was willing to sponsor it. In February 2014, a New York City council member proposed a bill requiring that a doctor is present for every youth football game and that only a doctor can decide whether or not a player should be tested for a concussion. The bill stalled and didn't reach the floor for a vote. But it was clear that a national movement had emerged. States across the country were passing laws establishing concussion protocols for football games and practices. In California, the state legislature passed a bill to limit high school football teams to two full-contact practices a week during the off-season.

"It's ridiculous," said another father. "It's part of this sissy-fication. I had at least five concussions myself and I played through all of 'em. You got high drop-out rates, kids on drugs, headed to jail, violence, poverty—these ain't the problems. It's concussions? Get real. For some kids this the one chance they got. This the activity that keeps 'em outta trouble, gives 'em father figures. You gon' take it away? Mischief is the easiest thing to find."

"All that concussion stuff is not from these little guys," a third father said.

"You can't handle this right here, how you gon' handle life?" said the first father. "You think the hits hard out here? Wait till you see the hits life'll give you. This right here's where you build that mental toughness. That shit is key. Mental toughness."

The Pop Warner organization depended on this belief that the benefits of football outweighed the risks—so much so that league officials seemed to deny the reality of the risks. In June, in the midst of a heated national conversation about football's impact on the brain, Pop Warner hosted a panel discussion about health and football, titled "Eat Smart, Play Safe." Yet concussions were not a focus of the presentation, rather a single health issue among a wide array of topics. A poster board with a diagram of a brain declared how football promoted cognitive development: alertness, focus, mental engagement. When the discussion, after more than half an hour, finally turned to concussions, a neurologist on the panel, Dr. Majid Fotuhi, explained that people underestimate the brain's resilience. The long-term damage from concussions, he told the audience, sets in only if an athlete does not address it, "like a car that is damaged and you do not fix it." He claimed that sufficient sleep, regular exercise, omega-3 DHA supplements, and a healthy diet will cause the brain to grow and can work to balance out the potential long-term damage a kid suffers from a concussion. "If somebody has a concussion, it's not over," he said. "The brain is malleable, the brain is fixable, especially if you're young." He did not back this up with any specific evidence.

ooooo

THE PEE WEES lined up for the year's first set of hitting drills. A few parents pulled up their phones to record video.

"This is what it's all about," said one boy's auntie. "Once you hear those sounds . . ." She smiled wide and wagged her head in satisfaction. "I love this."

Two Pee Wees stepped to the center of the tackling stage. They were new to the team this year and neither had worn football pads before today. Both boys were big for their age, but their helmets and shoulder pads, which seemed to swallow them up, made them look much younger now. The boy with the football held it loosely between his palm and his forearm. The boy on defense stood straight up, awkwardly, with barely a bend in his knees and his arms down at his sides.

"Come on! Look like football players!" Esau shouted, and the boy on offense tucked the ball into his chest and the boy on defense crouched a bit lower.

"Set! Go!"

The boys jogged toward each other but a second before the collision they both slowed, nearly reaching a full stop by the time their bodies met. The boy on offense turned to the side and ducked his shoulder and the boy on defense lunged sideways and wrapped his outstretched arms around the ballcarrier's shoulders, like a toddler catching a beach ball.

"What, y'all don't wanna hit?" Esau said. "You ain't ready for no hitting. You been playing basketball all summer. You ain't ready for no contact."

The next two participants brought much of the same. They slowed before the collision, as if mutually agreeing to lessen the impact.

"That's soft!" Oomz said. "Why you scared?"

Donnie was next on defense. He eyed the ballcarrier and chewed his mouthpiece. Within a month, he'd chew his mouthpiece so flat that he'd need a new one. He was, his teammates all agreed, the most aggressive boy on the Pee Wees. All summer, he'd picked fights with teammates for the smallest reasons: for stepping on his toe and not apologizing, for accidentally elbowing him in the stomach during practice, for laughing too hard when somebody made a joke about how short or slow he was. Usually Oomz or Isaiah had to step in and pull Donnie away, and Esau would yell at him to calm down. But today, the first day of pads, brought an outlet for that anger. And now his teammates, hopping on their toes and rubbing their hands together, were excited to see what Donnie could do with a free pass to hit somebody as hard as he could. The ballcarrier, a skinny 11-year-old, nervously tossed the ball from one hand to the other.

"A'ight, let's go Donnie!" Esau said.

He crouched low and ran hard at the ballcarrier, who veered to the right side of the stage. Just before contact, the ballcarrier slowed down and ducked his head and turned his shoulders, bracing for the hit—but it never came. Donnie had run so hard that he overshot the mark, running right past the front of the ballcarrier, hitting the boy with only his left arm before losing his balance and tumbling to the ground.

"Awwww, come on Donnie!" Esau said with a chuckle.

Donnie slapped the ground with his hand and shouted, "Fuck!"

"It's a'ight, Donnie," Esau said, still laughing. "I know you ain't scared to hit, but you gotta control your body. Can't just be running around with ya head down. You wanna hit 'em but they tryna not get hit. Ain't just about who the maddest. Gotta getcha feet squared."

"A'ight," Esau went on. "Who's next? Ummm . . . Oomz. Isaiah."

"Ooooo-weeee!" Andrell shouted.

∞∞∞∞∞

It's natural for a boy to slow down and brace himself right before crashing into another body. The instinct is to avoid the collision, to limit the impact, to protect the body and prevent any possible pain. This mind-set, as Oomz put it, was soft, and one purpose of Hell Week was to drive it out and install new hard wiring. The veterans on the Pee Wee squad, the 11- and 12-year-olds with four or more years in pads, had shed their discomfort for contact through hundreds of hits, and on the tackling stage they embraced the violence. The veterans aimed to maximize the impact. They accelerated into the collision. They reveled in the sound of their hits. Their excitement for contact drowned out the fear. Some boys, like Oomz and Hart, claimed that they'd liked the violence from the start, that something in them had been drawn to the roughness of the collisions, that the hitting had always felt comfortable. "A lot of 'em get that first hit and, *man*, they can't get enough of it." Coach Vick said. "Once you get that bell rung, it's like a light goes on. And once that light goes on you'll never be able to turn it off again." Other boys, like Isaiah, admitted that they'd been scared at first; that they'd once shied from contact, and then gotten used to it, and then eventually learned to enjoy it. For the parents watching from the fence, it was clear that there were two types of boys on a football team: those who were *hitters*—a complimentary term perhaps second only to *football player*—and those who were not.

The Pee Wees didn't know if Marquis was a hitter. Esau called him to the stage and put him on defense. Oomz was the ballcarrier.

"Set, go!"

Oomz ran straight ahead and made no jukes. He crouched low, so his chest nearly brushed his knees, and got even lower a step before the impact. Oomz was the hardest boy on the team to tackle. He ran hard and aimed to punish those who tried to tackle him. He was short and thick, and with the way he ran low to the ground, it was like trying to tackle a tree stump. Marquis ran straight at Oomz, kept his hips square with Oomz's hips, and didn't shy from the collision. He crouched nearly as low as Oomz, then ducked even lower and punched his shoulder pads and helmet into Oomz's chest with a *pop!* He kept his legs pumping even as the boys seemed to stalemate, then with his arms wrapped around Oomz's waist, he dipped him to the ground.

"Yeah! Yeah! There you go, Marquis!" his father Ramsey hollered.

His teammates cheered and his coaches clapped. "I didn't know if Marquis could hit," Isaiah said later. "But it looks like he could hit."

The hits became harder and louder as the week went on, and the Pee Wees grew closer and more excited for the start of the season. They practiced every day that week, and each day confirmed the boys' belief that there was much talent on this team. A sense of urgency gripped them. It seemed to radiate out from Isaiah and Hart and reach every boy. Some days, they reminisced on the losses of the previous season, and they vowed that this season would be different. Almost nobody missed practice. Many arrived early. Their eyes stayed locked on Esau as he described the new plays he'd created. Few goofed around during practice, and those who did faced Oomz's anger. They ran laps and pushed through punishing 100-yard sprints without complaint. By the middle of the week, it became clear that the boys believed this was an important season. Some of them, like Isaiah, Oomz, and Hart, thought about it morning to night every day that week. They fantasized about the great plays they would make. They imagined the wins and the celebrations. It consumed them like a romance. It remained on their minds as they stripped off their pads, traveled home, showered, ate dinner, and sprawled on the couch as their mother or father watched television, which was filled with images of fires, tanks, shields, guns, and scores of angry people barely older than they were, bandanas over their mouths, running from billowing tear gas in Ferguson. Their parents watched the images with strained faces, understanding, praying things would change this time, perhaps wondering if the cost of progress was always blood.

ooooo

ON THURSDAY, THE second-to-last day of Hell Week, the sun dipped below the horizon of brick towers during practice for the first time all summer. Mr. Hart, Marquis's father Ramsey, and Dorian's father Dwight stood side by side at the fence watching their boys run and hit. They were all big men and they all worked in law enforcement. Dwight, with his chiseled arms and chest beneath his gray V-neck, was a Port Authority police officer in New Jersey. Ramsey—who, with his offensive lineman build, bald head, and beard, looked like Rick Ross—drove a bus on Rikers Island. Mr. Hart, short and round and solid as a boulder, had been a correctional officer at Rikers for 27 years. He'd been a dutiful guard who rarely missed work, until the knee injuries that sidelined him in March. He had been on his back at home for months, but he returned to Betsy Head in time for the summer practices.

The coaches and parents gave him a hero's welcome. His booming voice had been missed, Coach Chris said. Among Mo Better parents, Mr. Hart and his wife were the center of gravity. They'd attended nearly every practice since their son had joined the team four years earlier. For the anxious fathers who complained about the coaches' decisions and worried about another losing season, Mr. Hart was the voice of reason, calm, and optimism. He brought energy to the park, and his energy caught on among other parents.

"Andrew! Andrew!" Mr. Hart shouted at his son. "You gotta extend the arms and drive him back! Gotta block him! Gotta get the ball to your quarterback before you can block! Yeahhh! Yeahhh Andrew!!"

"Hell Week, baby! Hell Week! Let's get it!" Ramsey added.

"Good block, son!" Dwight yelled. "Good run, Isaiah!"

Dwight had nearly pulled his son from the team after last season. Why commute an hour for each practice only to lose so many games? There were plenty of teams closer to his home in New Jersey. But Chris had persuaded him to stay. It was an off year, Chris had told him, and we plan on fixing it. Dwight decided to give Mo Better one more chance, but "this will be Dorian's last year here unless they do something special," he'd said in the spring. Now Dwight believed that they really might do something special.

"They shouldn't lose a game this year," he said to the other fathers. "The talent is there. It's just a matter of putting it together and executing."

"I come all the way from Queens to come out here," Mr. Hart said. "They got the talent. The coaches just gotta get it together. We are stronger. We are stronger. We ain't giving nothing up."

"Y'all know I'm coming from Queens, too," Ramsey said. "Coming all the way out here for this 'cause I heard this is the place to be. What happened last year?"

"They should've gone undefeated last year, but they fell apart at the end of games," Dwight said. "Brick City, East Orange, and Montclair—they kept it close through two, three quarters, then got tight or something and the other guys pulled away."

The Brick City game, Dwight and Mr. Hart recalled, was particularly painful. It was a brutal contest, and the teams looked evenly matched.

"It was six to nothing for most of the game," Dwight said. "But they lost confidence in the end. It's up to the coaches to keep them together and organized at the end. Sometimes they got a bit disorganized. They lost thirty-something to nothing."

The fathers went quiet and watched the action on the field. The park was buzzing. Latino men played softball in one corner. West Indian men played soccer on a patch of grass in another corner. Five kids on bikes rolled up and down the dirt mounds at the edge of the grass. Three boys played baseball with an aluminum bat and a mini basketball. A group of girls practiced cheerleading moves. Several people jogged around the track. Dozens played handball, cricket, or basketball on the caged-in blacktops.

"One more play!" Coach Chris shouted at the Pee Wees. It was past 8 p.m. and the sun had nearly set.

"It's already getting dark! What's the difference? Ain't this hell week?" Ramsey shouted.

"I just got here!" Mr. Hart shouted. "I just got here! 10 more plays!"

"Sun's still out!" said Ramsey. "Come on, coach, nobody goin' home!"

"C'mon, coach! S'posed to be Hell Week!" Mr. Hart said. Isaiah took a handoff and Dorian met him in the hole and they collided with a loud *pop!* "Now we hear some rattling!"

THE BOYS GATHERED around Coach Chris before the last practice of Hell Week, a Friday. It had been a good week, and all were hopeful about the team's prospects. The day was overcast and light rain was in the forecast.

"What a great day for football," Chris told the boys. "When it rains this field is perfect. It kills the dust."

Their first preseason game was on Sunday, and the Pop Warner season was a few weeks away.

"Start thinking big," Chris said. He'd given versions of this speech before. It was one of his favorites. "You don't have to get a job; get a business, own something. Start thinking big. You don't have to get an apartment; buy a building. Start thinking big. You don't have to get an eighty; get a ninety. Start thinking big. Start thinking big."

Chris had high expectations for the season. So high that he'd already begun thinking and speaking about the team's game against Brick City, whom he considered Mo Better's main rival. Brick City had risen to the top of their league in recent years. "They came out of nowhere," Esau said. "Back when I played, I never heard of them. They just came up. Back in my day, we didn't lose in the regular season." Brick City dominated the league now the way Mo Better had for two decades. Last season, nearly all five of their teams had won regional championships and made it to Florida for the Pop Warner Super Bowl. It was an organized program. The players marched off their bus single file, quiet and disciplined, with their blue bags. They were fast, strong, and hungry, and they reminded some of what Mo Better used to be. That angered Chris—*used to be.*

"The division that we're in, the black and blue division, they have no respect for us!" Chris said to the boys. "They don't fear us no more! They're already giving it to East Orange and Brick City! They lost respect for us. Only way we gon' get respect, we gotta take something from them. We gotta take their heart. Knock them out!"

The Junior Pee Wees' 35–0 loss to Brick City last season still bothered Chris. His boys had gotten the ball within 10 yards of the end zone four times and Brick City had stopped them from scoring on all four. With each stop, the boys lost spirit, and by the fourth quarter they seemed to have given up. Brick City specialized in a running game that spread the field, unlike Mo Better's old-school, inside smashmouth style. They ran to the outside and, in the fourth quarter, they overpowered and sprinted past Mo Better's tired defenders. Though the team had fought hard and kept it close for much of the game, the finish had been an embarrassment.

All week, Chris had already been preparing the Pee Wees for Brick City's attack, showing defenders how to line up to contain the outside runs. When he caught a boy joking around and not paying attention, he shouted, "See if you smilin' when we playin' Brick City!" before making the team run a lap.

"I'm sick of these dudes," Chris continued. "They lost respect for us. It's bothering me. It's a matter of being real physical and nasty about our business. They not gon' believe it until we shut them down. Everybody gotta be nasty and on the edge. We all gotta be like razors, all of us. Nobody getting around us this year. When they get wide on us, I want you to knock they asses into they fathers' laps. That's the attitude we gotta have."

Chris stomped around the circle as he spoke, going up to each boy and looking him in the eye. His arms flapped up and down to accentuate his sentences. His voice was fiery and his cadence found a rhythmic groove.

"All our national championships and all that good stuff, that don't mean nothing now. I want some new stuff. I'm tired of talking about the past. I want some new stuff."

ooooo

IF THIS WAS the year Mo Better returned to Florida, Chris believed, it would be because they had a weapon no team could stop. Halfway into practice, he and Esau watched Isaiah take a pitch and speed around the corner, graceful as a cheetah.

"Man, I love number two," Chris said to Esau. "Number two could get to the outside. They catch him, we can tip our caps. He could put fear in people."

"Every time outside, they ain't gon' catch him," Esau said. "Ain't nobody in Pop Warner faster than him. He's too fast."

Yet Chris and Esau harbored a fear about the season that they kept from players and parents. None of Isaiah's talent mattered if the team wasn't able to suit up at least 16 players every game. Youth football participation was down across the board, they knew. Just that week, they'd learned that two prominent non–Pop Warner Brooklyn programs, the Warriors and the Chiefs, had decided to merge because neither had enough players. Many of the Pee Wees had friends on those teams. Some Pee Wees had played for them previously. The news surprised the boys but not Chris. Each week at practice, he checked with Esau about numbers.

"How many you got?" he asked him on the last day of Hell Week.

"Sixteen," Esau replied.

Chris pursed his lips and nodded silently, nervously.

– 13 –

STOP DANCIN' AND RUN SOMEBODY OVER
August–September 2014

IT WAS A MILD SUMMER, MUCH DIFFERENT FROM THE previous one, which had been very hot and violent in Brownsville. This summer, through June, July, and early August, the days had been mostly warm and breezy, and there was mostly peace—fewer shootings than locals anticipated. The NYPD set up temporary lights near the street corners and housing projects most known for violence. More uniformed officers and marked cars patrolled the streets at all hours. "Since they've been posting the police like that, you haven't been hearing gunfire as much," Coach James said.

But he didn't give all credit to the police. There had been a greater, singular force behind the scenes in the weeks after Poppa's death. James, like many locals, gave the majority of the credit to Coach Gary. From the minute he learned about his nephew's murder, Gary set out to prevent retaliation. He met with Poppa's crew and tried to calm them down. He told them he understood their anger, but controlling it meant they had the power to control whether or not another one of them would be killed. This talk wasn't always enough.

Gary knew the streets, and those who ran them respected him and his family. Over the years, he'd taken scores of neighborhood boys under his guidance. "I don't have sons," he said. "I have daughters. I always wanted sons. So many kids don't have a father figure and that's why they fail." The only way to prevent more violence, he believed, was to target and influence the boys most likely to continue the cycle of revenge shootings. It was a strategy community leaders across the country were using. Rudy Corpuz in San Francisco's Hunters Point, James Clark on Saint Louis's north side, Ameena Matthews in Chicago, Andre Mitchell in Brooklyn's East New York, and others elsewhere intervened when emotions ran highest in the hours and days after a murder. Gary missed many practices over the summer, but now, with the season a week away, he was back at Betsy Head.

He arrived at the park around 7:30 a.m. on this Saturday in late August, before most of the players. Mo Better's three teams had an early bus trip to Teaneck, New Jersey, for their third and final preseason scrimmage. Gary paced in front of the long green bench, greeting boys and parents as they arrived. He owned a catering business and wore a Bluetooth earpiece even early on a weekend morning. Some boys strolled into the park munching on breakfast sandwiches from the corner store down the street. Most arrived with nothing other than cleats, a helmet, and football pads.

"Who hasn't eaten anything this morning?" Gary asked the boys gathered by the field. More than half raised their hands. Gary turned to the other coaches and whispered, "We gon' have to stop by the store and get them something, otherwise they might not have nothing in their stomachs 'til we get back here in the evening." The coaches often pooled their money to feed their players. Sometimes, Gary paid the whole bill himself, which is what happened the previous week, following Mo Better's trip to New Jersey for their first scrimmage of the year.

The coaches, focused on making sure every kid was on the bus and collecting the $10 fare from their parents, hadn't thought about breakfast on that first trip. One boy had only a handful of sunflower seeds. Two other boys split a Snickers bar. Another boy said, "I didn't eat anything for breakfast, but I drank this whole bottle of Sprite, so that'll keep me energized." Many took the field later that morning without having eaten anything since the previous night's dinner. Despite that, Mo Better's three teams beat up their competition. They played several Pop Warner programs that day, in a rotating "jamboree" format. Among the dozens of teams across multiple age groups, Mo Better's Pee Wees emerged as the most impressive bunch. The defense didn't allow a single touchdown. The offense scored on nearly every possession. And Isaiah lived up to the hype. "They never seen speed like that before," Dorian's dad Dwight said. "Just hit the corner and was gone. Nobody could catch him. He made it look like a video game. They showed they're a force to be reckoned with." The dominance brought back memories of the program's golden age. During one of Isaiah's long runs to the end zone, the announcer exclaimed into the microphone, "Mo Better's doing their thing!" When the boys retuned to Brownsville, Gary got them burgers, pizza, and chicken wings from the store.

Memories from the golden age came rushing back again a few days later, during Mo Better's second scrimmage, a Thursday-night affair at Betsy Head against Brooklyn United, a new program in Brownsville. The coaches had taken the matchup personally. Brooklyn United had sprouted up in Mo Better's territory and recruited kids who would've played for Mo Better. "When we play somebody around here, we need to dominate them," Chris told the boys before the game. "I'm gon' put it in street terms: I wanna kick they ass. They coming in our house. They coming with that talk, that bravado, that swag. It's like you gotta kick everybody's ass on your block. People feared coming to Betsy Head when we played here. They didn't wanna come to the pit. The way they came in was not the way they came out." Brooklyn United had posted information about the scrimmage on the program's Facebook page. "They thought Mo Better was slippin' and they wanted to show that they were the real king of Brooklyn youth football," said one Brooklyn United parent, Jason. "Our people were doing a lot of talking." Hundreds of locals showed up. Like the old days, fans circled the field and, when the games got started, the dust kicked up and seemed to swallow the park whole. "The dust was everywhere," Naz's father Repo said. "I was chewin' dust." Brooklyn United didn't play in Pop Warner but in a league without weight limits. The running back on their Pee Wee team was more than 200 pounds; one of his teammates, around 185. Mo Better's heaviest boy was less than 140 pounds. "They were bigger but our boys didn't care," said Repo. "They wasn't scared. They just ran around them. They tore that team up. Tore 'em up!" The Pee Wees scored five touchdowns and allowed none.

As the boys lined up in front of the yellow school bus on this Saturday morning, they were still talking about that dusty Thursday night.

"I didn't expect much," Isaiah said. "They talked a lot and they thought they were nice 'cause they beat local teams. But we was way better."

"I thought they was gonna be good 'cause they was big," Chaka said. "But they was mad slow. They came in thinking they was gonna be a dog, but they came out like a cat."

"Everybody was bigger than us," Isaiah said with a smile.

"That one dude, I can't even get my arms around him," Oomz said. "But I ain't need to 'cause I just hit him so hard he fell over—*boom*!"

The boys chuckled.

"Isaiah, 'member that one run?" Hart said.

"When I chucked somebody?" Isaiah said.

"That was baaaaad!" Hart said, bringing his fist to his mouth like he'd just heard a dope line in a rap battle.

"You said—*dooogggggg*!" said Oomz, lowering his shoulder to mimic Isaiah's run. "And the guy fall back!"

"You a power back and a speed back," Hart said.

"I coulda cut it back, though," Isaiah said, shrugging his shoulders. "If I cut it back I woulda scored."

ooooo

THE BUS WAS loud and every seat was filled. The Pee Wees took up the first few rows, the Junior Pee Wees sat in the middle, and the Mitey Mites were in the back. It was loudest in the back.

Mo Better had only enough money to rent one school bus this week. It barely fit all of the players, and left no room for the coaching staff. Chris, Esau, Gary, and most of the others carpooled with parents. When the bus driver turned on the engine, Elsie was the only coach on board. She sat at the front, her hands over her ears and a look of horror on her face. "Where is Vick?" she said. "We have all this noise, and if Vick ain't on this bus, I'm getting off."

To her relief, he stepped onto the bus a few minutes later. A chorus of "Shhhhh!" rippled through the rows as the boys noticed his presence. Vick was grimacing as he dragged up the steps, and his eyes, unusually shifty and downcast, suggested his mind was elsewhere. Then, as if waking from a dream, he quickly shifted his demeanor. His face straightened and his eyes locked in on the boys before him.

"Quiet down!" Vick boomed, and the boys all went silent. The bus rolled forward, onto Saratoga Avenue headed north. Vick stood in the aisle, his hands on the seat backs. A tan bandage was wrapped around his right palm. "Dear God," he said, "put a shield around this bus, around all the cars trailing behind us. We ask that you get us there safely with no hurt, harm, or danger. All in agreement?"

"Amen!" the boys shouted.

"One, two, three—"

"Mo Better!"

"Mitey Mites, you should be eating, because in five minutes, you will be reading," Vick said, as he made his way down the aisle, before taking his seat in the last row. And five minutes later: "Mitey Mites! Start reading! I don't care what you reading, just start reading."

Vick had started making his Mitey Mites read on bus trips nine years ago. "The talking was driving me crazy," he said. "If they reading, they not talking. My mother told me the day you stop reading is the day your brain starts to deteriorate." The Mitey Mites all knew how seriously Vick took this policy, and those who'd forgotten to bring books had improvised to avoid punishment: several boys were reading the *Amsterdam News*, a free local newspaper they'd picked up from the corner store next to Betsy Head. The front page of the paper featured a photo of a protester in Ferguson, Missouri, holding up a sign that said, "Don't Shoot." The thick headline read: "UNREST"

By the time the bus reached the highway, the Mitey Mites were calm and quiet. Some whispered and giggled in their seats, but most had their eyes on their reading material.

Vick leaned back against the window and stretched his legs into the aisle. He closed his eyes and sighed deeply. Twenty minutes later, he was back on his feet. He stopped at each row of Mitey Mites.

"What are you reading?" he asked a boy, who looked up at Vick with big, scared eyes.

"I'm reading *Charlotte's Web*."

"What's the spider's name?" Vick said.

"Wilbur."

"Wilbur is the name of the pig. What's the spider's name?"

"Charlotte."

"Very good."

He turned to the next boy.

"Puerto Rico, what did you read?"

"*Goosebumps*," Puerto Rico said with a big grin and excited eyes.

"What is it about?"

"There's a boy named Chris and he likes puppets and the puppet is alive and—"

"OK," Vick interrupted, nodding his head. "Very good."

A few rows later, a boy held up a thin hardcover book. Vick opened it and read the first page. His shoulders slumped and an exasperated look came over his face.

"Don't get on my bus with this baby book," he said to the boy. "It says right here: age two to six. How old are you?"

"Eight."

"You see how big the words are? Don't be getting on my bus with this baby book. You shouldn't be reading these big words."

In his mind, though, Vick did not blame the boy. The boy's book choice, Vick later said, "goes to show you that nobody's pushing this kid." Yet Vick didn't fully blame the parents either. Perhaps they were doing their best. Perhaps they couldn't afford to buy him new books and didn't have time to take him to the library. Perhaps they were overwhelmed by their circumstances. Vick had eight kids and he believed that he'd tried his best with each of them. Two of them were in college. One was an accountant. Another worked for the city. But those were only the success stories. A few days earlier, his 23-year-old son Donte had called him from Tulsa County Jail in Oklahoma. He had been arrested on armed robbery charges. "He asked if I could help him make bail. He said, 'Dad, my bail is four hundred thousand dollars.' I said, 'Nigga, I ain't got four dollars.'"

Vick's life was unraveling. A few months before Vick was scheduled to graduate, his vocational school, Micropower Career Institute, shut down. Federal authorities charged school administrators with fraud, accusing them of issuing illegitimate visas. Vick hoped to transfer his credits to another school, but he wasn't sure if any other school would oblige. He had been in the process of getting an internship, a requirement for his degree, but he learned that many hospitals didn't want to work with students from his school anymore. "I'm worried I have to start over from scratch," Vick said.

He didn't have enough money to start over. He had already invested all he had in his schooling. With that in limbo, he went back to looking for work. He picked up some temporary gigs with a former Mo Better parent who worked as a construction contractor. It was enough to pay the bills. In recent weeks, Vick had worked on a warehouse project in lower Manhattan. While soldering pipes, he scorched his hand. The jackhammering wore on his back, which was now in constant pain. "I'm too old for manual labor," he said. "But I don't know what else I can do."

Meanwhile, Vick's girlfriend had kicked him out of her apartment. He'd been looking for a new place to live for several weeks now, which was not easy in New York City, not even in east Brooklyn—especially for a renter unable to afford even $500 a month. He was now staying at a classmate's house.

The stresses weighed on Vick's mind. Back in his seat in the last row of the bus, he slept for the rest of the ride.

ooooo

The Pee Wees leaned their foreheads against the bus windows. "Yoooo, look at," said Oomz. The field's artificial grass was a lush green with bright white lines. The building behind the field, which housed a basketball gym and locker rooms, shone with fresh blue and cream paint. A forest thick with pine trees stood on one side of the field. Train tracks ran along the other side. "This is beautiful," said Hart.

The Pee Wees marched off the bus. Many of them wore their freshest pair of sneakers: Isaiah in LeBron XIs, Oomz in Air Jordan IIIs, Chaka in Air Jordan VIs. They lined up on a paved path that snaked through the woods and onto the field. Birds chirped. A woman in black tights jogged past. Oomz's eyes followed her. "She got that badonkadonk," he said with a mischievous smile.

The morning was windy. Many of the boys had their hoods over their heads and their hands stuffed into their pockets. Chris walked beside the line of players like a general assessing his troops.

"Take the hood off ya head," he said. "When we travel we take the hoods off our heads."

"But we from Brownsville!" Oomz shouted sarcastically.

"We ain't in the hood," Chris said. "We out the hood. This is not hood activity."

On the field, the Pee Wees slipped on their pads and formed a circle for stretching. A freight train chugged beside the field with a low rumble. The boys reached down to stretch their hamstrings, pulled their legs up to stretch their quads, sat down and twisted their torsos to stretch their backs, and brought their feet in and leaned forward to stretch their groins. They counted to 10 in unison for each stretch. The train chugged on, its front end and back end out of sight. Donnie had started counting the cars but gave up after 20.

"Yo, how long is this train, though?" Hart said.

"What if it never ends?" Chaka said.

"Nah, man, it's gotta end," Oomz said. "Everything got an end."

"Isaiah, you think you faster than that train?" Time Out said.

"Isaiah faster than you, though," Hart said, and the boys laughed.

"See, it's different kinds of speed," Time Out said. "I'm zero to forty real quick. Isaiah zero to sixty real quick."

"Isaiah zero to one hundred real quick!" Hart said. "For real, though, we gon' give up less than twenty yards today. They not going nowhere." He paused for a second, then added, "All right, I'ma stop being cocky. We gon' give up less than thirty yards."

As the boys spoke, they stopped counting out loud and some ended their stretches early before the whole group reached 10.

"C'mon, we gotta do it as a team!" said Oomz, suddenly serious, his voice loud and sharp.

"Now you wanna talk about the team?" Time Out jabbed. "Now you wanna talk about the team? Now you wanna talk about the team?"

"'Member when you quit?" Naz joined in.

"But now we a team, huh?" Time Out said.

"Why'd you quit anyway?" Hart asked.

"He couldn't take how Andrell was yelling at him," Time Out said.

Oomz sat quietly, frowning, looking at the ground, shaking his head.

ooooo

ISAIAH GOT THE ball on the offense's first play. He ran toward the middle of the line, then hopped outside around the edge. A defender met him 10 yards upfield and Isaiah accelerated, lowered his shoulder and bucked the boy onto his back, and his teammates and parents let out a collective "Wooooo!" He raced down the sideline and dove into the end zone. On the next possession, Isaiah got the ball again, on a sweep to the outside. He sprinted around the corner and ran 50 yards, untouched for another touchdown.

It seemed at first that the day would be a repeat of the first two scrimmages. But then the yards became more difficult. Teaneck's defense stuffed Mo Better's runs and its offense pounded forward for good gains. After each play, Oomz bent over with fatigue and walked slowly to the huddle. He complained to his teammates that he'd hurt his hand when it smacked into a helmet. On some defensive plays, he barely moved. Late in the first half, a Teaneck runner burrowed into the middle of the defense, right through Oomz's arms, on the way to a long touchdown. It was the first score the Pee Wees had allowed all preseason. The boys on Teaneck's sidelines jumped up and down and shouted in joy. The Pee Wees dropped their heads and slapped their arms to their sides. A few shouted at the ground in anger. Some looked at the sky and shook their heads. By the time halftime came, Mo Better's early success felt distant.

As the Pee Wees sipped water on the sidelines, though, the frustration seemed to have worn off. Several of the boys were laughing with their helmets off. Oomz toyed with a roll of athletic tape, ripping off pieces to wrap on his facemask. Isaiah kept his helmet on. He had seen this before: the way his teammates would shrug off their poor play and drown their disappointment in a barrage of humor. He believed it was their way of suppressing the pressure and urgency of a tight game—as if by making light of their struggles they could avoid the pain of failure. He believed this was why they lost so many games last season. A few boys complimented Isaiah on his touchdowns. He nodded solemnly at them but did not speak. Oomz ran up to him and jumped on his back. "You killin' 'em out there, boy!" he told Isaiah. Isaiah pushed Oomz off and looked at him sternly.

"You gotta stop crying, though," Isaiah said.

"But my pinkie!" Oomz said with a wide grin.

"You too busy jokin', boy."

"We playin' good, man."

"We should be smackin' 'em."

Then Isaiah turned to the rest of the team and said, "We playin' like they Brooklyn United!"

The boys fell silent. Esau stepped to the front of the group.

"He right," Esau said. "Y'all seem hungover out there. Like y'all was drinking last night or something. All y'all backs: stop dancin' and run somebody over. You don't take somebody heart by juking. Run some-body over. Stop dancing. That's not for y'all. We on offense next. We just gotta run it down they throat."

∞∞∞

ISAIAH AND OOMZ took pride in being running backs. Running back is a tough and glorious position. A running back gets the ball behind the line of scrimmage and has the whole field before him with all 11 de-fenders seeking to crush him, diving at his knees and launching them-selves at his head. "Running back is the best position," Oomz said. "You get a handoff, right? You got vision, you got everything in front of you." A running back can sprint around the defenders or make quick cuts to juke by them, but most often a running back must lower his shoulder and bang helmets. Advancing through each level—from Pop Warner to high school to college to the pros—meant defying the odds and avoid-ing catastrophic injury on hundreds of these carries. The average NFL career lasted less than four years; the average for a running back was around two and a half.

Modern NFL and college football relied increasingly on quarter-backs and passing. But youth football remained old-school. Strategies were simple and teams often won because they had the fastest, strongest, and savviest runners. Running back was perhaps the most prestigious position at this level, the one that drew the most eyes over the course of a game. Running backs got special attention at Mo Better. Coach Vick spent much of his time at practice pulling aside his young prospective backs to teach them the fundamentals of the position while the rest of the team worked on blocking and footwork drills. Mo Better had earned a reputation for producing great running backs, from Dajuan Mitchell to Curtis Samuel. The coaches expected this year's Pee Wees to defend that legacy.

Oomz opened the second half at Teaneck with a punishing seven-yard run, right up the middle, dragging three defenders before falling to the ground. On the next play, he ran to the outside, and it looked like he might try to beat the defensive back to the sideline, but then he slowed—eyes scanning the bodies around him, mind reading the possible moves—and sliced back to the middle of the field, trapping the defensive back behind a blocker, before sprinting back to the outside for a 30-yard run. The offense pounded the ball further down the field, eating up yards with each run, until Oomz blasted through the line for a five-yard touchdown.

"Oomz comin' to play!" Vick shouted from the sidelines.

On defense, Oomz was energized. On a third down, he blitzed up the middle and smacked Teaneck's running back three yards behind the line, a hit so hard the boy's head snapped back and his back hit the ground with his legs still in the air.

"Let him know it's real in Brownsville, Oomz!" Vick hollered.

"That looked like his father almost!" another coach said.

"That boy don't even want the ball no more," Vick said.

Oomz reached a hand down to help the boy up, but the boy didn't try to get up. The referee and several coaches jogged over to him. As in most youth football games, there was no doctor on the sidelines. Many programs barely scraped together enough funds to pay referees and league fees, hoping each week that the concession stand made enough cash to cover the game-day expenses. A medic on hand was considered a luxury. And so, the coaches knelt beside the boy, asking him questions about his name and the day of the week. A majority of injuries, according to Coach Chris, initially appear worse than they are because kids are kids and football is rough and most 11-year-olds are still getting accustomed to playing through bruises and bumps. After a few minutes, the boy pushed himself up to his feet and slowly walked to the sideline. The coaches concluded that he did not have a concussion.

Mo Better scored touchdowns on the next two possessions. Teaneck didn't move the ball past midfield. On the sidelines and in the stands, Mo Better's coaches and parents savored the success, joking and smiling, growing more and more eager for the start of the regular season the following week. Some parents, already thinking about the drive home, discussed whether they should avoid the Verrazano-Narrows Bridge because wasn't Al Sharpton leading a "justice for Eric Garner" march there today? A few parents scrolled through their phones between plays.

With the scrimmage winding down, Isaiah took a pitch, stiff-armed a defender, and ran down the side of the field for another big run, bringing more cheers from Mo Better's bleachers. From the corner of his eye, Isaiah spotted a defender racing toward him. Isaiah thought the defender had an angle on him, so he throttled down, considered cutting back inside, then decided to just outrun him. But the boy had made up ground, and he dove at Isaiah's legs. His helmet slammed into Isaiah's left knee and Isaiah toppled out of bounds, into Teaneck's sideline. Isaiah felt a sharp pain pierce his knee. He grabbed the knee and groaned. The crowd went silent.

"Coach! Coach! Your running back, coach!" Teaneck's coach shouted to Chris, who ran with Esau and Andrell to Isaiah, who lay on his back and feared the worst. Chris pressed his fingers on the sides of Isaiah's knee and Isaiah told him where it hurt. Chris bent Isaiah's knee, slowly, slightly, gently, and Isaiah told him when it hurt. The coaches helped him to his feet and Isaiah limped to the sideline with his arms on their shoulders, putting almost no pressure on the injured leg. He sat on a metal bench behind the sideline and held a cold water bottle to his knee.

ooooo

THE MOOD ON the bus home was jubilant, full of laughter, optimism, and declarations like, "Man, I be gettin' like one hundred texts from girls a day!" But Isaiah sat quietly near the front, staring into the screen of his mother's iPad. He didn't know if he'd be able to practice on Monday. He'd hidden from his teammates how worried he was about the injury. When he'd limped from the field to the bus, he told everybody he was fine.

"You good?" Oomz asked. "You gon' be at practice?"

"Oh, hell yeah," Isaiah replied.

In truth, he did not know how badly his knee was damaged, only that he could barely walk. His thoughts bounced between hope and dread. In his mind, he relived that final play, imagined all the ways it could have gone differently, if he had cut inside here or accelerated there. On the field, Isaiah was a technician and a perfectionist. Unlike some

of his teammates, he did not see football as merely a chaotic and violent jumble of bodies. There was a science to anticipating an opponent's
strategy and movement, and there was an art to applying that science in
the midst of the chaotic and violent jumble of bodies. On his mother's
iPad, he watched a recording of the game he'd just played. He rewound
and re-watched his mistakes more often than his highlights. He saw the
holes he had missed, the tackles he should have broken. He rewound
and re-watched until he understood the error, memorized it, and identified the tools he needed to fix it on the next try. Watch the outside
linebacker's first step on an off-tackle handoff before bouncing out or
slicing in. Look for the cut-back lane when the safety goes too wide
on a pitch. It calmed Isaiah to review the footage, and the thought of
becoming even more dominant excited him. Yet all this preparation and
improvement would mean nothing, he thought, if he couldn't get back
on the field. He stared into the screen and tried to lose himself in the
video, watching himself glide across the grass.

– 14 –

WHAT THEY'VE BEEN WAITING FOR
Early to mid-September 2014

THE NIGHT BEFORE THE SEASON'S FIRST OFFICIAL GAME, Isaiah got a reprieve. His knee, diagnosed as mildly sprained, had improved steadily, but Isaiah knew it was far too weak for a game. After a frustrating week of limping around Betsy Head, he planned to suit up in pads and play at least some snaps at line, where he could limit his running. The team had only 16 players, the league minimum, which meant Isaiah had to play at least 10 snaps to avoid a forfeit. More than that, though, Coach Chris expected him to play. All week, Chris had told him he'd have to "tough it out" and "play through the pain." A hobbled Isaiah was still a better option than some of the team's less-talented players. So, Isaiah steeled himself. He lay in bed and visualized the game.

Then his phone buzzed. Coach Chris had called to tell him that the game was canceled. Their opponent didn't have enough players and had to forfeit. "I was mad and happy at the same time," Isaiah said. "It was like a weight off."

His knee healed to full strength over the following days. By the time practice rolled around the next Saturday, Isaiah was running and cutting like he had been all summer. On his way home, his mind on the game less than 24 hours away, he stopped by the corner store to get a sandwich. Oomz was already inside, waiting for the deli man to finish cooking his order. They slapped hands.

"Let's blow 'em out," he said to Oomz.

"Mm-hmm," Oomz hummed.

Coach James walked in a few seconds later.

"Y'all make sure to rest up today. Stay off ya feet," he said. "School's 'bout to start too, so make sure you start getting ya homework done before practice."

The boys nodded.

"Oomz, you still going to that school over here next year?"

"I don't know," Oomz said. "My mom tryna get me into a junior high up by where she's at. She want me to get out of here."

"Well your mom, she's doing the right thing."

ooooo

THE WEEK AFTER the forfeit, Hart was eager to finally play a real contest. The night before game day, he had trouble falling asleep. He woke up feeling energized, pulled off his blanket, shuffled down the stairs, and ate a bowl of Cinnamon Toast Crunch and a handful of jelly beans. He felt he'd been cheated out of a game last week, and so this week, he said, "I gotta play twice as good." He made a bet with his father: if he got at least two sacks, his father would take the family to Olive Garden after the game.

After breakfast, Hart and his father went into the bathroom and Hart stepped on the weighing scale. He was 122 pounds. He got dressed in his pads and uniform and stepped back onto the scale: 130.5 pounds, half a pound below his weight limit. This was cutting it close. His father was nervous about the official weigh-in before the game all through the drive to Franklin K. Lane High School on Jamaica Avenue, on the border between Brooklyn and Queens. They pulled into the parking lot at 10 a.m., three hours before kickoff.

The Mitey Mites were on the field. The morning was hot. The sun reflected off the windows of the high school's main building, a towering brick colonial-style structure with white columns just behind one set of goalposts. Elevated subway tracks ran behind the other. The smell of hot dogs and burgers floated around a concession tent, where Coach Gary and his cousin worked the grills. Parents and players filed into the stands, with Mo Better's contingent gathering on the north end of the bleachers and the Elizabeth, New Jersey, visitors on the south side. Hart had a sheen of sweat by the time he found several of his teammates in a circle playing with a small arcade basketball on a cement walkway beside the bleachers. He put down his pads and bag and slapped hands. The boys showed off dribble moves, tossing fadeaway jump shots at an imaginary hoop. The ball went around the circle, each boy trying to one-up the last boy's moves. When the ball got to Oomz, he dribbled it between his legs twice, spun around, and just as he was punctuating his turn with a twisting finger roll, a voice behind him called out, "Yoooo!"

It was his father, Big Oomz, walking over with a scowl and shaking his head. He was a tall, lean man, with a shaved dome, square jaw, and day-old stubble. He wore a black T-shirt and gray sweatpants. He grabbed Oomz's arm and pulled him out of the circle. "Time to chill out and get focused," he said. He led Oomz to a cement bench in the shade of the bleachers and sat him down beside his grandmother. "Getcha mind right," Big Oomz told him.

The other Pee Wees stopped playing too. They picked up their pads and bags and found an open area in the dark hollow beneath the bleachers. Giant tires, steel pipes, and sticks of plywood littered the space. The boys sat on the tires.

"I can only imagine how hot that turf's gonna be," said Hart.

"Everybody's gonna have a couple of turf burns," said Isaiah.

"I be hopping right up, though!" said Hart.

"Yeah, it's no thing," said Isaiah.

"Yo, we gon' bust these fools," said Donnie.

"We busted them last year," said Time Out.

"We did not bust them!" said Naz. "It was a tough game. We won by one point. We probably woulda lost that game if it wasn't for all they penalties."

The cheers and groans in the stands above them echoed within the cavern, and the stomping feet shook the bleachers with a metallic rattle. Hart sat silently now. He looked at the ground and bobbed his head as if listening to music on headphones. He prepared his mind for the violence to come. He was the kind of boy who smiled a lot and asked a lot of silly questions and showed giggling excitement over the smallest joys: a turkey and egg sandwich from the corner store, finishing a book report, a new pair of football gloves. But on the field, he seemed like a different kid. He possessed a roughness. Sometimes that roughness accidentally seeped out on the playground at school, in games of tag or basketball, and his teachers had to tell him to go easier on his classmates, who were smaller and meeker. In a few hours, though, he could release that energy. His fingers tapped the tire. On the field, he told himself, he was unstoppable; he was a destroyer. He was stronger than any other boy on the field, he told himself. No other boy could block him and any boy who stood in front of him would get drilled with a heavy shoulder to the sternum. This was a violent game, and Hart aimed to be the most violent boy on the field.

ooooo

IT WAS A good show from the start. On the first play, Isaiah fought off a blocker and tackled the Elizabeth running back five yards behind the line of scrimmage. On the next play, the ball slipped out of the quarterback's hands and Marquis dove onto the fumble. Five plays later, Time Out scored the Pee Wees' first touchdown of the season with a four-yard run. They got the ball right back when Oomz sliced through the line and hit the quarterback, knocking the ball loose and recovering it himself. Three plays later, Isaiah jogged into the end zone for an easy touchdown.

By now, it was clear this was a very uneven fight. The Mo Better Jaguars were certainly bigger and more athletic than the Elizabeth Packers. They were more skilled, too. But on top of that, they also seemed far more disciplined and focused. The Brownsville boys on the sideline stood shoulder to shoulder, watching and cheering with their helmets on; they shouted "pass!" and "run!" and "fumble!" to their teammates on the field. By contrast, the Packers across the field were down on their knees or sitting on their butts, fiddling with their shoelaces or the turf, their helmets on the ground beside them. The game quickly became a blowout. Mo Better's offense plowed down the field on each turn, with Oomz pounding through the middle and Isaiah sprinting around the outside. Elizabeth's offense struggled to even get the ball across the line of scrimmage, as Hart and Donnie blasted through the front lines on each play. And those runners who made it past the front lines were quickly picked up and thrown to the turf by Isaiah and Oomz. They slapped hands and patted shoulder pads after big hits. The hard game face Isaiah had worn earlier was gone. By the third quarter, he was smiling behind his facemask after many plays. This was the performance he had hoped for. On defense, he was flying around the field, drilling people to the ground. On offense, he was cutting, stiff-arming, and running people over. The field seemed wide open, every square inch accessible to him. The game felt easy and fun.

On one play, he blitzed around the edge of the offensive line, lowered his shoulder, and smacked the quarterback to the turf. Isaiah let out a shout and stood over the quarterback, looking down at the boy and flexing his arms. The referee ordered him not to celebrate like that again. When Isaiah returned to the huddle, Oomz began laughing at him. "Isaiah was feelin' himself," Oomz later said. "He's so calm and chill in real life, but in games he's so intense." Isaiah carried himself with a fierce swagger on the field. On the first play of the third quarter, he took a handoff and raced toward the outside. Two defenders read the play well and cut him off in the backfield, so Isaiah cut away from them, angling his sprint away from the line of scrimmage, losing ground from where he had started. The defenders chased him deeper into the backfield, before Isaiah accelerated straight toward the sidelines and turned the corner, beating the defenders to the outside and zooming past the rest of the defense for a long touchdown. When he reached the end zone, he dropped the ball and pretended to rip open his jersey to reveal an imaginary Superman logo underneath—a touchdown celebration Carolina Panthers quarterback Cam Newton had made famous. He posed that way for a few seconds, as if the whole world was watching him.

Coach Esau and Coach Andrell turned to each other with awe in their faces.

"Esau, that's not fair," said Andrell, smiling wide. "That's not fair! Come on, don't do that. That's not fair!"

On the kickoff that followed the touchdown, Oomz booted a dribbler that bounced to a heavy-set boy 20 yards downfield. Naz met the boy halfway and grabbed him around the thighs, unable to take him down. Oomz, sprinting down the middle of the field, recoiled into a crouch then launched himself at the boy. *Smack!* Their helmets crashed and the boy fell onto his back and immediately put his hands over his face, squirming in pain.

Ooooohhhhh! the crowd boomed.

Esau and the Elizabeth coach ran onto the field and knelt beside the boy.

"What's wrong?" Esau said to the boy.

The boy pointed at his earholes.

"What's your name?" the Elizabeth coach said to the boy.

The boy did not answer for several seconds.

Players on both teams took a knee. After a few minutes, the coaches helped the boy to his feet. Parents and players clapped as the boy walked slowly off the field. Oomz got up from his knee and looked over at Coach Vick on the sidelines.

"Coach Vick, I saw you there," Oomz said. "That was for you."

ooooo

THE SUN BEAT down on the bleachers. Isaiah's older brother, Shaq, held an umbrella over himself and their mother, Roxanne. They sat in the top row so the umbrella didn't block anybody's view. Roxanne filmed the game on her iPad, as Isaiah had asked, so that he could review the film that night. The parents a few rows below them provided a running commentary of the action on the field, shouting encouragements before each snap and critiques after the whistle.

"Get that quarterback, son!" shouted Mr. Hart, always the loudest voice in the stands. "Yeah! Yeah! That's my boy!"

"Good play, Andrew!" Mrs. Hart added after her son's second sack. "Let's go!"

"Watch the run, Dorian!" shouted Dorian's father Dwight. "There it is! Good hit, son!"

"Two hands on the football, Marquis!" Marquis's father Ramsey shouted. "Run through those arm tackles!"

"Let it loose, Naz!" Naz's father Repo shouted, as his son dropped back to pass. "Let it loose!"

And when the spiral landed in Chaka's hands for a long touchdown, Chaka's uncle John shouted, "You the man Chaka! You the man!"

"Hell of a call, Esau!" shouted Repo.

"Our tax dollars goin' to good use!" shouted Ramsey.

Roxanne and Shaq watched quietly for most of the game, several rows behind many of the other Pee Wee parents, who sat in a pack in the front rows. They greeted and smiled at the other parents when they arrived before the game, but otherwise kept to themselves. They clapped after good plays and shook their heads after bad ones. Mostly, they talked to each other, with Shaq explaining the nuances of the game to his mother. Whenever her son was on the field, Roxanne leaned forward with her elbows on her knees, eyes locked on jersey number 2. She had been massaging her son's injured knee most nights, hoping to strengthen it for the beating it would take. She held her breath during the tense seconds when her son had the ball and exhaled heavily when he popped up to his feet after getting tackled. She watched with an intensity that built with each play, and when her son crossed the end zone for a touchdown, she rose to her feet and broke her silence with a jubilant cheer—"Go Isaiaaaaahhh! Yeah Isaiaaaaah!"—before returning to her silent perch.

She had been amused to learn how important football was in America. How thousands of people filled the stands to watch Shaq's Lincoln High games on Friday nights and Saturday mornings. How television cameras stood on the sidelines and behind the end zone and local news stations replayed highlights of these teenagers running around in jerseys that seemed too big for them. How grown men and women became so angry after a dropped pass or a missed tackle, and how some even cried in the stands after losses in big games. She learned that these passions ran deep across the country and that there were high schools and colleges spending millions of dollars on this sport, for stadiums, coaches, weight rooms, bus trips, and uniforms, instead of on books, teachers, and field trips to historical monuments. She had heard about communities near and far devoted to football as if it were a religion, gathering in parking lots hours before games and investing their emotions into the outcomes. When she thought about those communities, they reminded her of her Seventh-day Adventist friends, who spent their Saturdays worshiping in church from early morning to late evening.

In Brownsville, football was not the end but the means. Football offered a path to escape the neighborhood. Addressing the team one evening, Brooklyn borough president Eric Adams said, "When you're holding a football, you don't have a gun in your hand. When you're running down the field, you're not running from the police. If you can put a ball through a hoop, you can wear a black robe and sit on the Supreme Court." To Harry Edwards, the renowned sports sociologist, this mind-set is rooted in socioeconomic reality. Public school classrooms are overcrowded, extracurricular programs are being cut, college tuition rates are rising, grants are limited. Sports, Edwards said, can make a kid think and care about his future. Sports can be the hook that keeps a kid in class and keeps his mind focused on setting and reaching goals. It would be unrealistic to think that without sports in a boy's life he'll "focus on everything else," Edwards said. "You've got to fix everything else first."

Though Roxanne had learned to like football, she did not like everything about it. The violence worried her. She'd read about the scientific research on brain damage and about the NFL's assurances, in response, regarding the sport's safety. But while she was unsure about the exact dangers of football, she was absolutely certain about the benefits her son would gain if he went to a good high school and then college after that.

Because football was important in America, she recognized that Isaiah's skills made him valuable in the eyes of those who could help him.

Many of the parents in the stands felt the same way. Dwight, Repo, Ramsey, and Mr. Hart all said they'd be thrilled to see their sons rise through a big-time Division I college and into the NFL. But they all also said they'd be thrilled to see their sons rise through an Ivy League college and into law school or medical school or whatever profession the boys chose. These were middle-class men who had risen from low-income households and, like every parent, they hoped to see their own children reach even further than they had. It wasn't that they believed football was necessary for their sons to find that success; they simply believed that football could help propel their sons forward through an environment where every advantage might be the one that makes the difference.

Beyond that, these men loved the sport and were happy to see that their sons shared that love. It was a tough sport that taught a boy to do his job right even if that meant taking a hit. It stripped away fear, or at least instilled the courage to fight through fear. Proud to see their boys exhibit these virtues, the fathers shouted their enthusiasm from the front rows.

Just in front of them, standing alone on the walkway, leaning against the fence, Big Oomz was seeing his son play for the first time. He watched intently and calmly, the expression on his face stoic and unchanging. When his son broke a tackle and hammered up the field for an eight-yard run, the men behind him cheered.

"There you go, Oomz!"

"That's what I'm talkin' bout, Oomz!"

"Keep poundin' 'em Oomz! They can't stop you!"

Big Oomz, though, stayed quiet. He slowly nodded his head. A small, slight smile crept up his face.

ooooo

BIG OOMZ WAS happy that his son played football and that he was a smart, respectable boy who did well in school. He credited his son's mother and grandmother for this. But he also believed there were some bits of wisdom that only he could pass along to his son. He taught the boy to keep his shoulder pads low and accelerate at the point of contact. He taught him to keep both hands on the football when running through traffic because there was nothing more shameful for a running back than fumbling.

He had repeated these and many other lessons earlier that day as they stood in front of the bleachers before the game. Big Oomz crouched into a running stance and held out his left arm, his open palm smacking an imaginary defender's helmet. "When you stiff-arm, you gotta push off and not just hold your hand there," he said. His son looked up at him, nodding, eyes focused and intense. "You gotta punish 'em for tryna tackle you," Big Oomz said.

Oomz had spent most of the week at his mother's apartment in Fort Greene. He'd been admitted to the new charter school a few blocks away. Big Oomz didn't have the final say on where his son went to school, but here, beside a football field, was his jurisdiction. Here, he could teach his boy the lessons he needed to become a man. And, to his eyes, his boy had a long way to go.

Late in the third quarter, as Mo Better continued to dominate Elizabeth, Big Oomz watched with a look of contempt on his face. He was not impressed with Mo Better's performance. This was a weak opponent, and in his day, Mo Better would have dropped 50 or 60 points by the end of the third quarter. The boys he saw on the field were skilled, yes, but they were not so tough and not so passionate. They had nothing on the Boogeyman, Pup, and the rest of his guys. Back in Big Oomz's day, every boy in a Mo Better uniform could bring the lumber. They took pride in their hitting and the fear they instilled in their opponents. Big Oomz felt a shiver of nostalgia thinking about those days, when he was the best player on a great team. He scored four touchdowns some games. One game, he scored on a run, an interception, and a fumble recovery. "We were always playing these big white boys upstate," he said, "and we would always whoop them." It wasn't just that his teammates were tougher and faster than those white boys; he believed he and his guys were so good because they loved football and took it more seriously than anybody else. "We played football every day," he said. "Not a day went by I wasn't playing. After practice we'd go out to the projects and play." They played in the courtyards, in the streets, on the blacktops, in alleyways, and in narrow, dimly lit, paint-chipped hallways.

It wasn't the same these days, he believed. "These kids, they inside with the computer all day," he said. "These kids not getting out as much." He saw his son spending free time playing video games and watching TV. No wonder his son wasn't as fast or as tough. Big Oomz pondered if the coaches were to blame. He had doubted these coaches since his return to Brownsville.

The win he was witnessing now meant little. Big Oomz clapped and nodded, without much enthusiasm, when Chaka caught a touchdown in the fourth quarter. He clapped and nodded some more when his son burrowed through the line for the point-after conversion. (After a touchdown in Pop Warner, teams could try for an extra point by punching the ball into the end zone, or go for two points by kicking it through the goalposts, though few teams at this level had any boy skilled enough to do so.) Because of the lopsided score, 33–0, the referees had the mercy rule in effect through the second half, which meant the game clock didn't pause for any reason. After the game finished, the Pee Wees gathered at midfield, peeling off their jerseys and shoulder pads, smiling and giggling, recalling the day's highlights.

"I saw that block!"

"They couldn't touch you!"

"Man, you really hit that guy!"

Though they were savoring the feeling of victory, the celebration was tempered. The boys had not jumped up and down or pumped their fists or hollered out when the final whistle blew. They had expected this outcome.

Big Oomz walked toward the group. He held a folded black umbrella, which he pressed against the turf like a cane. He lifted the umbrella and tapped its tip on Oomz's shoulder. Oomz turned and looked up at him.

"I'm leaving," Big Oomz said. "You ridin' with ya mama. You coming to the house later?"

Oomz nodded. His father left.

The next week's game was in East Orange, New Jersey, against the East Orange Wildcats. Two buses would pick up the boys and coaches in front of Betsy Head Park early Sunday morning. Oomz and his father decided that Oomz would spend Saturday night at Big Oomz's place, which was a short walk to the park. After practice on Saturday afternoon, he went to his grandmother's house and waited for his father to come by and pick him up. His father didn't show, so he stayed at his grandmother's house that night.

∞∞∞∞

SUNDAY MORNING WAS chilly and windy. Oomz got to the park around 7 a.m. He wore his football pants, red and white Air Jordan IIs, and a T-shirt. He'd forgotten to bring his hoodie. He was grumpy.

"Yo, you not cold?" one of his teammates asked him.

"Yeah, I'm cold!" he hissed.

He dropped his bag on the long green bench and rubbed his hands together. A 10-year-old Junior Pee Wee nicknamed Philly, because he'd just moved to Brooklyn from Philadelphia, put his bags down nearby. He looked over at Oomz and said, "Y'all playing today?"

Oomz shot back a look of condescension—lips pursed, eyes dead, head tilted to the side.

"Nah," he said. "We just got these pants and brought all our equipment and got up early and came over here—"

"All right, all right, all right, all right, all right," Philly interjected. He paused, and something on Oomz's face caught his attention. Squinting, he locked in on the scar below Oomz's right brow, which pushed his right eyelid slightly lower than his left one—an old playground injury. Philly said, "Why ya eye look like that?"

"'Cause it look like that!" Oomz scoffed.

"You mad negative this morning, boy," Philly said.

Oomz turned away from Philly and walked over to Donnie, who'd missed the last two practices because he'd gotten in trouble at school for an angry outburst after his teacher called him out for talking in class. It was a classic Donnie tantrum: a hard face, lots of shouting, balled fists—

the posture of a drunk man at a bar who'd just seen somebody make a pass at his girl. Donnie hated to be disrespected.

"Long as you here for the game, that's what matters," Oomz said, nervously counting how many of his teammates were present as he headed for the bus, fully aware that a single absence meant an automatic loss.

Coach Chris stepped on after the players, who had filled the seats and settled into a zone of fidgety excitement, some singing along with the music playing on Oomz's phone. It had been an eventful week for Chris. The Democratic primaries were on Tuesday, and he'd been campaigning through the summer. In late August, he'd switched his allegiance in the 55th District state assembly race from Lori Boozer to Latrice Walker, a lawyer who specialized in civil rights cases against the police department. He liked both candidates, but he was savvy enough to sense the likely winner. And indeed, on Tuesday, Walker easily won the election, with 40 percent to Boozer's 23 percent. The week only got better from there. On Saturday, Mo Better alumnus Curtis Samuel rushed for more than 100 yards, and fellow Mo Better alums Brandon Reddish and Wayne Morgan, both defensive backs at Syracuse, had strong games. As Chris stood silently at the front of the bus, waiting for the boys to quiet down, he was smiling. He felt good about the future.

"Yo!" Coach Esau shouted. "Shut up! Stop talking! Turn that shit off! Get in your seat!"

The bus was silent. Chris cleared his throat.

"Yo, anybody know what domestic violence is?" he said.

A boy in the back shouted, "Like Ray Rice!"

A video had recently emerged of the NFL running back punching his fiancée in the face in an Atlantic City hotel elevator. The league had suspended Rice indefinitely, and the story was all over the news.

"Yo, forget Ray Rice," Chris said. "You think he was the first one? That goes on in stories you don't hear about, in a lot of families you don't hear about because the people involved aren't celebrities. That could go on in some of your families. My father did that to my mother. I'll never forget what I saw. I still remember what it felt like. That could go on in any of our families."

His voice turned soft.

"What's the biggest emotion we as men have to control?" he said.

"Anger," several boys replied.

"Louder!"

"Anger!" the boys on the bus shouted in unison.

"Louder!"

"Anger!"

"Some of y'all sitting here right now know exactly what I'm talking about, 'cause it happens in our families," Chris said. He spoke slowly, matter-of-factly, as if they were all sitting around his living room shooting the shit after a long day at work. "My dad was in jail during my city championship game for domestic violence. Then he had the nerve to tell me after how I could have played better. All that stuff you go through at your age, it has an impact on your futures. They can predict if you're going to be a criminal now based on your reading level. How many people we know at Rikers Island right now?"

A bunch of boys nodded, some hummed "mm-hmm," several raised their hands, and Marquis said, "My dad works at Rikers Island!" Chris quickly waved his hands, holding in a laugh as he realized the boys hadn't recognized that his question was rhetorical. "Don't put your hands up," he said. "Don't say anything. I'm not trying to put your business out there."

The whole time Chris spoke, Oomz stared out the window, impatient to get moving.

ooooo

AS THE BUS crawled through thick traffic, the boys took in the sights out the window, keeping up a steady commentary. Prospect Park. Barclay's Center. "Do you think Jay-Z is in there?" "He probably don't even stay in Brooklyn no more." Tall, unfinished towers, steel beams exposed, cranes and scaffolding hanging off the side, men in hard hats and orange vests gathered at the base preparing to begin the day's work. Brooklyn Bridge to the left. Statue of Liberty beyond it in the distance. Lower Manhattan rising high above the choppy waters. Packs of Canal Street pedestrians seeping around unmoving cars like floodwater. Old men smoking cigarettes leaning against light poles. Refrigerated transport vans, hazard lights flashing, double-parked on narrow one-way side streets. Young men in hoodies unloading crates from the trucks, stacking them on dollies, and rolling them into stores. Old Chinese men and women hawking fresh fish and vegetables on the sidewalk. Rhythms many generations old, through changing skylines, clothing styles, and car models.

Soon the bus escaped the slog of the city's streets, zipping through the Holland Tunnel and popping out onto the clear highways of New Jersey, passing lush parkways and quaint towns with clapboard houses and brick churches with sharp steeples, then winding through dark green swamps and waterways, over a rusted bridge, barges in the river, smokestacks in the distance, tractor trailers and gravel mounds on big lots, warehouses and refineries beside railroad tracks. The boys cringed at the fishy smell that wisped in through the open windows.

ooooo

IT WAS ANOTHER easy win. The Pee Wees were in no rush to get back to Brooklyn. Their pads were off, their sweat had dried, and their stomachs were full from the hot dogs and sunflower seeds the adults had bought them after the game. They walked slowly, with much swagger and laughter, across the stadium's cement concourse and onto the parking lot, where the bus waited. Big Oomz stopped his son and a few of his teammates for a photo. Their wide smiles disappeared. They posed with hard faces tilted back and their hands holding up peace signs. After Big Oomz got the shot and put his phone back in his pocket, the smiles returned. The team marched together in a long, strung-out pack and began filing onto the bus.

"That was Oomz!" Donnie shouted from the back of the group. "That was Oomz that put somebody in an ambulance! That was Oomz!"

Naz leaned his head out the bus window and yelled, "Brotha, how you break that boy leg?"

Oomz shrugged.

The Pee Wees congregated in the back of the bus, which quickly filled with the musty scent of sweat-soaked socks and undershirts. A dozen of them huddled around Isaiah, who had the game recorded on his mom's iPad. They knelt backward on seats and leaned across aisles. Isaiah held the screen out so all could see.

"Yo, watch me on this," Oomz said, as the screen showed the opening kickoff.

The boys burst into cheers when Oomz knocked an opponent to the ground with a powerful block.

"Yo, Oomz, what you do to that kid?" Hart said.

"I said put 'im in a coffin!" Oomz said. "Did y'all just see that hit?"

The boys were giddy seeing themselves on screen. Here was a record of their hard, unnoticed work. Here was Dorian beating the runner to the outside, forcing the runner towards the mass of Dorian's teammates in the middle of the field. Here was Hart driving a defensive lineman back nearly 10 yards. Here was Chaka sprinting 30 yards downfield and laying a block on the only defender left between Isaiah and the end zone.

"Oh, we out! We out!" Naz said as Isaiah broke into the open field.

"Oh, Isaiah gone!" Time Out said.

"That was my block!" Chaka said.

"Yeah, good blocking," Isaiah said. "That was real good blocking."

Chaka, beaming now, leaned in closer to the screen.

"Took it to the crib!" Chaka said.

"To the house!" Isaiah said.

Isaiah had been dominant again. During a punt return, he picked up the ball with four defenders just a few yards in front of him, then stiff-armed one defender, ran around the rest, and raced 80 yards. On one defensive play, Donnie grabbed the quarterback and Isaiah ran up, snatched the ball from his hands, and went the other way for a touchdown.

The bus ride home was a din of jokes, horseplay, and music. As the bus crossed the Manhattan Bridge and the city skyline began to light up in the encroaching dusk, Isaiah danced in his seat, rocking his shoulders side to side, raising his voice over the wind flapping through an open window, rapping with his teammates, "Bitch caught a body bout a week agooooooo!"

"Week ago!" echoed Oomz, standing, arms swaying, the volume all the way up on the phone in his hand.

The boys danced and laughed all the way to Brownsville. Counting the forfeit, the team was 3–0. The hardest games were yet to come, but those matters were for Monday.

– 15 –

EAST ORANGE
Mid-September 2014

THEY HAD DONE EVERYTHING RIGHT THAT WEEK.

The coaches didn't need to remind the boys what was at stake. The East Orange Jaguars beat them soundly last season. The Mo Better boys missed tackles and blocks. They kept the game close for two quarters, then fell behind, and when they fell behind, "they had terrible body language," Esau said. "They looked like they gave up." The East Orange Jaguars were tall and fast, the boys remembered. But looking back, the Pee Wees still believed they had been good enough to beat them—they just didn't have the heart to do it. "Last year we did bad," Time Out said. "I learned a lot of lessons from that loss and the other losses: don't put anybody down; lift everybody up. We all pointed fingers. This year, though, I think is gon' be my favorite year. We got every skill—defensive, offensive, speed, agility, passing. We all know these two games coming up. We really wanna kill them. The playoffs is coming and we gotta make it in." The East Orange Jaguars and Brick City Lions were their next two opponents. As Coach Chris had trumpeted all year, the Pee Wees had to get past Brick City and East Orange if they hoped to reach the regional championship game. East Orange had won the league title in Oomz's and Hart's age group last year and looked even better this year. Some Mo Better parents had heard that a few players from last year's second-place Brick City team had jumped to East Orange.

The boys arrived at the week's first practice serious and eager. For the first time all season, they had full attendance. They put on their pads in silence—no joking around, no proclamations about how badly they'd beat their opponents. Around them, the sounds of the park played on, like any other day, as if oblivious to the gravity of their endeavor. The train rumbled by. Children shouted in the distance. A basketball bounced. A bicycle chain spun. A car stereo thumped. Sneakers pounded the hard rubber track. A boom box bumped a Kendrick Lamar song. Stroller wheels squeaked. A dirt-bike engine hummed. Metal hooks on shoulder pads and metal buttons on helmets clicked and snapped. And soon, those helmets and shoulder pads were colliding, adding to Betsy Head's symphony.

Practice was hard and physical. The linemen crashed into each other with game-day intensity. Hart and Donnie set the pace. Donnie threw his body into the offensive line full throttle on every play, driving through the blockers even after Esau blew his whistle. Within the first hour of practice, Donnie had gotten into three fights. At one point, after he grabbed Oomz's neck in an attempt to tackle him, Oomz threw him to the ground, then Donnie hopped up and the two boys traded swings, both missing on right hooks before teammates pulled them apart. Hart, meanwhile, slammed a teammate to the ground on nearly every play. It was easy to identify the boys who were lining up against Hart because the backs of their jerseys were brown with dust.

The boys competed with such intensity that Esau had to tell them, "Yo! We're not trying to kill our teammates! Linemen, you hear that? Save that for Sunday." But Esau knew this was a good problem to have, and he couldn't keep from smiling when he saw the boys getting after each other. His team, he could tell, was taking this game as seriously as he was. He had thought up new tactics. He taught the Pee Wees a new trick that he called "polar": the offense lines up and the quarterback loudly calls "Go!" a few times in an effort to get the defense to jump offside. It was the sort of thing college and NFL teams did, but it required a level of discipline beyond what most Pee Wee teams had. The first time these Pee Wees attempted it, Chaka took off when Naz called "Go!" His teammates looked over at him. "Come on, Chaka!" Oomz said. "Hold your water, man!" But by the end of practice they had mastered the trick, as well as its strategic partner, the "quick snap": the center hikes the ball to the quarterback on the first sound—on "Ready!" instead of after "Ready, set, go!"—and the quarterback sneaks through the sleeping defense.

They also learned the new plays Esau had created in recent weeks: a reverse pitch to Isaiah, an option pitch to Marquis, a deep pass to Chaka after a fake handoff, a run up the middle on a direct snap to Oomz. The boys practiced these plays with urgency. "Everybody, get set!" Isaiah shouted when they broke the huddle. "Get set! Hurry up!"

The parents along the fence cheered on the offense's evolution.

"Esau pulling out all the plays!" Repo shouted. "That's what I'm talkin' 'bout!"

"They look like they wanna do something this year," Mr. Hart added. "They lookin' sharp. Focused."

"We'll find out what they're really about this week," Ramsey said.

The intensity kept up through the week. On Thursday, the team's day off from practice, Time Out and Marquis set up a video chat on their phones and did push-ups and sit-ups together in their respective bedrooms. Oomz and Donnie played tackle football with other boys at the park. Isaiah re-watched footage of the previous week's game. Hart worked on his defensive line moves with his father in their cement backyard. For this important week, the coaches were able to pull together enough funding for two buses, which was a relief to the Pee Wees because it meant that the Mitey Mites, scheduled to play at 10 a.m., could leave earlier on their own bus while the two older groups followed after another hour of sleep.

Friday's practice was perhaps the best they'd had all year, Esau said to Andrell. When Esau had the boys line up for sprints, not a single one complained. Not even Oomz. "Y'all run hard!" Oomz shouted to his teammates. "Let's go! Everybody run hard!" The park was nearly empty by then. Just a few Mitey Mites waiting for their parents to pick them up, four men kicking around a soccer ball, and these 16 middle schoolers and their two 20-something coaches remained on the field past 7:30 p.m. The sounds of football, of hitting and shouting and cleats thudding on hard dirt, carried across the park until practice was done and the players gathered around their coaches. Esau felt good about his team's chances.

"They running back, he's a strong little guy, but y'all strong too," he told the boys. "Y'all should fuck him up."

"He ain't been hit like y'all gon' hit him," Andrell said.

"They got athletes just like us but not better," Esau said. "Y'all gotta make plays. Football comes down to who makes plays. Ain't gonna be no clowning when they on the field."

He sensed that his Pee Wees had matured much since last year. He saw in them more resilience and confidence. But he knew their resilience and confidence had not yet been tested this season.

"Ain't nobody scored on us yet," he told his team. "If somebody scores on us—it's OK. It's OK. I'm gon' yell at you, 'cause it's what coaches do. But it's gonna be all right. People gon' score on you in football. Don't drop ya heads. Don't drop ya heads. Come back and get it back."

He paused as the train rumbled by.

"Listen, I wanna tell y'all something," he continued. "Chris gon' say all this and make this a big deal about East Orange. But they nowhere near better than y'all. I get upset when I think that they beat us last year. They cocky—they similar to us but they not better than us. We gotta punch 'em in the mouth. We should block them the fuck up. We should not lose to this team."

ooooo

THEY HAD DONE everything right that week, but when game day dawned, everything seemed to go wrong.

The Pee Wee team's school bus was supposed to leave Betsy Head at 7:30 a.m., but it didn't pull up to the park until 9:00, after an hour of frustrated coaches making frantic phone calls and restless players, like Oomz and Donnie, letting off steam by punching one another on the arm to see who could hit harder or racing to snag a bouncing football. "Stop playing!" Esau said more than once. "Y'all playin' too much!" Twenty minutes into the trip, as the boys gawked at the gold-plated columns of the Brooklyn Public Library, Esau noticed that the bus was making a wrong turn on the Grand Army Plaza roundabout. "Yo, bus driver, where you going?" Esau said. After a brief exchange about which way to go on Flatbush Avenue that left Esau rolling his eyes, he directed the driver, "Bridge is that way. You gotta go north."

An hour later, the bus reached East Orange, a suburban town with a familiar story: mostly upper-middle-class and white half a century ago and now mostly black and working class thanks to years of white flight and racist housing policies. The bus rumbled through tree-lined streets and past houses with short fences and long porches before turning into the parking lot of Paul Robeson Stadium. Many boys were looking out the window. They watched a group of East Orange Jaguars step out of a maroon van parked next to the bus. The talking stopped, and the boys on the bus stared silently. Heartbeats accelerated.

The Pee Wees pretended not to look at the East Orange players standing by the maroon van, and the East Orange players pretended not to look at the Brownsville boys walking into the stadium. Two 30-something men, with dreads and blue-and-red East Orange Jaguar shirts, leaned against the fence encircling the field. As the Mo Better Pee Wees walked past, one of the men said, "Y'all ready?" They ignored him and made their way to the empty far end of the bleachers. "There ain't no room for errors today," Hart said to his teammates, their eyes all on the field. The Mitey Mites had lost badly, and the Junior Pee Wee game was already off to a bad start for the Mo Better side. It was overcast and blustery. On a patch of grass behind the end zone, right in front of Hart and his teammates, their imminent opponents, the East Orange Pee Wees, lined up in front of a photographer for portraits—on a knee, football in arm, the customary pose.

"They look mad big," said Chaka.

"I'm nervous," Time Out said. "I just wanna see how they hit."

"If we lose this game—I'm not saying—but if we lose this game we gotta beat Brick City to get in the playoffs, huh?" Chaka said.

"If we lose this game, we gotta win the rest of our games," Time Out said.

East Orange's Pee Wees were bigger because more than half of them qualified as "older/lighter." While 9-, 10-, and 11-year-olds had to begin the season at 130 pounds or less to play Pee Wee, 12-year-olds were eligible if they weighed less than 110 pounds. Successful Pop Warner teams usually relied on a core group of older/lighters—their experience, skill, and strength. Every middle schooler knew how much of a difference one year could make during this prepubescent stretch, how seventh graders were so much more physically mature than sixth graders. It had been a group of older/lighters who had carried Mo Better's greatest teams to championships. This year's East Orange Pee Wees, an East Orange parent told Hart's father, had 14 older/lighters. Mo Better's Pee Wees had three: Chaka, Time Out, and Isaiah.

As if the Pee Wees hadn't been shaken enough that morning, they encountered near catastrophe less than an hour before kickoff when Hart realized that he was missing a cleat. He'd left it on the bus, but the bus was no longer in the parking lot. Panic spread through the boys and their parents as it occurred to everybody that the team would have to forfeit if one of their 16 players didn't have two cleats. After a nerve-rattling 30 minutes, by some miracle the bus pulled into the parking lot with barely two minutes to spare before the weigh-in cutoff time. With everybody in purple and yellow already on edge, the first big game of the year got started.

∞∞∞∞∞

IT WAS A hard-hitting game from the start. Mo Better opened on offense, and the East Orange defense swarmed Isaiah eight yards behind the line on the first play, then stuffed him for no gain on the second play. On third down, Naz threw a pass and East Orange intercepted it. Mo Better's defense responded by knocking the East Orange offense back several yards on their first two plays. On third down, the East Orange quarterback threw a pass to a receiver deep down the field. The ball wobbled high in the air, floating slowly down toward Chaka, who seemed in position for an easy interception, but he jumped too early and the ball breezed over his fingertips and into the arms of the receiver, who jogged into the end zone. 6–0.

This would be a game of turning points, and here was the first one, decided by inches, filling East Orange with confidence and affirming the anxiety and dread that had hovered over Mo Better all day. Chaka slapped his thighs and brought his face to his hands.

"Keep ya head up!" Oomz said to his teammates as they jogged to the sideline. "Keep ya head up!"

The teams traded big hits, and both defenses held firm. Mo Better's offense clawed forward, fighting hard for each yard. Oomz up the middle—loss of one yard. Marquis around the edge—loss of five. Isaiah on a pitch to the outside, stiff-arming a defender in the backfield then sprinting past two more before getting drilled into the sidelines—a tough three yards. He wasn't used to getting manhandled like this. Neither were Oomz and Hart. But here they were, getting knocked backward, unable to move their opponents the way they wanted to. It was a humbling, discouraging feeling being physically overpowered like this, especially for those accustomed to doing the overpowering. These East Orange boys were strong, athletic, and tough. When Isaiah, Oomz, or Hart hit them, they hit back harder on the next play. For the first time all season, their opponents didn't fear them. Hart noticed some of his teammates turning hesitant. He saw some of them wide-eyed and stiff in the huddle, far from the casual cool they usually projected. The sense of dejection seemed to carry from the boys on the field to their parents in the stands, who weren't used to seeing their offense struggle.

"They not blocking man!" Repo shouted. "Getting blown off the fuckin' ball!

"If we block, we win!" Ramsey shouted.

"We need to take that touchdown back!" Mr. Hart shouted.

"Ay, let's go coach!" Repo shouted. "Let's pay these bills before they put us out."

After recovering a fumble, Mo Better had the ball at midfield, but the defense drove them back again. The East Orange defenders were attacking aggressively, anticipating the snap and rushing into the back-field. Needing 18 yards on third down, Esau called "polar." East Orange jumped offside. Esau called it again, and East Orange jumped offside again. The two penalties, for a total of 10 yards, seemed to rattle the defense, and on the next play Naz connected with Marquis for a 15-yard pass. Esau called for a similar play, and when the defense converged on Marquis, Naz released a long throw to Chaka, who sprinted past the coverage and dove for the ball 30 yards downfield. The Mo Better parents erupted in cheers, slapping hands and grinning until they realized the referee had ruled that the ball hit the ground, the pass incomplete.

"Come on ref, that was a catch, baby!" Mr. Hart shouted. "Come on ref! Jesus!"

Esau tried the play again, but the defense saw it coming and intercepted the throw, and the Mo Better parents went silent.

Back on defense, Isaiah sensed that his teammates were falling into the bad habits that had plagued them the previous season. Their heads were down and their shoulders were slumped. On second down, when the East Orange running back cut up the field and around the corner, they missed tackles and got swallowed up by blockers. It seemed the running back had a clear lane all the way to the end zone, but Isaiah, springing from the other side of the field, chased him down, grabbed him from behind, knocked the ball out of his arm, and whipped him to the ground. Isaiah jumped onto the loose ball. He pounded his chest and held the ball up in the air as his teammates ran over and tapped his helmet, and he kept pounding his chest until he realized the referee had ruled that the runner had stepped out of bounds before fumbling.

Angry shouts rained down from the Mo Better side of the bleachers.

"Come on ref! That's terrible!"

"You're costing us the game!"

"You're killing us!"

East Orange moved the ball effectively now, with outside runs and short passes. With the second quarter winding down, they marched easily toward the end zone, but they ran out of time. They were five yards away when the clock hit zero. Isaiah understood his team had escaped disaster.

"Only six-zip," he said to his teammates at halftime. "Come on, guys. Relax."

"We are in a dog fight," Hart added.

While the boys passed around water bottles, Esau ran through the adjustments for the second half. He had studied the moves of his opponent in real time, tracking formations and tendencies. East Orange was talented, but Esau believed they were winning because they had attacked weak points in his team's strategy. East Orange's defense had been bullying through Mo Better's offensive line, and the runners had no space to move. Mo Better's old-school power-running attack, which packed the offense tightly around the ball, was getting blown up by defenders blitzing through the middle. Esau shifted around the blocking strategy to protect the inside, and announced that they'd pass the ball more in the second half, to keep the defenders off-balance. On the other side of the ball, East Orange's offense had found a good rhythm by the end of the first half, as its quarterback learned the holes in Mo Better's pass coverage. East Orange ran a modern spread offense, with three or four receivers split out, widening the gaps between the defenders. Because Pee Wees rarely passed the ball, Esau's team hadn't practiced much pass defense. And because the defenders suddenly had to now think about how to defend the pass, they reacted slower to runs. Esau shifted the defense's alignment and changed certain players' assignments. He threw out much of his old game plan and built a new one from scratch.

It didn't seem to work at first. East Orange glided down the field early in the third quarter. It looked easy for them. Running backs cruised through big holes, receivers found wide-open spaces down the field, linemen drove off the defenders coming at them. But then, with East Orange around 25 yards from the end zone, Mo Better's defense tightened, stopping the offense for three straight plays, and now it was fourth down with eight yards to go. The Brooklyn parents stood and cheered. The boys on defense pumped themselves up.

"Let's go!" said Isaiah, his voice cracking into a higher pitch. "One stop! One stop!"

East Orange broke the huddle, and two receivers split out on each side. Isaiah, from his outside linebacker spot, shifted left and back a few yards, positioning himself closer to the inside receiver. His eyes were on the quarterback. On the snap, Isaiah drifted back slowly, as the inside receiver ran straight up the field. Isaiah watched the quarterback scan the field, from right to left, for two seconds, three seconds, four seconds, five seconds, until their eyes met, and by the time Isaiah realized where the quarterback was throwing the ball it was too late. Isaiah leaped high but the ball flew over his head and into the arms of the inside receiver, who had cut to the sideline. First down. Isaiah cursed and slapped his hands. He stared at the ground. He didn't want to see his teammates' faces, but he knew he had to eventually, so he brought his head up, tapped his chest, and said, "My bad," barely loud enough for any of them to hear. Their shoulders were slumped again, and they wore looks of frustration and disappointment.

On the next play, the East Orange running back went up the middle, broke three lackluster tackle attempts, and scored. 12–0.

Mo Better got the ball back on the 26-yard line. On the first play of the drive, Oomz was tackled six yards behind the line, and then the referee blew the whistle to mark the end of the third quarter. East Orange had held the ball for all but one play. Esau and Andrell looked at each other in shock.

"Quarter just started ref!" Esau shouted.

The Mo Better parents complained too. They accused the ref of running the clock too quickly. They yelled that the ref was terrible, incompetent, a cheat—until the referee, tired of the barrage of insults, said to Esau, "Yo, coach, if you don't quiet them, *you* gotta go." And Esau turned to the parents in the bleachers behind the sidelines and told them to quiet down, and they did. For a minute. And then they turned their anger toward Esau.

"We gotta pay this rent, man!" Repo shouted. "'Cause they about to put us out!"

"This game hanging in the balance right now!" Mr. Hart shouted.

"Winners never lose, Esau!" Repo shouted.

Esau pretended not to hear. Naz jogged over to him to get the play call: going deep to Chaka. "Let it loose," Esau said. "You've made this throw a hundred times. Let it loose and make him go get it."

It wasn't a perfect throw. Naz didn't release it as cleanly as he'd hoped. The defenders had broken through the line, and Naz had to quickly shuffle backward before winding up and letting it loose. The ball came out too high and was underthrown. Chaka had to stop and turn, waiting for the ball to fall. The cornerback was on his hip and the safety had scurried over to help. The three boys stood bunched together looking up at the ball. They all jumped, but Chaka jumped highest and snagged the ball out of the air, shook himself free from the others, and raced down the open field for an 80-yard touchdown.

The Mo Better crowd went wild, stomping the bleachers, shaking cans filled with pennies, whooping and clapping, raising their arms in the air, expressions of euphoria and amazement on their faces.

Esau called time-out. The offense gathered around him. The score was 12–6. This point-after try was significant. If Mo Better could make it 12–7, they would need only a touchdown to win. Esau laid out the plan: After the time-out, the players would jog onto the field and get into a huddle. Then they would break the huddle and walk slowly to their positions. And then, with the defense relaxed, they would run the quick snap and Naz would scoot up the middle for the score.

It was a brilliant call. The defense had been timing Naz's pre-snap cadence all game, and Naz had fooled them with two polars. The defenders were on edge now, thinking about the cadence and the polars and the touchdown they'd just given up and *boom*—they'd hit 'em with the quick snap. Esau had saved it for the ideal moment.

They'd practiced this many times. They'd gotten the rhythm down. And it all looked normal and well rehearsed when the offense jogged onto the field. "Get in the huddle," Esau shouted to them, just as they'd scripted. They began to circle together, calmly, just as they'd scripted, and it was all going according to plan.

But then—

"Huddle!?" Repo shouted from the stands. "Get on the ball! We just came out a time-out!"

All game long, Esau had ignored the second-guessing, the back-seat coaching, the "Throw the ball to Chaka!" and "What kinda defense is this!" and "Too predictable, Esau, too predictable!" All season long, he had ignored the whispers that he was too inexperienced to be coaching the program's best team, that the coaching at Mo Better wasn't as good as it used to be, that he was the reason these talented boys had under-achieved last season. It had weighed on him and weighed on him, and now the program's best team was staring down defeat, and if they lost, he knew the blame would fall on him. But if his boys could just get this one point and then get a stop and then score again—

Esau turned around, faced the bleachers, and shouted with all his might: "Yo, shut the fuck up, man! Shut the fuck up! Nobody can't coach like that! Chill!"

Silence. Everybody went silent. The boys on the field, confused, looked at one another then looked at the sideline. The parents, shocked, looked at one another then looked at the sideline. All eyes were on Esau.

Standing beside him, Andrell said, calmly, almost in a whisper, "Esau, yo, chill."

The boys lined up on offense. The eyes returned to the field. The ball was snapped and the defense stopped the play.

ooooo

ESAU GREW UP down the street from Betsy Head Park. On days when he had football practice, he'd look out his window and wait until his teammates had run three laps, then he'd head over and slide in with them for the final lap. He'd pump his arms fast while his legs moved at a walking pace to fool his coaches into thinking he was running hard. His teammates followed his lead. "We knew all the tricks," he said.

He was short, but he worked hard and was built like a fire hydrant. He was a good hitter, had a sharp intellect, and served as captain on some of Mo Better's most successful teams. To Chris Legree, Esau was a natural coach. Though he was young, he was mature beyond his years, wise and stoic. Maybe most importantly, as one parent put it, "he knows how to call some motherfuckin' plays."

Chris saw Esau as a good role model for his players, a cool young man who knew the streets but had avoided the paths that some of his old friends had taken. One day that summer, one of those old friends showed up at the field and caught up with Esau while the Pee Wees did their laps before practice. After some small talk, Esau asked, "You still doin' what you been doin'?"

"Yeah," the friend said, shrugging his shoulders and looking at the ground.

"Do something where they can't take your freedom away from you," Esau told him. "All money ain't good money. Remember that."

Esau was more like a brother to his players than a father. Boys did not fear Esau as they feared Vick, but they related to him, confided in him, and believed that he understood them, that he remembered what it was like to be their age and face the challenges they faced. He knew all the tricks, after all, and he shared those stories with his players. He sat with them on the back of the bus and gave them advice on their girl problems. He clowned them when they said something absurd. He talked to them like colleagues, like men. "Esau always real with you," Oomz said. Once, when Naz mentioned that he was getting a ride home from a game with his "step-pop," Esau corrected him: "Yo, that's your father," he said. "Just 'cause another man made you, don't mean he take care of you. Your father is the father figure in your life."

Esau was father to two boys, whom he raised with his girlfriend. The older boy, 8-year-old Taquan, was not his biological son, but Esau cared for him as his own. He was 24 years old but, like others in Brownsville, had grown up fast. He'd entered the adult workforce at the peak of the Great Recession and struggled to find a job. A Mo Better parent helped him and Andrell get jobs at a casino in Queens. He scheduled each week's practices around his work calendar, which meant that Esau and Andrell often spent their Friday nights coaching a bunch of preteens at the park. Coaching took up much of his free time, but he was happy to make the sacrifice. He loved the game, he loved his players, and his players loved him.

But Esau felt he had much to prove. His first year as a head coach had been a disappointment to many parents. And while the Pee Wee season had gotten off to a good start, he received little of the credit. He discovered the coach's curse of being blessed with a talented team: when they did well, it was because of the players; when they did poorly, it was because of him.

Now, though, his team clearly did not possess more talent than its opponent. East Orange was bigger and more athletic. East Orange had more players. East Orange had more older/lighters. East Orange was the defending league champ, and Mo Better was not about to beat them solely on the strength of their physical abilities. If Mo Better were to win this game, it would be on the strength of their bright young coach.

Esau wanted it badly.

It was 12–6, seven minutes left in the game, the ball back with East Orange at the 50-yard line, first down and 10.

"Let's get that ball back!" Mr. Hart shouted. "Who want that ball? Who want that ball?"

"You gotta want it, baby!" Ramsey shouted. "You gotta want it! It's the fourth quarter!"

The ball went to the running back, and a wall of blockers formed in front of him, bulldozing around the corner and up the field. Isaiah, from the opposite side, took off in pursuit, sprinting hard diagonally across the field, angling to catch the runner in time. At the five-yard line, Isaiah dove at the runner's legs, but the distance had been too great and the runner strode into the end zone. The cheers from the bleachers churning his stomach, Isaiah rolled onto his butt and sat still for a few seconds, looking at the ground between his knees, trying to convince himself that the game was not yet over.

But the game was over. When the clock hit zero, the scoreboard read East Orange: 19, Mo Better: 6.

By the time the Mo Better Pee Wees had composed themselves and gathered their bags from the sideline, the older boys in the next game were warming up on the field. Isaiah, Hart, Oomz, Donnie, Chaka, Naz, Time Out, and the rest of the boys walked across the field toward the parking lot in silence. Several teenage East Orange Junior Midgets laughed when they noticed this downtrodden group.

"Get off our field, Mo Better!" one boy shouted.

"Bye-bye!" said another.

The Brownsville boys pretended not to hear.

– 16 –

TO MAKE IT IN THE JUNGLE
Late September 2014

It was only a youth football game, only a youth football season. There was no money at stake, no write-up in the newspaper, no legion of fans emotionally invested in the outcome. Coach Vick had had former players get murdered, go to prison, point a gun in his face. His own son was in jail, unable to make bail and awaiting trial. One boy on the Junior Pee Wees was now homeless because his family's house had burned down. A 12-year-old boy who played for Brooklyn United had gotten shot in the leg over the weekend. Coach James had torn his rotator cuff three weeks ago and was unable to work for the foreseeable future and unsure how he would take care of his family. Two kids, brothers who'd played on Vick's Mitey Mites last year, had just been sent to foster care after allegations of abuse. Nobody needed to tell Vick that a youth football season was not important in the grand scheme of things.

But still, Vick was pissed. He was a competitive, proud man who was not used to losing many football games. Sunday in East Orange had been disheartening. He was angry throughout the 10 a.m. game, as his Mitey Mites put up what he thought was a weak effort. He was angry as he watched the Junior Pee Wees lose by a wide, embarrassing margin in the 11:30 a.m. game. He remained angry though the 1 p.m. main event, as the Pee Wees' hopes of a dream undefeated season dissolved. He was angry on the bus ride home, which always took too long after a loss, and all Sunday night, as the games replayed in his head, as he reflected on the recent weeks, and as he wondered how things had fallen apart. He was still angry when he strolled, slowly and stiffly, into Betsy Head for the week's first practice.

He wore a black polo shirt, jeans, and a scowl. He pulled his gray bucket hat low on his brow, then cracked his knuckles. The bandage was still wrapped around his hand.

"It's gon' be an ugly practice," he said. "I'm going back to the old-school. I'ma go all the way back to Jersey to get embarrassed like that— I'ma bring it back to the old-school."

It was the toughest practice the 7-, 8-, and 9-year-old Mitey Mites had had all season. First they ran wind sprints. Then they did push-ups with their legs propped up on the red cement steps for added difficulty. Then they did 100 or so yards of crab walks, scurrying on all fours from one end of the park to the other. They did up-downs, dust billowing as they chopped the ground with their feet and flopped to their chests. They ran around the track, over and over. When they didn't follow Vick's directions fast enough, he ordered push-ups. Less than an hour into practice, the Mitey Mites were exhausted. Their legs churned as if they were in water. They bent over, hands on knees, at every break. They sucked air and their faces looked pained.

Standing out of Vick's earshot, the other Mitey Mite coaches, James and Oscar, wondered aloud if he was pushing the boys too hard, if he was perhaps taking out his own frustrations on them. But who were they to tell him how to coach his team? The man was a legend at this park. If Mo Better had a Mount Rushmore, Coach Vick's face would be on it. He had coached at this program far longer than they had and he was, without doubt, its most widely respected figure. The assistant coaches let Vick do his thing.

Vick believed his boys needed a jolt. After opening the season with a win, they'd lost the next two games. Vick had never lost three games in a row.

"I got a reputation to maintain," he said.

He sensed his reputation was slipping, and he was right. Across the program, his former players whispered that Vick had lost some of his fire. Hart and Oomz both said that Vick had calmed down in recent years. Vick's son, Vick III, said that he didn't see the same passion his father once had. Coach Vick missed practice more often. Coach Vick didn't demand as many push-ups. Coach Vick didn't yell as frequently or as loudly. Simply, Coach Vick didn't care as much. The string of losses had shocked Vick into realizing it. He hadn't been his old self this season, he now believed.

"I've been distracted," he said. "Very distracted."

He'd been laid off from the warehouse job and was back on unemployment checks, looking for work. But now, as his players sprinted across the field, he felt his spirits rising. He observed 9-year-old Puerto Rico, chubby and slow, pumping his legs harder than anyone else, busting his ass for a team that might not win two games this season. After the loss in East Orange, as he lit a postgame cigarette, hand cupped to block the wind, Vick had said, "Only one that came to play today was Puerto Rico."

ooooo

PUERTO RICO WAS always smiling, even though he was not ignorant to the turmoil around him. His mother, Alicia, had hoped to move the family to Miami before the school year started, but the plan fell through. The boy was familiar with stumbling blocks. He'd been born a sick child, with a kidney disease that caused intense pain in his abdomen and sometimes kept him from peeing for days at a time. He'd had six surgeries in his young life. Alicia had canceled the move to Miami because her son's ailment had worsened during the summer, keeping him in bed.

Because of his early health complications, Puerto Rico couldn't walk until he was three and didn't talk until he was three and a half. He seemed so fragile. His mother hovered over him everywhere he went, and whenever he stumbled she would catch him before he hit the ground. But she worried that her instincts to protect him would only hold him back further. She did what she could to help him catch up. She signed him up for swimming and karate classes. She read to him every night and taught him to read herself, and by the time he was in kindergarten, he was the smartest kid in his class. When he was in third grade, he was reading at a sixth-grade level.

When he was six, he asked his mother to let him play football, and she agreed only because she assumed he would quit after a few weeks. As she watched the first practice, she was even more sure that he would quit. Alicia's brother was in the Air Force, and the practice reminded her of a military boot camp. Puerto Rico had never been yelled at before and had never done anything so physical and exhausting. She was sure he would cry. Instead, he was smiling when he ran off the field after each practice, and before practice he would urge Alicia to hurry up and get ready because he didn't want to be late.

During one practice, Puerto Rico collapsed. At the hospital, the doctor told Alicia that there was a clog in his system preventing oxygen from getting to his brain. They performed emergency surgery. The following week, Puerto Rico begged Alicia to let him go to practice and kept begging until the doctors cleared him to play three weeks later. During the last game of that season, Puerto Rico played on the offensive line and was getting beat up by a boy nearly twice his size. Every play, Puerto Rico would drive into the boy and, nearly every play, Puerto Rico would end up on the ground. On a snap late in the fourth quarter, though, Puerto Rico drove into the boy once more, and this time he drove so hard that he toppled the boy onto his back.

By Puerto Rico's second year on the team in the fall of 2013, he and Vick were close. Alicia sometimes asked Vick to speak with her son whenever she was especially worried about him. Usually it had to do with Puerto Rico's relationship with his father. After a practice that season, Puerto Rico told Vick he was upset that his father's girlfriend was pregnant with a boy who would be named after his father. He wondered if his dad was ashamed of him because of his disease—if that was why his father was not among the fathers at Betsy Head to watch practice. This was an emotional period for the boy. When teammates or classmates bothered him, he tried to fight them. He cried more than he ever had. Many days he didn't want to go to football. He made excuses, said his back or stomach hurt. He talked back to his mom and acted up at home.

Over those months, he had many long conversations with Coach Vick after practice, and by the following spring, the anger that seemed to overcome him had faded and he was again a playful, obedient, optimistic boy. His temper had been tested that spring. One day at school, a classmate punched him in the face in the hallway, and Puerto Rico refused to hit him back. A teacher saw it happen, and the boy was expelled. When Alicia asked Puerto Rico why he didn't swing at the boy, he said that his martial arts instructor had told him to avoid fights. He ended the school year with perfect attendance and the highest mark in his third-grade class.

Yet the boy couldn't catch a break. On Labor Day 2014, his favorite uncle, the one in the Air Force, died. Puerto Rico took the news hard. Mother and son flew to Florida for the funeral a few days later. There, Alicia learned that her brother had been accused of attempted rape and locked in jail. He had gotten into a fight with another inmate and been sent to solitary confinement, where he killed himself. She didn't tell Puerto Rico these details. He was back at practice as soon as they returned to Brooklyn.

ooooo

WATCHING PUERTO RICO, Vick felt a pang of shame for his spell of self-pity. In his head, he repeated to himself the words he'd said to countless kids: *Toughen up . . . Be a man . . . Losing's a part of life . . . Don't like how it feels, you gotta do something about it.* He recalled a day that summer when a small boy at his first practice started crying because the drills were too hard. "You not no boy anymore," Vick had said to him.

"Suck it up. You not no boy. You're a big dog now. Say, 'I'm a big dog.'"
"I'm a big dog," the boy said, meekly and through sniffles. "Say, 'I'm a big dog!'" Vick repeated, his voice stronger, more self-assured. "I'm a big dog!" the boy shouted, wiping his tears on his sleeves then heading back into the mix.

The Mitey Mites were running laps now, a single-file line with Puerto Rico at the head. Vick jogged beside them. When they finished the lap, the coach led them back onto the field and told them to get into a circle. He counted to 10, and when he reached 10, the attempted circle looked more like a horseshoe. Vick ordered them back to the track.

The Pee Wee parents, standing along the fence at the edge of the track, looked on with approval, smiling to one another and joking about "ol' Coach Vick bringing that Mo Better discipline back." But Coach Chris, watching from the other side of the field, was anxious. He walked to James and Oscar and said, "He gotta calm down. I gotta talk to him." At the next water break, Chris went to Vick and told him to "turn it down."

Vick gathered the team and told them he appreciated their hard work today. This would be a hard week, he said. This was Brick City week. It was also homecoming week. The teams would play at South Shore High School, Chris's alma mater, and Chris had invited every former player he could think of. It was the biggest, most anticipated game day of the year, and Vick didn't want to get embarrassed. "They coming," he said. "I'm tellin' you right now—they coming to Brooklyn, and one of the worst feelings in the world is getting beat up at home."

∞∞∞∞∞

IN 18 YEARS, Chris had never before told Vick to calm down. It was a sign of the times, Vick believed. He'd noticed a shift in how parents expected their kids to be treated. "Used to be, 'Coach Vick, do what the fuck you want,'" he said. Nearly every week, parents and players from those days dropped by Betsy Head to tell Vick how big of an impact he'd had, instilling work ethic and discipline.

Vick knew not every parent liked him. Specifically, there was a certain type of father he always seemed to come across—an absent, or sometimes absent, father who didn't show up to a single game or practice but heard all about Coach Vick from his son or, worse, his son's mother. The father, hard with envy, would usually show up at the year-end banquet and mug at Vick, and then Vick would ask the man to step outside and say something like, "Don't let this suit fool you. I don't appreciate this disrespect and I'll do what I gotta do." Or, instead of mugging at him, the father would greet him with over-the-top graciousness, hearty back slaps, and big promises. These men annoyed Vick more than the ones who mugged at him. "They come up to me and say, 'Coach Vick, I appreciate what you've done. I just wanna tell you I'ma be around more and let me know if you need my help,'" Vick said, before adding with a tone of disgust, "If I need your help?"

This came with the territory, and Vick expected it. What he did not anticipate was the type of parent that had emerged in recent years: present, active, loving ones who couldn't stand to see their sons wincing in pain and heaving for air during a tough practice. These days, Vick heard that parents were complaining about him, telling Chris, "Coach Vick is too mean." "These parents pacify their kids more," Vick said. "It's a generational difference." He wondered if some of them had threatened Chris with lawsuits, if maybe that was why, after all these years, Chris felt the need to tell him to calm down.

Vick respected the parents who let their kids struggle, who understood the value of pain and resilience. In the long run, Vick believed, their kids would be the ones who navigated past Brownsville and past college and rose up through the cold, hard professional world. And in the short term, he knew, their kids would be the ones who won football games. To Vick, the parents of the Pee Wee boys were a good example. "Look at all those fathers over there," he said, gazing across Betsy Head the evening before the Brick City game. As always, the fathers stood along the fence watching their boys, cheering their hits, chiding their mistakes, demanding effort and improvement. The evenings were darker now, and the park lights were on. A cold and vicious wind kicked up the dirt and blew thick clouds of dust all across the park. The fathers covered their faces with their hands, hats, or shirt collars. "It's hoodie weather right now," Dorian's father, Dwight, said.

These fathers were of the same mind as Vick. All week they'd been discussing the headline NFL news: star running back Adrian Peterson had been indicted on child abuse charges for hitting his 4-year-old son with a switch.

"It's bullshit," Marquis's father, Ramsey, said. "I don't think he did anything wrong. I just whooped Marquis ass the other day." Marquis had talked back at home, he said, so he got the extension cord. "He begged me not to use it," Ramsey continued. "No! No! Please! Please!" His wife told him not to use the extension cord—"Too much. Too rough," he recalled his wife saying. "Use the belt instead." And when he got the belt, Marquis let out a relieved sigh before bracing himself. "You see," Ramsey said to his wife. "He ain't even scared of this!"

Fear was the whole point, Ramsey said to the other fathers. "I'm trying to put the fear in him," he said. "If he don't fear this, it ain't do nothing."

Not all the fathers agreed with corporal punishment. Mr. Hart said that he didn't hit his children, but he respected a parent's right to decide how to best discipline his child. His own father had hit him, and he believed that it helped keep him in line. "But it was a different time," he said. Dwight said that he didn't hit his kids either, but he understood "that to a man who was disciplined that way, that's how he will discipline his own kid. If you exposed to only one thing, you'll stick to what you know."

The fathers nodded in unison. This was a sensitive topic, they all knew. It was a personal, in-house philosophy, the men believed, and they were hesitant to criticize how another man raised his son. Four years old was probably too young, the fathers along the fence agreed—especially these days.

"From the outside, it looks really bad," Dwight said.

"It's a different time," Ramsey said.

Ramsey's mother began beating him when he was around 4, he said. They lived in Far Rockaway, Queens, in a neighborhood filled with distractions. "Drugs and girls and criminals," he said. He remembered getting into the shower after beatings; the soap burned his wounds. "The scars helped me remember not to fuck up," he said. "It built my character."

Ramsey took off his sunglasses and wiped them on the white T-shirt under his hoodie.

"If a kid is disrespectful, disobedient, acting up, I'd rather he get a few scars now than end up committing a crime later, end up in jail or dying, because what can you do then? Can't take that back. You only get one try. Like a lion raises its cubs to make it in the jungle, a man gotta raise his son."

Ramsey considered himself a man of initiative and action. He had big dreams for his son and he knew the margin of error was thin. Marquis was competing—for a spot in a private high school, admission to an elite university, a white-collar job offer—with rich white kids whose parents had the money and connections to bail them out of jams and hook them up with fast-track opportunities. To keep up with those more privileged, Ramsey was always thinking ahead, always making moves. In the spring, he'd sent his son to this youth football team with pipelines to some of the city's top high schools. In the summer, he'd signed his son up for football camps at some of those high schools.

It was his nature to try to take control of situations, and the Pee Wees' loss to East Orange had prodded this aspect of his character. "That shit bothered me," he said. "It bothered me." Another loss would likely doom their playoff chances: Brick City was also 3–1, having lost to the same opponent, and jockeyed with Mo Better for the second of two playoff slots in the division they shared with undefeated East Orange. On Monday morning, the day after the game, he sent Esau a long text message—a "love letter," Ramsey called it—saying that he appreciated Esau and everything he was doing, and then asking if Esau would allow him to help out. He volunteered to work with the linemen. Ramsey had played on the line back in high school, and the line had been the team's weak point against East Orange. Esau accepted the offer, and that evening he told the team that Marquis's father would be joining his coaching staff.

"I know y'all don't know me," Ramsey told the team. "I don't know y'all. But I watched the game, and discipline is one thing y'all need."

Ramsey's impact was immediate and loud. When one boy was slow to put his pads on before practice, Ramsey said to him, sarcastically, "Wassup, boss, long day at work?" When the boys did their warm-up jog around the track too lackadaisically for his taste, Ramsey shouted at them to speed up, and when they still weren't going fast enough, he joined them, setting the pace at the front of the line. With Esau's approval, he devoted the first half hour of practice to conditioning. He had the boys do bear crawls across the field. Oomz, Donnie, and Chaka sucked their teeth and half-assed the drill, moving slowly and then, when Ramsey wasn't looking, standing up and running forward a few yards, then dropping back down before Ramsey caught them cheating. When Ramsey did catch them cheating, he yelled at them, and when Oomz talked back, Ramsey yelled even louder and Esau yelled at him too, demanding that Oomz show Ramsey respect. It was a hard practice, focused on blocking and tackling. The boys did full-contact hitting drills for the first time since Hell Week. They finished the night sore and dirty.

Now it was Friday, the evening before the Brick City game, and the boys were in full pads, still blocking and tackling. Usually, practice was relaxed the day before a game. Players usually wore shorts and T-shirts and jogged through plays. Tonight, though, they were smacking one another to the ground, dust billowing into the air and floating up into the lights above the field. When a boy made a mistake, Ramsey called for push-ups. Fifteen push-ups. Twenty push-ups. Twelve push-ups. Forty push-ups. And then, one time, Ramsey kept shouting "Down-up!" as the boys counted past 50, then 60. He kept shouting "Down-up!"—even as the boys were barely able to lower themselves more than a few inches and barely able to push themselves back up—until they reached 100. And then it was back to hitting. It was the toughest, most physically demanding practice of the year. If a boy didn't hit the ballcarrier hard enough, Ramsey told him to go again. "My man, soccer season is over," he said to one boy.

"You better be ready for war!" he shouted at the boys. "You better be ready for war!"

Chaka didn't hide his frustration. He wasn't always in the mood to hit, and when he went up against Oomz during a tackling drill, he weakly threw his arms around Oomz's waist, slipping off as Oomz powered through.

"Do it again, Chaka!" Ramsey shouted.

But Chaka kept walking to the back of the line.

"Do it again, Chaka!"

Chaka ignored him, eyes straight ahead, hands on his hips.

Ramsey began a lecture about discipline and how Chaka and the rest of his teammates lacked it. Chaka turned his head to Ramsey and, with cold eyes, yelled, "So?!"

"Shut the fuck up," Esau said, without raising his voice.

He walked up to Chaka and stood face-to-face with him.

"What's your problem, man?"

Chaka said nothing, avoiding eye contact.

"You got a problem. What is it?"

No answer.

"I'm asking you a question. Talk."

Still nothing. The other Pee Wees glanced over, careful not to hold their stares too long, pretending to mind their business. Of all the boys on the team, the coaches believed that Chaka had both the most long-term athletic potential and the highest short-term risk of falling to the streets. He was very tall for his age and very thin, which, to Coach Chris, meant that he had a "good frame" to build on once he started seriously lifting weights in high school. The boy was more skilled at 12 than his older cousin, Brandon Reddish, had been, and that young man was now a starting defensive back at Syracuse University. Chaka was a sweet boy, generous and warm with those he cared about, usually shy and polite with adults. He carried an innocence and curiosity that occasionally pierced through the cool swagger he presented to the world. He was an impressionable boy, and this worried his coaches. They often saw him hanging with older kids at the Betsy Head playground on weekends and evenings when he didn't have football. He'd show up to practice with fly new clothes, and when teammates asked how he got them, he turned defensive.

"Every time I see him in the park he wearing a new pair of sneakers," Donnie had said before one practice.

"That's 'cause he rob people," Esau joked.

"I don't rob!" Chaka corrected, with an aggression that caught Esau off guard. "I got money!"

When Donnie asked him how he got his money, he wouldn't dignify the question with a response. Esau knew Chaka well enough to know that he turned cold at the slightest hint of disrespect. He was a boy who valued respect above all and knew enough to give it in return. So, on the night before the Brick City game, Esau's voice was calm and direct.

"Show some respect, man," he said to Chaka. "Would you ever act like that to your father?"

Chaka shook his head. Esau could sense the boy's icy shield beginning to melt.

"That shit ain't cool, man. Football's about more than just catching the ball. You gotta block and you gotta tackle. So what's your problem?"

"Nothing."

"You obviously have a problem. He was yelling at you to do it again and you just kept walking. What is the problem?"

"I didn't want to go."

"Why not?"

"I can't tackle him."

"What do you mean you can't tackle him?"

Chaka shrugged.

"Who is Oomz? Who is Oomz?"

Another shrug.

"Exactly. If you afraid to tackle Oomz—come on, man."

Chaka nodded his head. He went to Ramsey and apologized. They shook hands and practice continued.

ooooo

THINGS FELT PRECARIOUS.

Isaiah stood at the front of one of the two lines, gripping the ball in the crook of his right arm, as Oomz crouched down at the front of the other. Isaiah had been running hard and hitting hard all week. While some of his teammates complained at first about how hard Ramsey was on them, Isaiah kept quiet and did the work. Eventually, his teammates stopped complaining and followed his lead. "We need this shit," Isaiah said. He was stunned by how badly they'd been beaten. He watched the East Orange game over and over, nitpicking through the film. All week, his brother, Shaq, walked past his room late at night and saw him sitting up in his bed, eyes locked on their mother's iPad. "He watched it like twelve times," Shaq said. "At least once every night since." Isaiah welcomed Ramsey's insight and passion, and he believed a hard practice like this was exactly what his team needed. Ramsey shouted "Go!" and Isaiah ran forward and Oomz angled toward him and their helmets collided with a loud smack as Oomz tackled Isaiah to the ground.

"Woooo!" the parents along the fence howled.

Isaiah pushed himself up to his feet slowly. He adjusted his helmet and took a few wobbly steps in the wrong direction.

"Yo, you got a headache?" Andrell said. "You walking to the wrong line."

"I'm good," Isaiah said, turning around and heading to the other line.

Along the fence, Dwight turned to the other fathers and said, "They gon' have concussions before the game. All of 'em."

"It's hitting season!" Mr. Hart said.

"We ain't gonna have nobody for the game tomorrow," Dwight said. "We gotta cool off."

How hard to push when the margin for error was gone? Nobody was certain. After more hitting and a set of wind sprints, practice was over. The boys walked off the field tired and covered in dust. In less than 24 hours, they would play Brick City—the biggest game of the year.

BRICK CITY
Late September 2014

TODAY OF ALL DAYS, DONNIE DIDN'T WANT TO BE LATE. He'd heard Coach Chris hyping the Brick City game for many months, and now it stood as a bona fide must-win game. He'd heard Esau remind the Pee Wees at practice that they had only 16 players, the required minimum, and needed every boy to show up. He'd heard his teammates say, over and over, that they had to win this game to make the playoffs. He'd heard parents talk about how this was homecoming week and a lot of people were going to be there and you didn't want to embarrass yourself by losing in front of all those people during homecoming. With the other Mo Better age groups already eliminated from contention, Esau's team was again the program's last hope for postseason success.

Donnie told his older cousin, who was accompanying him and his 8-year-old brother Tarell to the game, that it was important they left early. He'd reminded her the night before, he'd been the first in the apartment to wake, and all morning he'd prodded her and Tarell to hurry up. Donnie's cousin had attended South Shore High School, the location of the game, and she had no trouble getting them there from the Castle by bus. They arrived at the field around noon, five hours before the Pee Wee game and two hours before the Mitey Mite game. The bleachers were still empty. They were the first ones there, and it felt like the whole stadium was theirs.

Donnie and Tarell dropped their bags at the top of the bleachers, kicked off their rubber slippers, and ran onto the field in their socks. They brimmed with excitement and energy. Donnie didn't like to spend time at home, where it was often crowded, hectic, and messy. He craved open space, and now here was 120 yards worth of artificial grass to run around on. They tossed around the football they had borrowed from their older brother. They chased each other, zigzagging around orange cones that randomly dotted the field. They hopped onto a gymnastics balance beam on the track and tried to walk from one end to the other. When he reached the end, Donnie jumped off and ran back onto the field. Then he stopped, crouched down, and casually leaped into a front flip, landing on his feet, before running to the 50-yard line and plopping onto the ground, where he sat with his arms looped around his knees, grinning and giggling. Tarell ran over and took a seat next to him. Donnie was glad to see his brother smiling.

Lately, Tarell had been getting into more fights at school and throwing more tantrums at home. "He just be mad at all the stuff we don't have," Donnie said. "I be mad too, but I be better at dealing with it now than he is. Like I be thinkin' bout how the anger goes away. He not really old enough to think things like that." One recent day at Betsy Head, Tarell took his anger out on a boy he knew from the neighborhood. Tarell was playing tag with several others when this boy showed up, placed his backpack and a cup of applesauce on the ground, and asked if he could join. Tarell shouted, "No!" and began making fun of the boy's clothes, a maroon polo shirt and black slacks. They traded insults. Then Tarell picked up the applesauce and slammed it down, brown mush exploding on the dirt. The boy claimed he knew karate and got into a karate pose, and Tarell made fun of that too. "I'll knock the shit out of you!" Tarell said to him, and the boy replied, "You think I'm scared of you?"

Oomz, Donnie, and some other older boys at the park paused their football game to watch.

"It's about to get lit!" one boy said. "Tarell 'bout to get beat up. That boy mad bigger."

"Tarell don't get beat up," Oomz said. "I've never seen him beat up."

Soon they were swinging at each other. Though the boy in the maroon shirt was bigger, Tarell hit harder, and after a few punches, Oomz and Donnie broke it up.

"I woulda knocked him out," the boy said, his face twisted in anger, as Donnie calmly guided him away from Tarell. "That lil' boy keep saying my mama got crabs in her vagina. He live on the street! He eat on the street! I bet he gon' eat that applesauce on the ground!"

Tarell pointed at the boy, laughing loud enough for him to hear, saying to the other boys, "Look at that kid! He think he know karate! His mama nasty!"

Donnie had tried to get tougher on Tarell, hoping it would harden him, make him better able to shrug off the nice clothes and new toys other kids flaunted. One evening, Tarell showed up to Betsy Head in full pads without knowing that there was no Mitey Mite practice that day. Donnie, who did have practice that day, punched him in the chest for being irresponsible. "'Cause you never be listening!" Donnie shouted at him in front of all the Pee Wees.

But now, as he and Tarell sat at midfield, Donnie wondered if maybe all his brother needed was space and calm, grass and quiet, time away from the sounds of gunshots and elevated 3 trains. He looked at his brother and couldn't see a trace of the anger lingering within him. He saw a pure smile, a smile so wide and free that sweat dripped onto Tarell's teeth. It was the first Saturday of fall but more than 80 degrees, the hottest day in weeks. The sun was high and the sky was clear and bright. Other boys began to arrive. Donnie and Tarell greeted them, then returned to the to the bleachers, where their cousin was changing her baby's diaper.

"I'ma get so many tackles, it's not even funny," Donnie said to her. "I'ma hit somebody. I'ma hit they helmet off."

From the top of the bleachers, Donnie and Tarell watched the stadium come alive. A ceremonial vibe soon took hold of the place. The stands filled quickly. Former Mo Better players hugged and caught up. Brownsville old-timers gathered on the walkway sharing stories. Down at the base of the bleachers, Coach Chris held court, regaling a crowd with tales of his glory days at this very stadium. He told them about how he played so well here because he knew the crosswinds, how he loved throwing to the east end zone because the wind was usually at his back, how he'd tossed many long bombs to his brother Ricky, the fastest kid on the field, thanks to his understanding of the wind. The people in the crowd listened with smiles, nods, and wide eyes, they laughed at his jokes, and when he said he had to move on to greet others, good host that he was, they slapped him on the back and told him they looked forward to seeing some Mo Better wins today. "Great day for football, huh?" Chris boomed as he worked his way through the people. "Great day for football!"

The day's joy dissolved once the football got going. Brick City dominated the Mitey Mite game in the morning, and then ran up a huge lead in the Junior Pee Wee contest before the second quarter was over in the early afternoon. The Pee Wees watched this devastation from under a big oak tree behind the west end zone. Esau had corralled them there to keep them cool in the shade and far from the distractions of the bleachers. Frustration, anger, and gloom simmered in the stands. Parents and former players complained that Mo Better had fallen behind its competitors in Newark and East Orange. The golden years were long gone, went the whispers. On the Brick City side, where the shirts and hats were blue and silver, there was confidence and pride. For the second straight year, Brick City was proving its superiority over the legendary Brooklyn juggernaut. "They was really feelin' themselves over there," Oomz observed. When the Mo Better Pee Wees had crossed the bleachers on their way to the oak tree, a Brick City coach said to them, "Y'all know y'all not scoring." The boys had kept on walking, without saying a word, until they reached the tree, at which point Naz said, "They coaches crazy. Can't believe he said we not gonna score."

"I bet we do score," Oomz said. "I bet Isaiah scoring."

"*They* not scoring," Naz said. "How 'bout that?"

The boys stewed under the tree, their faces serious, quietly chewing sunflower seeds.

Time Out broke the silence: "If we lose—"

"Stop talking about losing," Isaiah interrupted, his voice harsh and loud. "I don't wanna lose!"

Esau was on edge, too. He felt the pressure of the game, knew the season hinged on this day. He chided the boys for eating sunflower seeds: "That shit'll dehydrate you!" He chided Oomz for roughhousing with friends at the park earlier that week and mildly spraining his ankle in the process. Oomz aggravated the injury during tackling drills at practice on Friday night, and now he sat on the ground, his shoes off and right leg stretched out as Andrell wrapped his ankle in athletic tape.

"Yo, remember, we can't afford any injuries today," Esau told the team. "We only got sixteen. You just gotta get up and walk off. One injury and it's a forfeit. So unless something is broke, you gotta just get to the sideline."

The worry lingered at the back of every player's mind. A single play, one awkward fall or blind-side hit or overextended stride, could end the game and cost the season. Many anxieties fogged their minds—about dropped passes, missed blocks, and fumbled balls; about making the mistake that ruined the season. Dreadful images from the week before pushed against their confidence. Isaiah tried not to think about the first-down catch on the deep out route. Chaka tried not to think about the touchdown pass that floated over his head. Naz tried not to think about the interceptions. Esau tried not to think about the *Shut the fuck up!* moment. Hart, like every one of them, tried to clear his mind and lock into the present: the long field in front of him, the teammates in purple jerseys packed around him under the goalpost, the rattle from the stomps on the bleachers, the smell of hot rubber rising from the turf, the rush of traffic on the street behind him, the stern and sullen face of Coach Vick, who stood before them with fire in this throat.

"We gon' go out there and y'all gon' represent the hood today," he declared. "I got my behind whoop today. I ain't never ran from an ass whoopin. But I got my behind whoop today. I need y'all to whoop that behind for me."

More than 100 yards away, Brick City's Pee Wees stood packed around the opposite goalpost, nodding along to their own coach, who maybe had fire in his own throat. They too had lost to East Orange, they too believed that the fate of their season depended on this game, and they too had a hood to represent. Dorian's father, Dwight, had summed it up well during the hard and dusty practice the night before: "They're similar to us," he'd said to the other fathers. "Just change the uniforms and it's like . . . " But he couldn't finish the sentence.

ooooo

BLOCKING AND TACKLING—these were the fundamental and essential skills in football. At many practices, over many years, Coach Chris had stood before his players and asked, "What are the two things you gotta do in football?" And his players answered, "Block and tackle." All year, from the first practice in spring to the one on Friday night, the boys had dedicated scores of hours to mastering these two skills. They had practiced in T-shirts and in shoulder pads, on rubber dummies and on each other. Blocking and tackling were what separated a good athlete from a good football player. Chris had seen many boys—strong and fast boys with nimble legs and soft hands, who dominated their peers in sandlot football games—lose interest in the sport once they realized how much more there was to football than throwing, catching, and running with the ball. Blocking and tackling were fundamental and essential and rooted in violence. There were collisions on every play, and a boy who did not enjoy these collisions could not enjoy playing football. The violence was inherent to the game; it could not be avoided. And when Oomz kicked off the ball to open the first quarter, the 11 boys in purple and the 11 boys in white charged forward, and, like two armies meeting on a battlefield, the sides smashed together in a collection of individual collisions. Isaiah and his counterpart slammed into each other with a loud *pop!* and with such equal force that they bounced off of each other and stayed on their feet, and when the whistle blew they stared at each other for a few seconds, perhaps out of respect or contempt.

The defenses stood firm to begin the game. Mo Better drove the Brick City offense 10 yards back and then recovered a fumble. Brick City countered with an interception. The first quarter ended without a score. In the second quarter, Mo Better's blocking began to hold, opening lanes for the star running backs. The offense marched, gaining its rhythm. With Oomz clearing the way, Isaiah ran to the outside for 30 yards, bringing the offense past midfield. On the next play, Isaiah cleared the way for Oomz, who burst for eight yards, but as he lunged through the defenders, fighting his way forward, the ball popped loose and a Brick City boy dove on it. The blue-and-silver side of the bleachers cheered at the clear fumble, but then fell silent when the referee ruled that Oomz's knee hit the ground before he lost the ball. That silence turned to groans and grumbles seconds later, when Isaiah ran 40 yards before stepping out of bounds at the two-yard line. On the next play, Oomz shot through the middle for a touchdown. 6–0.

On the last play of the first half, Isaiah drilled the Brick City quarterback, igniting *woooos!* and claps on the Mo Better sidelines as the clock ticked to zero. The Brooklyn boys ran off the field, toward the oak tree, hopping around and slapping each other on the shoulder pads. The boys from Newark moved slowly and quietly with their heads down, before glumly taking their seats in a shaded patch of grass beside the bleachers. "Look at 'em!" Andrell shouted. "Look at 'em walkin' around. They not used to bein' down. Let's take their heart." On the first possession of the third quarter, Naz faked a handoff to Isaiah, drawing the defense to the running back, then lobbed a deep pass to Chaka, who was so open that he raised his arm at the 25-yard line and pointed to the sky all the way to the end zone. Joy had returned to the purple-and-gold side of the stands. After converting the point-after, Mo Better led 13–0.

It felt like Mo Better was on the verge of a blowout. The boys on Brick City's sideline appeared defeated, slouching and shaking their heads. Mo Better had scored easily on two straight possessions and prevented Brick City from advancing past midfield. On its next chance, though, Brick City's offense began to chip through the defense. They spread the field, with two receivers on each side, and ran the ball to the right, away from Isaiah. The running back, who wore number 3 and had thin sweat bands on his lower leg, sliced through the defense for 20 yards, and then, on the next play, broke through three tackles for nine more yards. The Mo Better defenders bent over with fatigue and the Brick City offense rushed to the line, keeping up the fast-paced attack, but just as it seemed that the offense was rolling, the referee blew the whistle. The third quarter was over—after just eight total plays. Brick City's coaches, furious, shouted a flurry of questions at the referee. How did the eight minutes pass so quickly? How could the quarter end when their first offensive possession had barely begun? Why hadn't the ref, tasked with keeping time on his hand-held clock, updated them? "Ay, ref! We need to know the time on this side of the field!" shouted one coach.

But Brick City trudged on in the fourth quarter. Their running back with the leg bands scored a touchdown, and then, on the kickoff, they recovered the short on-side kick to regain possession.

"Fuck, man!" Andrell shouted. "Damn!"

With the score 13–6, Brick City had the ball at midfield, seven minutes left in the game. Less than half an hour earlier, Oomz had thought the game was over. He didn't say this out loud at the time, but he would admit it days later. "I thought we had them done," he would say. "It turned so fast." Now, his heart began to beat faster and he felt anxiety bubbling in his stomach.

"We just gotta hold 'em," Esau said to Andrell on the sidelines. "Right here."

"Isaiah! Oomz! Get me that ball back!" Andrell shouted to the field.

Brick City's offense continued its roll. Four yards. Six yards. Four yards. Eight yards. Nine yards. The same play, sweep to the right, over and over, and yet the defense couldn't stop it. When the running back with the leg bands hopped up from the turf, he walked back to the huddle with a swagger, bouncing on the balls of his feet, a bop in his step, the stroll of a confident athlete.

"They tired!" shouted a man on Brick City's side of the bleachers.

They were less than 20 yards from the end zone. Dripping with sweat, Hart leaned his head back, looked to the sky, and sucked in air with big breaths. Oomz rested his hands on his knees, his chest heaving. Even Isaiah looked winded, slowly dragging his heavy legs to his position on the field between plays.

"Y'all letting it slip away!" Andrell shouted to the boys. "Damn!"

On first down and 10, Brick City ran for a short gain, but a lineman was called for a holding penalty, moving them back 10 yards. It was now first down and 20. Brick City gained four yards on the next play, and then one yard the play after that.

"Fourth down!" the referee announced, and the coaches on Brick City's sidelines looked at one another in confusion.

"Third down!" a coach yelled. "It should be third down! We had that penalty! It should be third down!"

"It's fourth down!" the ref again declared.

Bewildered outrage rained down from the Brick City sidelines and bleachers.

"What?!"

"No way!"

"You can't let this happen!"

"The fuck is this?!"

"Come on, it's third down!"

The Brick City coaches pleaded with the referee. "It's fourth down," the referee stubbornly repeated, and then he blew the whistle for the next play to begin. The Brick City coaches, stunned and speechless, with no option but to accept the injustice, called on the offense to play on. Mo Better's defense held them short. Esau and Andrell looked at each other with gleeful, grateful smirks. Last week, the breaks had gone against them. Fortune could make all the difference, they knew, and they welcomed it to their side.

Up seven points with less than five minutes left, Mo Better could seal the victory by scoring again or by running out the clock. Isaiah got the ball first and pushed forward for four yards, the time ticking down to four minutes. Esau called a play for Oomz next, and Oomz lined up in the backfield with Isaiah in front of him. Oomz was confident and calm again, his adrenaline rising because he was about to run the ball. He had been eager for this game all week. His father had not hidden his disappointment after last week's loss. Big Oomz had told him that he and his teammates played soft, played unlike the Mo Better teams before them. "Y'all gotta step it up," he remembered his father saying. "I'ma go hard," Oomz replied.

ooooo

THE GAME AGAINST Brick City had been on his mind all week. He had plenty of time to daydream. His mother had transferred him to the charter school in Fort Greene for his sixth-grade year, and the bus ride took about 45 minutes. He now mostly lived with his maternal grandmother in East New York, and in the mornings, he took the B25 bus by himself to school. His paternal grandmother, Monique, who worked in Downtown Brooklyn, met Oomz outside his school in the afternoons and accompanied him home on the 3 train. If he had practice that day, he'd return to East New York to pack an overnight bag, head to Betsy Head, and then spend the night at Monique's house in Brownsville.

His father didn't like this new routine because Oomz was spending less time with him at Monique's house. His coaches didn't like this new routine because Oomz was late to practice more often. A few times over the past two weeks, he showed up 30 or more minutes late, still in the clothes he wore to school, and by the time he was dressed in his pads, he'd missed nearly an hour of practice.

"She got him going to school all the way up in Downtown Brooklyn," Esau said to Ramsey as Oomz strolled into the park the night before the Brick City game.

"Why he ain't going to school 'round here?" Ramsey said. "She crazy."

When Oomz's mother, Tasha, dropped by the park that evening, Esau complained to her that Oomz kept showing up late to practice since switching schools.

"Esau, you pick him up from school then," she proposed.

"You gotta take him back around here," he deflected.

"Nah, uh-uh, Brownsville ain't good."

"There's some good schools around here. The one he went to was pretty good."

"They got too familiar with him, and then it was just whatever."

Tasha believed that the shift from a Brownsville public school to a Fort Greene charter school would be an educational upgrade. As an added benefit, her son would be spending more time outside Brownsville; she didn't want him to become one of those young men who rarely left the comfort of his immediate surroundings. Though the new commute and routine brought inconveniences to his life, Oomz supported his mother's decision. He knew enough to know that he already had plenty going against him. His family didn't have much money, and he'd heard that many public high schools didn't properly prepare students for college. He knew that he was smart and that to escape his neighborhood one day, to rise further than anyone in his family before him, he needed to maximize whatever opportunities he encountered. This didn't mean getting lucky. To Oomz, escaping and advancing meant keeping himself on a certain path, a simple path: to get a good job he had to go to a good college, and to get into a good college he had to go to a good high school, and to get into a good high school he had to go to a good middle school. If his mother believed that this charter school in Fort Greene was the best middle school available, he was all for it. Oomz's mother had visited the school. It was clean and bright, and the administrators talked a big game. She'd heard good things about charter schools, from other parents and from news articles. She put her son's name into the lottery, and when he was selected, it felt like an easy decision.

Oomz and his mother had expected a rigorous curriculum, good teachers, and eager students at this new school. But they were soon disappointed. "My mom thought it was gonna be people who sit in they seat and do they work, but it's not," Oomz said. By his second week in class, Oomz had concluded that the school wasn't for him. The students were disruptive, and the teachers seemed overwhelmed and inexperienced, Oomz observed. Classes started and quickly sputtered into chaos, the teacher sitting impotently behind the desk while students talked and flirted and teased, not even pretending to fill out the day's worksheet assignment. "They ain't teach us algebra or nothing," he said. "Just teaching us division. They ain't even give us homework!" At his old school, Oomz got along with everybody and felt that his classmates respected both his charisma and his intelligence. At his new school, though, "there's always kids tryna start stuff," he said. "People always tryna fight. They just wanna start anything." Though he sometimes had a quick temper, Oomz wanted to avoid trouble. He talked his way out of having to throw punches, and because he was not releasing his anger, it built with each confrontation. One kid in particular kept poking at him. This was "a slow kid," Oomz said, who seemed to take offense at Oomz's efforts to bring order to the classroom: the way Oomz was in his seat before the bell, raised his hand to answer questions, and told other kids to be quiet while the teacher was talking. Oomz didn't dress or speak like a square, but he acted like one in class, and he believed that this kid thought he was showing off. Why else would this boy talk so much smack to him? He told his father about all this, and his father advised him that "if this kid says something to me or touches me, I'll hit him," Oomz said. A few days before the Brick City game, as the classroom descended toward anarchy, Oomz raised his voice and told his classmates, "Yo! Pay attention!" The kid turned to Oomz and growled, "Shut up!" Oomz felt the anger rise from his gut up to his head and he clenched his jaw and fists. He cocked his arm back and swung, but then pulled his hand back inches before it connected with the kid's face. The kid flinched and cowered, and the other classmates laughed. The kid didn't say anything to Oomz the rest of the week. Oomz told his father about how he'd scared the boy into silence without having to hit him, and his father was impressed.

ooooo

Big Oomz hadn't come to any practices so far, but he'd been at every game, quiet and brooding at the front of the bleachers. Now, as Oomz lined up for the play, the bleachers were rattling on both sides, with stomps and banging fists. Naz took the snap and held the ball out for Oomz to grab, and Oomz opened his arms and took the ball into his stomach. But, when he closed his arms, the ball squirted out and bounced onto the turf. A Brick City player dove on the ball and the Brick City side of the bleachers went wild. Two plays later, Brick City ran in for the touchdown and then tied the game at 13 with the point-after conversion.

On the sidelines, Oomz seemed close to tears. He bit his lip and stared at the ground, his hands on his hips. One by one, his coaches approached him.

"Get over it, Oomz," Andrell said. "Just make it better."

"Let's go," Ramsey said. "Your team needs you. Perform under pressure."

"Oomz," Vick said. "Listen to me, baby boy. You need to go out there, lay somebody the fuck out. You lay somebody out, I promise that'll make you feel better. This is the opportunity right now. Right now, put a block on somebody. You made a mistake. Go out there and make up for it right now. Hold ya head up. You a fighter."

The sun dipped below the trees on the horizon. A soft blue light engulfed the field. It was cool now, and a breeze flapped jerseys and leaves. Mo Better had the ball back and Oomz was on the field. On fourth down, with a few seconds left in the game, Naz dropped back for a Hail Mary pass attempt from midfield. Oomz, blocking to give Naz more time, leveled a defender and Naz threw the ball deep toward Chaka, but a defensive back intercepted it, then cut across the field, and as the seconds ticked down he had much space in front of him and it looked like he had a chance to score. But just as he was about to break free, Hart caught up and cut him down. The game would be settled in overtime. The Brick City side of the stands cheered loudly, keeping alive the energy they'd built in the game's final quarter. The Mo Better side was silent, tense—even Mr. Hart. He was standing with his arms crossed, as quiet and brooding as Big Oomz.

∞∞∞

To Mr. Hart, merely standing up still felt like a feat. He'd been bed-ridden or on crutches for seven months, and only a few weeks ago did he take his first steps out of the house without help. In those early months after his knee injury, he hoped to eventually return to his job. He had worked as a correctional officer at Rikers Island for 27 years and planned to retire at 30 years, which would mean a bigger pension to put his two kids through college and support his and his wife's retirement. Hitting 30 years was supposed to be the final step of a long climb from poverty to the middle class, an ascent that stretched back decades and spanned hundreds of miles. Mr. Hart's parents had grown up poor in Georgia before following the Great Migration trail north to Brooklyn. They settled in Bed-Stuy and built working-class lives. Mr. Hart's father was a cook at an oyster restaurant and his mother worked in a factory. They ran a strict household, where the punishment for misbehavior was a belt to the backside. They were active and caring parents, but Bed-Stuy was rough in the 1970s and '80s, and Mr. Hart hung out with troublemakers. As a teenager, he joined his friends on a few stickups. He never got caught; an armed robbery conviction would have prevented him from getting a job as a jail guard, irreversibly altering the trajectory of his life—his son's too. Just as a child is born into a family's accumulated wealth, a child is born into a family's accumulated troubles. But by luck or God or fate, Mr. Hart was not pulled into the criminal justice system.

He worked some odd jobs after high school, then decided to take the civil service test, applying for work as a police officer, a garbage collector, a correctional officer, and a bus driver, which was his first choice. Rikers Island guard was the only offer he got. For a young man with a working-class background and no college education, the job represented upward mobility. After five years, he could make more than his father made; after 10, he could make six figures; after 20, he could retire with a pension that paid half of his salary for the rest of his life; and after 30, he could retire with a pension that nearly equaled his full salary. A generation earlier, he might have found such an opportunity at one of Brooklyn's booming factories, but most of those factories were closed now. So, he went to Rikers.

The job was more grueling than he had imagined. Every day, he would patrol the cell blocks, absorbing a constant stream of shouted curses, thrown feces, and spit from inmates. He saw an inmate stab a pen into another inmate's eye. He saw an inmate dump a pot of boiling water onto another inmate's head. "His head swelled to the size of four basketballs," Mr. Hart recalled. The environment hardened him. Inmates who disrespected him paid the price. "You would just pop him in the face, write up a small report, and you'd be good," he said. Over the years, though, that changed. Mayor de Blasio pushed to grant inmates more rights. Around 75 percent of inmates at Rikers hadn't been convicted of a crime and were simply awaiting trial. De Blasio appointed a new Department of Correction commissioner who aimed to change the culture at the jail—less solitary confinement, less violence against inmates. "These days they're cracking down, and you could get in a lot of trouble for hitting an inmate," Mr. Hart said. "And so inmates act out more." He believed that these reforms were making the job more dangerous, that the bureaucrats making the decisions had no clue what it was like trying to keep order over angry and spiteful men, some of whom were surely planning to shank a guard at the first opportunity. Within a year, city officials reported that the number of stabbings and slashings at the jail increased by around 30 percent, the annual tally of injured guards rose by 104, and attacks on civilian staff tripled, from 17 to 54, even as the inmate population dipped by more than 5 percent.

So, while Mr. Hart had been hoping to get his 30 years, he concluded that he was getting out at the right time. He was on terminal leave now, receiving his salary checks for $6,000 a month until his vacation time was exhausted in November, at which point he would begin to receive his pension checks, around 60 percent of his salary. It would be enough to live a happy twilight.

He was still in his 40s, and he felt blessed to be able to retire before his kids were even teenagers. Those first few months after the injury, he'd thought about how unlucky he was to suffer such a debilitating freak accident, but his spirits quickly turned once he discovered the benefits of being a stay-at-home dad. Before, he and his wife, who worked as an accountant, had to juggle the standard responsibilities that emerged in every non-rich household with two working parents. Once Mr. Hart was healed enough to drive, he had all the time to take the kids to school in the morning, clean up the house during the day, pick the kids up in the afternoon, and prepare their meals in the evening. He quickly fell in love with how much time he got to spend with them.

He had worked hard to build this life. His kids went to a good public school and lived in a two-story, three-bed, three-bath, wood-paneled house with three televisions and a backyard in a quiet neighborhood. They had a fish tank in the basement and a basketball hoop out back. Their closets were stuffed with clothes and their walls lined with shoes. This was a long way to come over a generation.

Mr. Hart's son didn't act like a child born into any sort of privilege. Perhaps he developed this awareness thanks to the many hours he spent among boys who were not born into the same comforts, boys who needed double the effort to make up for their lack of fortune. Or perhaps because he had a father and a mother who had warned him about his privilege all his life, parents with the sense and devotion to send him to Brownsville in the first place. Success required a convergence of various circumstances working out in a person's favor. All Hart's parents could do was try to maximize their son's chances.

Hart's childhood was one of routine and stability, with the luxury of days blending together. There was Mr. Hart parked in the car-pool line one fall afternoon, no different from the fall afternoon before or after. There were Hart and his sister, Brianna, climbing into the charcoal Dodge Charger. They went to McDonald's and ordered 20 chicken nuggets, which Hart and Brianna dumped onto Styrofoam plates and shared while doing homework at the dining-room table. With practice in two hours, Hart was restless. He had four homework assignments, and his father said that they would not leave for Betsy Head until all the assignments were finished. First was a history reading. His father wiped down the kitchen counters and quizzed him on what he was learning while humming to the R&B music playing on the speakers in the background.

"That's crazy," Hart said. "Spartans were taught to steal but they were punished if they got caught. So you were allowed to steal just so long as you didn't get caught."

Hart spoke with an earnest wonder. He leaned forward in his chair, elbows on the table, peering down at the gray papers, his eyes quickly scanning the lines.

"Oh dang, that's crazy," he said, looking up toward the kitchen again. "To test their courage, their teacher sent them out with no light in the dark to run errands, and they would just have to do the best they can. Basically, what I'm picking up from this is the Spartan culture was survive the best way you can and don't get caught."

When he completed the assignment, Hart shouted, "Done!" and his father replied, "On to the next one!" Before beginning the next one, Hart took a break to practice his signature on a blank sheet of notebook paper, until it was nearly covered top to bottom, his name scribbled in several different styles. "I need to figure out my signature," he said quietly and seriously. A worksheet was next. And then two short essays, on a poem about a raven (not the famous one) and an article about an indigenous wood-carver in Alaska. Then, finally, a chapter from a book, *Beauty and the Beast*. Through it all, Hart tried, without success, to persuade his father to let them head out.

"I'll finish it tonight," he said.

"You're not gonna wanna touch that work after practice," his father said.

By the time the homework was done, they were running late.

"Go upstairs, put a shirt on, and take two puffs of ya asthma pump and get down here," Mr. Hart said. "Let's move. You're moving like a snail here. Got work to do."

Practice was starting in 15 minutes and the drive over took 30. Hart rushed up the stairs, his heavy feet pounding the hardwood. Kanye West's "All Falls Down" came on the speakers, and Mr. Hart turned the volume up. *It seems we living the American Dream. . . . The prettiest people do the ugliest things, on the road to riches and diamond rings.*

Traffic was light, and so was the mood in the car.

"I wanna go to Stanford," Hart told his father, as they passed the housing projects on Pennsylvania Avenue, which took on a red-orange tint under the setting sun. "Or Syracuse. I would love to go to Yale, but their football team is not that good. But if I got a scholarship then I would have to make the toughest decision: football or school. But I could be a star at Yale and they'll still hear about me and I'd go to the NFL."

"School first, then football," Mr. Hart said matter-of-factly.

He knew he didn't need to lecture his son about this. The boy had always seemed to take his education seriously. Recently, he'd joined an engineering club that made robots to compete in citywide competitions against other schools. Hart was the only black kid in the club. Most of the other kids were Southeast Asian, Chinese, or white. After a few weeks in the club, Hart contemplated shifting his post-NFL career path from law to engineering. "That's where the money will be at," his father told him. But at the same time, Hart knew his father understood his passion for football and supported his football dreams.

Mr. Hart had played football for many years after high school, not in an organized league but in the games his New York City Department of Correction team played against the New York City Police Department and the New York City Fire Department and against other corrections departments in Texas and Florida. He loved football. He loved that every play brought a new physical and mental challenge. He loved the feeling of knowing that an opponent feared him. Mr. Hart claimed that he'd never felt fear on a football field, and if this was true, it was a trait he had passed down to his son.

His son's era was different. While Mr. Hart only had to worry about the opponent across from him, his son also had to consider the long-term consequences of all those hits. Hart prided himself on keeping up with current events, and he'd heard about the national concern about what football did to the brain. Just that month, he'd seen on the news that NFL officials admitted in federal court that they expected nearly a third of retired players to suffer severe cognitive problems at "notably younger ages" than the general population. Less than a week after that news dropped, Hart read that a 16-year-old boy from Long Island had collapsed after a big collision and died three days later.

"A kid just died from a hit," Hart said in the car on the way to practice. He paused, fiddled with a loose thread hanging from his football pants. "If you do proper technique and all that, keep ya head up, you can keep yourself safe," he continued, then paused again, staring out the window at people in the cars on the highway, random lives with their own unknowable fears, dreams, and destinations. "I dunno," Hart sighed. "But still, you face a lotta danger playing football. I think it's changing, though. Like basketball. You used to be able to hand check a guy, use your hands. Can't do that anymore. Football changing, too. Not as rough as it used to be."

Hart was ambivalent about these changes. Perhaps they would in fact make the game safer for his generation. Or perhaps they would only make the game less interesting and less thrilling, pulling it away from the facets Hart enjoyed most. But Hart thought less about the future of football than he did about where he wanted to play football in the future. For now, still, it was a rough game that tested wills. Like his father, he loved that, and as his team gathered around Coach Esau with the score tied at the end of the fourth quarter, Hart looked across the field at the Brick City boys gathered around their own coach. Days later, when he thought back to this moment, he would wonder: When the talents were equal, what separated those who won from those who lost?

Shoulders slumped and heads were down in the Mo Better circle. The boys knew they had let the game slip away. Esau sensed this. He had seen this mind-set many times last season, a resignation that defeat was inevitable.

"We gotta become men now," he said to the boys, his voice sturdy and crisp. "We messed that up. We gotta become men now."

He looked at Isaiah, the boy who had carried them all season, the boy with number 2 on his jersey, and he said, "We going with two. Everybody else block. We got two plays: we gon' run to the left, we gon' run to the right. We gotta become men now."

Days later, when Hart thought back to this moment, he thought about the Spartans, and how here was Esau sending them off into the darkness, and they had to find a way to survive.

∞∞∞∞∞

IT WAS COLLEGE-STYLE overtime rules: one team got the ball first and then the other team had a shot to match or exceed their score, back and forth until a team emerged from a round victorious. Brick City won the coin toss and chose to begin on defense. Isaiah got the handoff up the middle on the first play, at the 10-yard line, but the hole he was supposed to run through was clogged, so he quickly turned and cut to the left, jogging parallel to the line, eyes scanning the field, locking on the empty stretch of grass between the cornerback and the linebacker. He burst into the open space, veering to the outside, striding past defenders, picking up speed all the way into the end zone. Beneath his helmet he almost laughed at how, after all that tension and drama, the score had come so easily. His teammates, hollering and smiling, engulfed him. The Mo Better side of the bleachers cheered, but it was a tempered joy, with guards up, the parents unwilling to release themselves, still pushing back thoughts of victory. 19–13.

Oomz felt relieved by the score. He had been pouting since his fumble, and when Esau was speaking to the team before overtime, Oomz stood in the back looking sad, his eyes off in the distance, his mind replaying his mistake. But now he was rejuvenated. From his inside linebacker position, he stared over the hunched lineman at the quarterback, and as soon as the quarterback took the snap and turned to hand the ball to the running back, Oomz ran into the gap in the middle of the line and hit the runner. Three more stops and they would win the game, Oomz couldn't help but think. On the next play, Brick City faked a sweep to the right, drawing the defense in that direction, clearing the way for a run to the left. Oomz bit on the fake and by the time he realized his error, the Brick City runner with the leg bands was yards ahead of him, nearing the end zone with no defenders in front. Oomz dove, his arms swiping at the runner, catching him on the ankle and tripping him to the ground, the outstretched ball landing at the one-yard line. On third down, Brick City's star runner went up the middle, into the pile of bodies, pushing forward. Oomz met him at the goal line, held his ground, and brought the boy down. Some Brick City players raised their arms, signaling a touchdown in hopes of influencing the refs. Parents in the stands did the same. When the referee peeled away the bodies, he found that the ball was just barely short of the goal line, nearly flush with it, save maybe two or three blades of grass. Everybody in the bleachers was standing now. Sharif Legree pulled out his phone and began recording.

The boys on both sidelines crept to the edge of the field in nervous anticipation. Fourth down from inside the one-yard line.

"Yo, Hart, I need a big one!" Andrell yelled.

"Best game I've had all year," the referee whispered to the volunteers holding the orange yard markers behind him.

"De-fense!" Mr. Hart chanted in the stands. "De-fense!"

The teams lined up, the linemen put their hands on the ground. Hart dropped into his stance near the middle of the line. He peeked up at the quarterback, then at the running back with the leg bands a few yards ahead, then at the offensive lineman just to his right, then at the one just to his left, then down at the ball, which was inches from his head, then back up at the quarterback. He had studied the quarterback all game. He thought he noticed something: The quarterback seemed to spend more time wiping his hands on the towel at his waist before plays when the ball was snapped on the second or third "Go!"—as if trying to lure the defense into jumping offside by slowing down his pace. When the snap came on the first "Go!" the quarterback wiped his hands on the towel with a single, brisk stroke. Hart had come to this conclusion sometime in the fourth quarter, but he thought maybe it was only his imagination; maybe his mind had formed a pattern that didn't exist.

Now, he watched the quarterback quickly brush his hands on his towel before crouching down and beginning his cadence.

"Readyyyyy!"

Hart stared at the quarterback's legs, through the space between the two linemen across from him.

"Seeeetttt!"

Hart rocked back, shifting more of his weight onto his legs, coiling like a snake about to strike.

"G—"

At the first sound of it, Hart shot forward like a battering ram, and by the time the offensive linemen reached up to block him, he was past them, in the backfield, driving his helmet into the chest of the running back, drilling him into the ground. He heard the explosion of cheers before he realized what he had done. He hopped to his feet, raised his arms, and let out a roar. His teammates surrounded him, hugging him, slapping his helmet and shoulder pads.

"That was crazy!" Donnie said.

"I love you, Hart!" Time Out said.

They celebrated on the field, jumping and screaming, and once they had let it all out, they gathered around Coach Esau, who seemed unable to speak for a few seconds and just stood there, mouth agape, looking at his boys.

"I'm so proud of y'all," he said. "Yo, I'm about to break into tears. Not even the win, but the way y'all fought back." He paused, then shouted, "Who got my back?"

"I got yo back!" the boys replied together.

It was getting dark, and the stands began to empty. Parents streamed onto the field and into the parking lot. Coach Vick pulled Hart into an embrace.

"You gon' remember this all ya life," he said to him. "That play right there you gon' never forget."

From where they stood, near the spot where Hart had made the game-winning tackle, they could not see the Brick City boys beside the bleachers on the other side of the field, sitting on the ground, hands covering their faces, many of them in tears.

– 18 –

NONE OF Y'ALL GON' DIE TONIGHT
Mid to late October 2014

OOMZ WAS IN A BAD MOOD. ANOTHER POINTLESS, DISAP-pointing day at a school he hated. He had woken up that morning consumed by a feeling of dread for the hours he was about to waste in the classroom. His mother had begun researching more schools, inquiring about whether any of the good ones would take him. His mood had turned increasingly sour throughout the day, and he arrived at Betsy Head with a mean look on his face. He felt his energy drained by his frustrations. He dressed in his pads quietly, trying to ignore the boys around him.

Their mood was joyful. Teammates reminisced about the big win. Parents held their phones over the fence and showed off photos from the game. Coaches joked about the mistakes on the field that made them maddest and about how all is forgiven in victory. Oomz kept his eyes on the shoulder pads he was buckling, feigning a deep focus on adjusting the straps under his arms. He resented this vibrant energy and felt trapped by it. He was more relieved than happy about the win. He was ready to move on from it. After the game, his father had told him he was proud of how the team fought but disappointed by Oomz's late-game fumble. Oomz couldn't shake the memory of that fumble. He felt guilty for becoming so consumed by his individual mistake instead of reveling in his team's achievement. He wondered if he should have skipped practice and gone home, but he figured he could clear his mind and lose himself in the repetition of football drills.

Practice did not lighten his mood. While his teammates ran their warm-up lap, Oomz alternated between walking and jogging. Chaka joined him. When Coach Ramsey spotted them, he ordered all the boys onto the ground for bear crawls—"crabbing," in the team's vernacular.

"Why we gotta do this?" Oomz said.

"It was you and Chaka!" Ramsey replied. "I watched you and Chaka damn near walk the whole damn lap. Y'all brought this on y'allselves."

Oomz crawled at the back of the pack. Every few yards, he stood up and complained to Ramsey that his back was sore. Ramsey ignored him, and the next time Oomz stood, Esau shouted, "Yo, Oomz, shut up and crab!"

"I just—"

"Shut up and crab!"

"Until somebody take the initiative to stop all the bullshit, we gon' keep doing stuff like this and not work on football," Ramsey said.

"None of y'all even been to the playoffs yet!" Esau said. "None of y'all!"

At 4–1, second in the division and with the hard part of their schedule done, the coaches hoped to keep the Pee Wees sharp in the weeks until what everyone assumed would be an inevitable rematch with East Orange for the league title. Unless Mo Better's Pee Wees lost two of their final three games, they'd beat out Brick City for the division's final playoff spot.

When Ramsey ordered them to drop for push-ups, Oomz lingered on his feet.

"Yo, get down!" Marquis said to him.

"Shut the fuck up!" Oomz replied.

Ramsey, eyes wide with fury, stormed over to Oomz.

"Ay! Ay! Get off this field if you gon' act like that!" he said, shaking his head and rolling his shoulders back.

"I didn't do nothing," Oomz said defiantly.

After 45 minutes of conditioning, the football work began, but Oomz's mood remained unchanged. During blocking drills, he was slow on his feet, shoulders slouched, head cocked to the side, as if broadcasting to the whole neighborhood that he was giving mini-mal effort. He brazenly stood out from his teammates, who hustled through drills and bounced on their toes, fast and crisp, in mid-season form. The coaches called him out, over and over, with both gentle en-couragement and harsh shouts, but he made no effort and showed no interest. On the next round of push-ups, Oomz, again slow to the ground, barely bent his elbows, dipping his body down only two or three inches. His head was down, eyes on the dirt, so he did not see his father enter the park, walk onto the field, and stand a few feet away. His face steady, his hands in the pockets of his gray hoodie, Big Oomz stared down at his son.

"Do the push-ups," he hissed.

Oomz's face shot up, his wide eyes meeting his father's. This was the first time Big Oomz had ever showed up to practice.

"You can't do no push-ups like that," Big Oomz continued. "Get down. Stop cheating yourself."

"My back hurts," Oomz murmured softly through his mouthpiece.

"So what? I don't give a fuck."

On the next push-up, he dipped his chest to the ground, and then again, and then again, until he was back on his feet and lined up beside his teammates for another round of blocking drills. Ramsey asked who wanted to go next, and Oomz's hand shot into the air. He drove Marquis five yards back with a bull rush, then drove him back even further on the next go, and after he knocked him to the ground on the third try, he peeked at his father standing behind him.

Something had changed in Oomz. He was running hard now, jump-ing to the front of the line for each drill, counting louder than everybody else during push-ups. When the coaches excused the boys for a water break, Oomz called for his teammates to gather in a circle first. "Yo, break it down! Hard work on three! One, two, three!"

"Hard work!" they shouted in response.

As the boys gathered by the light post, passing around water and Gatorade bottles, Big Oomz approached them.

"Y'all need to come together as a team," he said. He looked around at them, a serious and urgent look on his face, his hands still in his hoodie pockets. "Y'all lazy. Y'all don't do push-ups. Y'all don't stretch right. Y'all don't do drills right. Y'all don't even listen to the coaches. You won't ever start for no high school team. You don't got no energy. You don't work hard."

The boys looked up at him with reverence. They'd heard of him. They'd witnessed Miss Elsie point to Oomz and say, "His father, man, his father was a legend. He was so fast." They nodded their heads as Big Oomz spoke, their faces open and trusting, as if they were taking in some new, revolutionary gospel.

"Y'all gotta run hard. Run hard. Hard. You gotta work hard. You got the ball in yo hand, you gotta run all the way to the touchdown."

Twenty yards away, on the other side of the fence, Repo, Mr. Hart, Dwight, and the rest of the usual group of fathers looked on silently, shooting knowing side-eyes at one another. The man hadn't attended a single practice all year, they couldn't help but notice, and now suddenly here he was after the biggest win of the season, standing on the field, rambling on about some nonsense.

ooooo

BIG OOMZ KICKED a foot up on the porch's wooden railing and sunk lower into the lawn chair parked beside the front door. It was good to be back, out in the cool autumn air, watching the day pass. Motown soul jams poured out from inside his mother's house on Strauss Street, loud enough to carry to the end of the block. He closed his eyes and soaked in the music and the breeze, and he tried to push the stress out of his mind.

He was working now, but only part-time construction gigs. Many employers had turned him down for full-time jobs once they learned of his felony record. He tried not to think about the job applications he'd sent out and never heard back about. He tried not to think about the bills his mother and girlfriend were paying, and the shame he felt for not being able to help out as much as he wanted. He tried not to think about the years he had lost. He thought, instead, about his son, and this eased his mind into a calm satisfaction. His son was not as hard as he was at that age, but a boy didn't need to be so hard these days, Big Oomz observed. There was virtue in hardness, he believed, but it was also a heavy weight that a boy had to drag with him wherever he went.

It was a weight Big Oomz had carried since before he could throw a spiral. Coaches and parents often told him he'd be a football star one day, and he kept this dream in the back of his mind even in the years after he had stopped playing. He had never much thought about his future. Death or prison seemed inevitable to many teenagers growing up in Brownsville in the '90s. But now his future had come, and he wondered where his place was. He felt lost. In his life, he had found success in two endeavors: football and hustling. And he could no longer play football.

His son had more ambitions. Oomz talked about science, medicine, law, business. Big Oomz was proud of his son, maybe prouder than he would admit to the boy. There were nights when he thought about going to Betsy Head and watching his son's practice, but he was embarrassed to see the coaches, who'd once expected so much of him, and to see the other fathers, whom he did not know but who knew him, fathers who provided for and brought stability to their families. He stayed away those nights, and on the night he did go, he didn't want to stand with the fathers, but instead on the field, where he'd always been most comfortable.

He wondered if his best days, his happiest and most fulfilling days, were already behind him. He was not yet 30 years old. But how many people could point to a time in their life when they were at the top of their world? He gripped those memories tightly, the long touchdowns, the big hits, the nights in the upstate hotel rooms with his teammates.

Mo Better had cheerleaders back then, around the same age as Big Oomz, and on those road trips, 13-year-old Big Oomz and his team-mates would sneak the girls into their rooms. One time, a coach caught Big Oomz and Pup with girls in their room, and on the next trip, the coaches ordered that the doors had to stay open until lights out. The kids just broke that rule and locked the doors anyway, so on the trip after that, the coaches announced that they would patrol the hallways. Big Oomz and Pup climbed out their balcony and jumped to the next one, and the next one, until they reached the right room. A parent saw the balcony hopping, and the next season the coaches decided that Mo Better would not have cheerleaders anymore. "We couldn't look these girls' parents in the eyes if we kept bringing them on trips and all this kept going down," Coach Vick said.

Vick remembered those thrilling times too. He was a young man then, surrounded by young women whose sons adored him, and some-times those sons would see Coach Vick drop by their houses and their mothers would tell them it was time to go to bed. Vick wasn't the only one. "Sometimes there'd be drama," Vick said. "Sometimes you could tell something was going on. Like, why is coach so-and-so giving that kid so much playing time? Other times you'd have no idea. All that would go on at the hotels during trips and no one would have any idea, and then a parent would pop up the next season pregnant and a coach is over there with his head down and everybody is like, 'Oh coach was on that?'"

Sometimes Vick and a few other coaches would stay out all night partying and manage a big game hungover the next day. One night, Vick was out so late that he decided to go straight to Betsy Head, where the team was meeting for a 7 a.m. bus trip. He nestled himself at the top of the red steps to catch a couple of hours of sleep. When he woke up, the park was empty. It was nearly 9 a.m. "Luckily, one kid showed up late and I got a ride with him and his mom," he said.

Those were fast times, hard times, good times. They won many games and championships. Big Oomz missed those days. He knew they were long gone for him, at least, but perhaps this was the year the Mo Better Jaguars returned to glory.

The week after Brick City, the Pee Wees beat the Orange Tigers to improve to 5–1. The week after that, against the Jersey City Gators, there was Isaiah in the backfield taking a pitch on the right side. Three defenders predicted the play, converged on him seven yards behind the line, wrapped their arms around him—and then, somehow, Isaiah twisted his body out the tangle of limbs, pirouetted to the outside, ran three yards backward, looped around an oncoming defender, stiff-armed another to the ground, and sprinted past a third. Gone. Before he even reached the end zone, the spectators were on their feet, raising their arms in awe, laughing at the absurdity of what they had witnessed.

ooooo

LOWER MANHATTAN'S SKYLINE shined in the distance. It was dark inside the bus, and the coaches in the front slouched in their seats and closed their eyes, satisfied with the team's decisive win in Jersey City. The steel bars of the Manhattan Bridge whipped by as the old school bus rattled and hummed. Donnie prowled up and down the dark aisles. He snuck up beside a boy and punched him in the shoulder, then scurried to the back, before sneaking up beside another boy and punching him in the shoulder. Donnie snickered each time. The boys he punched rubbed their arms, gritted their teeth, and hoped Donnie was done messing with them.

In the second-to-last row, Oomz observed him with weary eyes. There were times when Oomz considered Donnie a kindred spirit, another moody boy who struggled to suppress a simmering anger. But Donnie couldn't control himself like Oomz could. Oomz's anger tended to be simple and predictable, igniting when a coach yelled at him or a boy teased him. It was often a restrained anger, one that he tried to keep within himself, seeping out in the tone of his voice, the slump of his shoulders, the fury of his tackles and blocks. Donnie, on the other hand, swung from euphoria to rage and back within minutes. At the start of the bus ride, he had gone up and down the rows telling jokes and trying to stump the other boys with brain teasers.

"I bet I can make you say black," he'd said to one boy.

"OK."

"What color is the sky?"

"Blue."

"I told you I could make you say blue!"

"Nuh-uh, you said you could make me say black."

"Ha ha! Got you! I told you!" Donnie cackled with a big gap-toothed smile, looking around to see if the other boys had noticed.

But soon the jokes and brain teasers seemed to bore him and his mood darkened. He stopped talking. "It's not as bad as it used to be, but sometimes I still just get angry for no reason," he later said. Sometimes his anger manifested as relentless shouting. Sometimes he simply shut down, staring blankly ahead, refusing to engage anybody who tried to talk to him. Sometimes he picked on people. He'd grab a boy's hat off of his head and make the boy chase him for it. He'd slap a Gatorade bottle out of a boy's hand. He'd go around telling other boys that a certain boy had lice. Tonight, he punched.

"Man, quit playing, Donnie," Oomz commanded, not the first time he'd said that to Donnie on a bus ride back from a game.

Oomz was leaning back against the window, his legs stretched out across the seat, watching Donnie's shadowy form shuffle up and down the aisle. Donnie ignored Oomz and went up to another boy and snatched the handheld Nintendo DS video-game console out of his grasp. Donnie held it behind his back.

"Yo, give him his DS back!" Oomz said. "You play too much!"

"Yo, I didn't do nothing!" Donnie contended, giggling as he looked at Oomz.

Donnie returned the device to the boy, then smacked him in the head with an open palm.

"Don't hit him!" Oomz said, his voice louder now.

Oomz sucked his teeth, stood up, and stepped toward Donnie, then punched him in the stomach. Donnie doubled over and Oomz grabbed him in a headlock and pulled him down onto the seat, pinning Donnie's head under his armpit to free his hands. He unleashed right and left hooks into Donnie's body, as Donnie tried to slip free.

"Chill! Chill! Yo, Chill!" Donnie groaned. "I didn't do nothing!"

Donnie swung his arms wildly into Oomz's sides, but Oomz kept on pummeling him.

"Yo, why you punching me?!" Donnie shouted.

Oomz pounded away without saying a word, beating on Donnie's kidneys and stomach.

"Time-out! Time-out!" Donnie shouted.

"Nah, no time-outs," Oomz replied calmly.

The boys' bodies banged against the bus's metal siding and slapped against the seats. The commotion got loud enough that it reached the front of the bus, and when Oomz saw Coach Esau walking down the aisle, he pulled Donnie to the floor, hidden from sight behind the seat backs.

"Yo, y'all keep it down," Esau said. "Why y'all can't be quiet?"

"Oomz fighting," a Pee Wee spoke up.

"Stop fighting," Esau said, before turning and heading back to the front.

Oomz let go of Donnie. Donnie retreated to his seat and slouched down with his arms crossed and an angry look on his face.

"Who said that?" Oomz said in a harsh whisper. "Who said my name?"

Nobody responded, but Oomz already knew the answer. He walked up to the boy, a normally gregarious and unassuming 11-year-old named Howard. "Don't put my name in ya mouth," he said. Then he started punching Howard in the body, wailing on him repeatedly, as the other boys looked on in silence. Howard curled up and took the punishment. When Oomz finally let up and returned to his seat, Howard began crying. He sobbed quietly all the way back to Brownsville.

ooooo

By the time Donnie got home, he seemed to have forgotten about the fight. He was a veteran of middle school fights, and by his standard, the tussle with Oomz barely qualified. Nobody was hurt or bleeding and nobody got in trouble. As always, the front door to the Castle was unlocked. Donnie dragged his feet through the lobby and into the elevator.

The panel with the buttons was covered with a thick red paste, which Donnie identified as tomato sauce. "Some kids rubbed a pizza on it," he said, shaking his head. "Stupid-ass kids." Music thumped from an apartment above—a Saturday night house party, Donnie guessed. His family lived on the fourth floor, but Donnie pressed the button for the third because the landing on the fourth was broken. He climbed a flight of steps and reached his door. Donnie didn't need a key because the door was broken. He grabbed the handle and shoved his shoulder into the door, and it popped open into a long, narrow hallway. The hallway led into a room. In one corner was a bed without sheets. There was no other furniture in the room, but on the floor were three large garbage bags with clothes spilling out. On the far side of the room, opposite the hallway, a doorless opening in the wall led into another room. On one side were a twin-size bed and a dresser with a small rabbit-ear TV on top. On the other side was a bunk bed, which is where Donnie and Tarell slept. Donnie dropped his shoulder pads on the floor and changed into basketball shorts. He sang along with the white man in the music video playing on the TV.

"Staaaaaay with meeeee," he crooned. "Staaaaay with meeeee."

The 3 train rumbled by out the open window. Donnie sang louder. Tarell didn't know the Mitey Mites had a game the next day, so the brothers stayed up until 3 a.m. They watched TV. They wrestled. They slap boxed. They played bloody knuckles, slamming their fists together until somebody's skin broke. They tried to hush their laughter because the rest of the family was asleep.

Their mother had recently gotten a job with the city's parks department and was saving up to move them out of the Castle. The family's long-term financial hopes seemed to rest on the broad shoulders of Donnie's older brother, a star running back at Grand Street High School. They were often reminded how tenuous these hopes were. A few months after his junior-year season ended, Donnie's brother had a kid pull a gun on him in front of the school. Things might have turned tragic, but a football coach standing nearby stepped between them and calmed the situation. "It can be dangerous out here sometimes," Donnie said. "Like, you can have no control over it. Stuff can just happen."

Donnie hadn't thought much about what he wanted to be when he grew up. "Maybe a football player or a lawyer," he said. "I heard lawyers make lots of money." He hadn't thought about what high school or college he wanted to go to. He lived day-to-day, finding fulfillment in the small pleasures he was able to scrape together: a handful of sunflower seeds from a teammate, beating his brother at one of their games, playing a prank on one of his friends. He was a decent student, but easily distracted, according to a counselor who worked with him. He avoided going to school whenever he could, staying home when he was too sleepy to get up or when it was raining too hard.

Late in the night, just as the boys were getting ready to go to sleep, the train once again rumbled by. "It used to bother me, hearing the train all the time," Donnie later said, "but it doesn't anymore."

ooooo

DONNIE AND TARELL were still asleep in their apartment when the Mitey Mites filed onto the bus at Betsy Head the following morning—a rare weekend when the three age groups didn't all play on the same day. Prowling the aisle, Vick greeted the boys with smiles, jokes, and high fives before working his way to the back, where he found a seat next to Coach Oscar.

"Ay, Vick!" Oscar said warmly. "How's the new place working out?"

Vick laughed excitedly and fished his flip phone out of his jeans pocket. He was still looking for a job and still living off of welfare checks, but he'd caught some luck. He found a small apartment in southeast Crown Heights for $250 a month in rent. For many years, he'd lived with a string of girlfriends, bouncing from one apartment to the next as each relationship ended. Now, for the first time in his life, he was living by himself. He was happier than he'd been all year.

"It's great, Oscar, it's great," Vick said.

"Nothing like having a place of your own," Oscar said.

"I'm loving it, man, I'm loving it."

He showed a photo on his phone of a small, dim room with chipped paint on the walls and plaster debris all over the floor.

"That's how it used to look," Vick said. "These are the walls when I first started."

He clicked to the next photo: a small, clean room with freshly painted maroon walls and a few pieces of furniture.

"Oh, got a lil' flat-screen there," Oscar said.

"Oh yeah. Oh yeah. I'm putting it together. Bad part about it is that now everybody wanna come over."

The bus went a few blocks then stopped in front of the Castle. A light wind blew stray papers and Styrofoam containers onto the street. Several of the garbage bags in front of the building had been ripped open. The sidewalk was covered in trash but empty of people this early on a Sunday—except for Donnie and Tarell stepping out from the Castle's front door.

Coach Chris had called their mother earlier that morning asking her why Tarell wasn't at Betsy Head for the game. Their mother said that Tarell thought that the game was canceled. Chris told her that they needed every boy to show up, and that the bus would pick Tarell up in about 15 minutes. She woke Donnie and Tarell and they groggily dressed and gathered Tarell's equipment. They slept on the bus all the way to Rahway, New Jersey.

Even with Tarell, the Mitey Mites were two players short of the minimum 16. Another forfeit loss to cap off the worst season of Coach Vick's career. But Vick and the opposing coach didn't tell their young boys that Mo Better had forfeited. Instead, the two teams played on as if the game counted. By the time he stepped onto the field, Tarell was wide awake and giddy, darting around like a pinball from his safety position in the back of the defense. He was the smallest boy on the field, yet the hardest hitter. He earned awed shouts from the crowd on three big hits within the first 10 minutes of the game. Late in the first half, he drilled a tall running back so hard that the boy flew two yards out of bounds before smacking the ground.

Donnie cheered the loudest, and all through the game he ran up and down the stands telling whoever was listening that the little boy making the big hits was his brother. "You know why he so strong? 'Cause I'm always bothering him," he said. "I'm always hitting him and pushing him. That's why he strong. When I was his age, I wasn't hitting like that. I wasn't as strong. My big brother never hit around on me like that. He didn't hit on me like I hit on my brother. That's why he got strength."

After the game, Tarell ran up and down the stands, excitedly babbling about how his team had won the game. A parent from the opposing team stopped him and corrected him: "The game didn't count," she said to him, in the sweet voice an adult uses when breaking sad news to a child. "You guys lost because you didn't have enough players." Tarell's face turned hard and he ran over to Donnie and told him what happened.

"But we won, right?" he said in an urgent tone. "That lady was wrong, right?"

"Yeah, y'all won," Donnie assured him. "That lady just jealous."

An adult who overheard the whole thing gave Donnie and Tarell a few dollars to buy food from the concession stand. Donnie got Skittles, cookies, potato chips, a Twix bar, and sunflower seeds, then counted the change the man behind the counter gave him. "Ain't these supposed to be ninety-nine cents?" he said, holding up the sunflower seed bag, which had a big yellow label on it that said 99 cents. The man behind the counter laughed.

"You a smart little guy, ain't you?" he said. "You are right. But we gotta make money here, too." Then he tossed Donnie a second bag, on the house. On the bus, Donnie offered a share of his snacks to all the boys seated around him. When a boy declined, Donnie countered, "Come on!" and pushed the Skittles bag closer to the boy's face until he agreed and fished out two Skittles. "Take more!" Donnie said.

∞∞∞

IT HAD BEEN a good year, the fathers agreed. The Pee Wees had finished the regular season with seven wins and just one loss, the second-best record in the conference behind the undefeated East Orange Jaguars. The team had lived up to, even surpassed, their expectations, and the fathers stood along the fence on this blustery Monday night reminiscing over the season and savoring Mo Better's return to the playoffs.

But even this long-awaited moment brought frustrations. The conference was split up into two divisions: Mo Better, Brick City, Orange, and the East Orange Jaguars were in the red division; Elizabeth, Union, Rahway, and the East Orange Wildcats were in the blue division. Traditionally, the two best teams in each division competed in the four-team playoff tournament. But league rules stated that only teams with more wins than losses qualified for the playoffs. Only the East Orange Jaguars, Mo Better, and Brick City, which finished 5–3, met that standard. Mo Better's coaches had never encountered such a situation. League officials decided that the reasonable solution was to include Brick City, the third-ranked team in the blue division, in the playoffs, and to eliminate all the red division teams from contention. From the officials' eyes, this was a fair setup: the league's second- and third-ranking teams, Mo Better and Brick City, would compete in a semifinal game for the chance to play the league's top team in the championship.

The fathers at Betsy Head saw it another way: while East Orange benefited with a free pass through the semifinals and Brick City benefited with a trip to the playoffs, Mo Better was stuck playing against a strong team that they'd already beaten to snag the coveted second-place playoff spot.

To make matters worse, unlike in the regular season, when programs kept the profits from concessions, in the playoffs Pop Warner got the profits. Without the concession money, Chris and his staff didn't have the funds to rent a field and pay referees, which meant that they had to relinquish their home-field advantage. Instead, the game would be played in New Jersey, on a field much closer to Newark than Brooklyn. Mo Better couldn't even afford a bus. The boys and their families would have to carpool.

"They don't want us to win this thing," Repo said.

"It ain't fair, man," Mr. Hart said. "It's us against the world. But I like our chances."

Despite the circumstances, the men at the park were all confident. They discussed travel plans for Florida; after their boys won the league championship, and then the regional championship, they would be off to the Pop Warner Super Bowl in Orlando. How much were plane tickets?

How long was the drive? Was Pop Warner covering the costs? What part of the country would their opponent come from? Texas, maybe, where the boys were big and tough? Or California, where the quarterbacks could throw the ball long? Or maybe they'd take on some track-star kids from Miami?

Their boys had beaten Brick City and grown as a team in the weeks since the East Orange game. Esau had crafted new plays specifically designed to slice through East Orange's defense. He'd spent many practices working with his boys on defending East Orange's passing attack.

"We gon' beat them this time," Esau told the fathers, who had no doubt this was true.

∞∞∞

THE NEXT EVENING, Tuesday, Isaiah and Coach Chris were at the park early.

"How you doin' in school?"

"I'm doin' good."

"You gotta be doin' excellent. Your standards gotta be high if you gon' do what you wanna do."

Isaiah stood on his toes, heels hardly touching the grass, arms at his side, chiseled and motionless like a statue. Thick veins popped along his forearms and calves, and his biceps bulged from under his T-shirt. The season had honed his body, his teammates often pointed out. They squeezed his arms, poked his abdomen, and joked about how he was already faster and more muscled than some of the high school athletes they saw. He took care of his body. He did dozens of push-ups at home, lifted his brother's barbells on occasion, and avoided any physical activity that might lead to freak injury. Like so many boys before him, he'd come to realize his body was a ticket to the life he wanted. Not just any ticket but perhaps the best ticket he'd ever have. A year and a half ago, he and his family hadn't even considered the possibilities that Chris was now telling them were all but assured.

"Now, if you had the choice, would you rather go to Poly Prep for football or Xavier for rugby?" Chris asked him.

Isaiah shrugged.

"I mean, they both good schools," he said. "Gym teacher, he wants you to go to Xavier. But Poly Prep, that's another level. I know you like to play football. You go there, you do well, you'll end up at Notre Dame."

Chris patted him on the back and walked toward the red cement steps, where a woman in a gray suit was sitting. She was a social worker waiting to meet with Chris. He walked with purpose, nodding at the locals jogging around the track, pointing to the teenager who used to play for him strolling by the park, waving at the fathers standing along the fence. A good year, he thought. The rumors of Mo Better's demise had vanished. His crop of superstar Pee Wees had astounded the high school coaches. Word was spreading, he said, that Mo Better was back. He flashed a big, warm smile at the social worker, patting her shoulder as he shook her hand. "A nice night, huh?" Chris said, hardly containing the excitement that had been coursing through him all week. "Thought it might rain tonight, but this is nice."

The social worker, Jasmine, had heard about Chris. She hoped the renowned Brownsville football coach would take under his wing some of the troubled teenagers she worked with. She was here today for one particular 15-year-old who'd punched a classmate who he said had bullied him. The classmate's mom pressed charges. The boy was suspended for a year and sent to an alternative school. "He's a good, quiet kid," she said to Chris. "But this one thing could really set him down a path that . . ." She paused to search for the right words.

"No, I know," Chris jumped in. "I've seen it too many times."

"I've heard about Brownsville," Jasmine said.

"What you hear?"

"Nothing good."

Jasmine had gotten the job in Brownsville just months ago, fresh out of New York University. People warned her about the neighborhood, she said. She'd grown up in a rough part of Youngstown, Ohio, and yet even she was intimidated by Brownsville's reputation. She took a cab to work on her first day, "for safety," she said. Her knowledge of the neighborhood to that point had mostly come through depressing and horrific news reports.

She'd heard about the 26-year-old man shot dead at a barbecue in June. The child struck by a bottle tossed out the window of an apartment in July. The 48-year-old woman dragged out of her home nearly naked by the police who stormed her building. The apartment complex on Rockaway Avenue that had turned into a rotting, boiling husk after the landlord shut off electricity, gas, and hot water and stopped throwing out the garbage bags in the middle of summer. Within just the past few weeks, she'd heard about the 22-year-old man beaten to death by a dozen men under the 3 train tracks on Livonia Avenue and about the three people shot in broad daylight near Thomas S. Boyland Street.

On her trips into the neighborhood that summer, she'd seen the police cruisers circling the blocks and the pairs of officers stationed on the corners. But it was fall now, the days shorter and colder, and the police presence had decreased. On this night, just one cop stood outside the bodega on Saratoga and Livonia.

ooooo

On Wednesday, it rained.

It was a miserable day, windy and dark and near freezing. The lights were on at the park when Donnie and Tarell arrived. Chaka sat shivering on the green bench.

"Cuz, it's way too cold," he said to Donnie while throwing a football to him. The ball thudded off Donnie's hands and fell to the ground.

"My fingers hurt so bad," Donnie said.

He and Tarell had stayed home from school that day "'cause it was raining," he said. The field was muddy and dotted with puddles. The harsh wind knocked leaves off the trees, pinning them against the chain-link fence. When Ramsey arrived, Donnie asked, "We still gon' practice?"

"Yeah, it's playoff week," Ramsey said. "Whatchu thinkin', man?"

"Are we gon' tackle today or nah?" Donnie said.

"My man, it's playoff week," Ramsey said. "We doin' everything!"

"Aw nah, man," Chaka said. "It's too cold!"

"We gotta play East Orange and Brick City again, huh?" Donnie said.

"Uh-huh," replied Chaka.

"But not if we lose, we don't play East Orange," Donnie added.

"We not gon' lose, boy," Chaka declared, looking at Donnie like he was crazy. "We goin' all the way."

Once all 16 Pee Wees had arrived, Coach Esau, as he did at the start of every practice, ordered them into two lines for their lap around the track. The boys, cold and stiff, half-heartedly shuffled into the lines. A quiet and stout 10-year-old named Jacob stood at the front of one of the lines, and Donnie had a problem with this. He marched up to him and said, "Yo, Jacob get in the back of the line! You don't know what you're doing!"

Jacob, caught off guard, shot back, "No!"

"Move!"

"No!"

Over the weeks of the season, as he grew more confident as a player, Donnie had increasingly taken it upon himself to serve as one of the team's leaders, alongside Oomz, Isaiah, and Hart. This impulse would sprout randomly, at this practice or that practice, and never with any sustained effort. Donnie would volunteer to lead stretches, even though he hadn't memorized all the stretches they had to do. He would order boys around, even though he didn't always know what to order. His teammates would usually roll their eyes and indulge him, go along with what they saw as his make-believe. But Jacob wasn't having it on this evening.

"Move!"

"No!"

Donnie pushed Jacob. Jacob responded with a right hook that caught Donnie on the chin, beneath his facemask. The punch sent Donnie into a rage. He unloaded on Jacob, shouting nonsensically and swinging furiously with both fists until their teammates pulled them apart.

"Donnie, calm down!" Esau said.

Donnie kept shouting.

"Calm down or go home!"

"I don't care! I'll go home!"

His eyes were angry and staring at the ground. His fists were balled at his sides. He stomped his foot as he shouted.

"If you go home, you gon' have to quit, and if you leave, we gon' have to forfeit."

"I don't care!"

Donnie pulled off his helmet and his pads and handed them to Esau. As he walked off the track, the rest of the Pee Wees began their lap, unsure if their season had just unraveled. But Donnie did not go home. He sat down on the long green bench and cried. For an hour and a half, he watched his 15 Pee Wee teammates practice. He tucked his arms inside his hoodie. He breathed deeply, just as his therapist had taught him. Slowly, he calmed down. "I was thinking, if I quit, how would the team feel?" he said later. "How would it be like? If I quit, we gon' have to forfeit. Without me or without anybody, we can't play. If one person leave or get injured we gon' have to forfeit 'cause we don't have enough people. I was gonna quit, but then I didn't."

He got up and walked meekly onto the field. He went over to where the linemen were doing drills with Ramsey and he stood several yards behind them with his arms crossed. He feared that the coaches would not let him back on the team. Ramsey called him over. He bent down so their faces were level. Donnie kept his eyes on the ground.

"I'm talking to you like a man, look at me like a man," Ramsey said, and Donnie brought his eyes up to him. "Listen, I don't want your nonsense out here. Go over to Coach Esau and apologize, then go run your four laps."

Donnie walked, still slowly and meekly, to where the backs and receivers were running through plays with Esau. Once more, he stood several yards behind them, his arms crossed. Esau ignored him. Minutes passed. Embarrassed and bashful, Donnie walked back to Ramsey.

"So what's up?" Ramsey said.

Donnie said nothing.

"Go run your laps," Ramsey said.

Donnie went to the track, picked up his helmet and shoulder pads where Esau had left them, and strapped them on. As he ran, he watched his cleats splash the puddles on the torn-up rubber and he felt a wave of gratitude. How close he'd been to throwing away everything he and his friends had done all year. How close he'd been to letting his anger ruin everything. But this time, he'd beaten his rage. He felt gratitude and pride as he ran through the cold, windy night.

ooooo

BY FRIDAY NIGHT, the field had dried, and the dust returned after the hitting began. It covered the purple mesh jerseys of the Pee Wees, who stood in two lines, facing each other, forming a stage for the tackling drill. It also coated the jeans of the tall, lanky, stone-faced man standing beside the coaches. The Boogeyman.

He'd begun showing up at practice a few weeks earlier, after he returned home from prison. He kept his distance at first, perched on a bicycle on the track for 10 or 15 minutes before riding off, waving to the coaches who called out to him. He had missed the game and the hard, dusty field. When he returned to Betsy Head for the first time in many years and saw the purple jerseys and the dust clouds, the memories rushed back. "It was blowouts," he said, his arms resting on the handles of his bike. "Forty, fifty, sixty to zip blowouts. Everything was zip. All season. Nobody scored on us. Went a whole season nobody scored on us." He had a bony face, piercing eyes, and wore a black do-rag, a white T-shirt, and blue Adidas track pants. Three of his friends, also on bikes, posted up around him. "This is everything right here," he said, as he watched the hitting drills. "Everything you want is here." And then, after a long silence, he added, "I miss the hitting."

"You hit hard—*boom!*" said one of his friends, a young man in a camo hat. "And you was fast, too. Remember that ring y'all got? Purple and gold. With ruby. That shit was big. You could play, man."

He returned to the park on a few more evenings. Sometimes, he perched on his bike beside his crew. Other times, he watched practice while jogging around the track. Once, he sat alone on the red cement steps, seemingly basking in the anonymity he had lacked as the most feared man in Brownsville. But tonight, a crisp evening in October, the last practice before the playoffs, he decided to cross the gate, greet the coaches, and take in the action up close.

His facial expression was blank, serious and studious, until there was a big hit, and then the Boogeyman's smile widened and he nodded his head.

"All right, all right," he said.

Then came another big, crunching hit, the dust blooming into the air.

Coach Chris looked over at the grinning Boogeyman and said, "That sounds like a Mo Better football hit that time!"

The Boogeyman nodded some more and kept up his smile. He didn't speak to the players, didn't pass on any of the hard-learned lessons he'd picked up over the years. He didn't want to make a scene. He only wanted to watch. The world, he knew, had moved on without him, had humbled him, and he was the one trying to catch up, trying to brush off the history that clung to him like the dust on the purple mesh jerseys. In this new world, the grinding wheels of progress seemed destined to erase both the sport he loved and the community he called home. This was a time of transition, and he wondered where he might fit in the chaos. The boys in front of him had no such concerns. This was their world, and they had no memory of any other.

"We goin' to Florida!" Oomz howled as he took his spot opposite Naz, who gripped the football in his right arm.

"Set! Go!"

The boys ran toward each other and collided with a mighty thud. *Ooooohhhh!*

Oomz drove Naz to the ground and their bodies smacked the dirt, kicking up a cloud of dust that seemed to swallow them whole. Naz began coughing violently and kept coughing as he got back on his feet. He bent over with his hands on his knees, spit out some dirt, and then continued coughing until he made it to his water bottle at the base of the light post 20 yards away and gulped down the dust caught in his throat. He poured water on his head to wipe the dust from his eyes and face. He patted dust off his shoulder pads and chest, then jogged back, still covered in dust.

All the boys were covered in dust when practice ended and they stood around Esau. It was a quiet night, the park nearly empty, the clouds of dust wafting past the stadium lights shining down on them.

Esau spoke about the upcoming game, spoke about focus and preparation, spoke about making the most of every opportunity. Then he told them about an old friend of his from the neighborhood.

"He just died in his sleep last night," he said. "Twenty-two years old. Nobody knows why. Take care of your bodies. You don't know, you just might not wake up in the morning." Then, sensing the dark turn he had taken and seeing the worried eyes of the boys around him, Esau added, "All y'all gon' wake up tomorrow morning."

"You should say 'God forbid,'" Chaka said in a shaky voice.

Esau looked around and saw boys more aware of death than middle schoolers should be.

"None of y'all gon' die tonight."

Two days later, on a bright and cool Sunday morning, the Pee Wees and their parents and coaches gathered at Betsy Head, split up into seven cars, and headed for Roselle, New Jersey. When they got to the stadium, they found Chris Legree sitting alone on the bleachers, smoking a cigar.

– 19 –

THE REMATCH
Late October 2014

THE BUS FROM NEWARK PULLED INTO THE PARKING LOT, and the Brick City boys marched out silently. Like the boys from Brooklyn they would battle later today, they came from a hardscrabble place with a tough reputation, a place in the heat of dramatic change, for better or worse.

They too came from a city with a progressive new mayor. When Ras Baraka took office in 2014 following Cory Booker's departure for US Senate, the city was struggling. It faced a $93 million budget deficit. Its unemployment rate was nearly 10 percent. Its failing public school system was under state control. Its crime rate was rising, with residents suffering through a wave of carjackings and the highest murder rate since 1990.

A quarter of the city's children had asthma—three times the national average—because of the exhaust from rail yards, incinerators,

298 — Albert Samaha

and dumps, and the procession of buses and ships flowing in and out of the Port Newark–Elizabeth Marine Terminal, one of the largest ports in the world. Baraka, a former high school principal and the son of poet Amiri Baraka, campaigned on the slogan "We are the mayor" and vowed to push back against the outsiders who seemed to be taking control of the city: the charter school networks, state oversight officials, real-estate investors, and political consultants. He declared that his "movement to transform Newark" wouldn't come at the expense of long-term residents.

Newark's struggles ran parallel to Brooklyn's struggles, which paralleled the struggles of the past century in Philadelphia, Baltimore, Cleveland, Detroit, Chicago, Milwaukee, Saint Louis, and Oakland. The cities shared a singular question about the fate of their communities: Was development possible without displacement? Or were these residents, and the communities they had built, the cost of progress?

Newark locals saw it coming. Over the past decade, private investors had swallowed up scores of cheap buildings and lots in the city's downtown. One partnership spent $130 million on 79 properties, with publicized plans to turn them into condos, charter schools, offices, retail space, a hotel, and a soilless farm. People priced out of Manhattan had already moved to Jersey City and Hoboken; the investors were betting that Newark was next. The city's residents sensed the gentrification crawling south, just as Brownsville's residents sensed it sweeping east across Brooklyn. From Brownsville, it took an hour to commute to Manhattan by train or bus; from Newark, the trip was 20 minutes.

The displacement had already begun in many other cities across the country. Low-income black and brown people, unable to afford homes in historically low-income black and brown communities, were settling into suburban neighborhoods that had been reserved for white people less than a lifetime ago. According to a study by the Brookings Institution, the number of people living in poverty in New York City and Newark decreased by 7 percent from 2000 to 2010. Over that stretch, the number of poor people in the region's suburbs increased by 14 percent. By 2011, there were three million more people living in poverty in America's suburbs than in its cities.

Roselle, New Jersey, a solidly middle-class suburban town for decades, was bruised by the recession and saw its economic divide widen. From 2000 to 2010, while the median household income increased by $7,000, the child poverty rate jumped from 8.5 percent to 14 percent. Over that period, a fifth of the town's white people left, replaced by black and Latino people, who now made up 81 percent of the population.

Whatever poverty existed here lingered quietly below the town's surface. It was poverty without density, poverty hidden behind the doors of moderately sized wood-paneled houses with driveways on winding residential streets, poverty without a robust public transportation system or easy access to social services or a convenience store and Laundromat at the end of the block. It was poverty in a place designed for middle-class comfort. Poverty still without the stigma of places like Newark and Brownsville.

As Oomz looked out the window of his mother's car, he didn't see the signs of the struggle that existed here. He saw only peace and lush green lawns, the images that he'd learned to believe represented achievement. He saw a place that felt far different from the place he knew best. When he got to the stadium, he noted how loud the birds chirped, pointed out a hawk gliding low in the sky, and excitedly stood over a gopher hole.

"Oh word, there're groundhogs and everything here," he said in wonder. "You buggin'. You buggin'."

He bent down and peered into the hole, then dropped in a pebble to see how far it would go. A cold wind nipped at his neck. He stood straight and looked up at the trees around him, squinting his eyes against the glare of the sun.

"I wanna play here," he said.

He felt excited and clear minded. He felt at peace. His mother had gotten him into a new school several days earlier. Like every school he'd ever attended, Mott Hall Bridges Academy was almost all black and brown, and most students qualified for free or reduced lunch. Though the school was in Brownsville, Oomz liked how much the teachers focused on life beyond the neighborhood. Around the start of each school year, sixth graders took a trip to walk across the Brooklyn Bridge into Manhattan. Seventh graders had to take a class on entrepreneurship. All but three students in the school's most recent graduating class of 75 eighth graders went on to high schools outside the neighborhood. The classes were challenging, Oomz said, and the students were diligent and chill. "They teach us more advanced stuff at this school," he said. "I feel like I really have to pay attention and I'm learning a lot. I actually like going to school again." Mott Hall had gained acclaim from local education officials, but it didn't have enough space for every child who wanted to attend. Like other charter schools, a child had to be selected from a lottery. Only a third of applicants made it in. The school shared a building with two other public schools, and on their way to class in the mornings, Mott Hall students, in their purple uniform shirts, often crossed paths with kids not lucky enough get picked. Oomz had been on the waiting list and only got in when another student left the school. "I think I'm on a good path now to do everything I wanna do," he said. "I just gotta keep my focus."

Oomz had been smiling all morning, but now, as he lined up with his teammates for the weigh-in, his face turned serious, the hard look he wore in the moments before big games. Big Oomz stood alongside him, dropping bits of advice to his fellow running backs.

"Use that power. Use that strength," he said to his son.

"Use the whole field today, man," he said to Isaiah. "Your eyes guide your feet."

Big Oomz took a step back and snapped photos of Oomz and his teammates. He had arrived at the stadium early, before the Pee Wees had even slipped on their pads. He was the only parent to follow the boys and their coaches down the bleachers, over a wooden bridge, and into a grassy area separated from the stadium by a creek and a wall of shrubs. There, he sipped from a paper cup and watched the boys practice their offensive plays. He'd been skeptical of Mo Better's coaches all year. The team's success had softened but not defeated his doubt. As he stood beside his boy in the weigh-in line, he said in a low voice still loud enough for others to hear, "Come play for me next year. I'ma train you, get ya speed up."

All his life, Oomz had admired his father, had wanted to play like his father. All his life, he had craved his father's approval and wisdom. All his life, he believed he needed whatever his father could give him. But today, as his father tried to plan their future, Oomz looked straight ahead and didn't respond. Father and son stood beside each other in silence as Oomz stepped onto the scale, stepped off, turned, and, without even a glance at his father, jogged back over the bridge to join his teammates. Big Oomz found a seat in the bleachers.

ooooo

SOON THE 16 Pee Wees were huddled together.

"Playoffs, baby!" Marquis said.

"Let's go! We gon' win this!" Isaiah said.

"I don't know why they even here!" Dorian said.

Esau stepped into the center of the circle and the boys went quiet. They hopped on their toes and shook the stiffness out of their hands and arms. They tightened the straps on their gloves and pulled their socks up to their knees. Every eye was on Esau, who stood before them scanning their faces, nodding his head.

"We got this game," he began. "Trust me. We just gotta put it all together. Like I told y'all, they can't fuck with y'all. You gotta believe that."

He paused. A gust of wind rustled jerseys and leaves.

"They don't want us to take this game," he went on, slowly and calmly. "They don't want us to go further. They don't want us here next week. They don't want no Brooklyn team in it."

Then his voice got loud and the pace of his words quickened. A year's worth of strain and care and frustrations and hopes came tumbling out. Esau recognized the magnitude of the moment and he sought to instill in his boys this same understanding, of the rareness of certain opportunities, the way they pass so quickly but linger so long and painfully in memory.

"Y'all goin' to war, I'm goin' to war with y'all! We goin' to war to-gether! This shit here is war! We goin' real fuckin' militant. We goin' to war today. We goin' to war today, a'ight?"

The boys clapped their hands, nodded, let out their shouts. They lined up, single file behind Isaiah. Esau marched up and down the line, bobbing his head as he preached, and soon his voice cracked and tears welled in his eyes.

"This shit is real emotional for me," he said. "Look at me in my eyes. I don't want y'all to go home today! I love y'all! Y'all see these tears? These tears real. 'Cause I love y'all. If y'all knock somebody head off, I'll knock they coach head off, and that's on my mother! Put it all on the line today and we'll have tomorrow."

He stopped pacing, put his hands on his hips, and looked to the ground. His boys stood frozen, eyes still locked on him.

"I got nothing else," Esau said. "I give everything I got for y'all. I need y'all to give everything you got for me. I love y'all. I love y'all, and I don't want to see y'all go home."

They marched ahead, silent, over the bridge and into the stadium, deadened to the noise stirring in the stands around them.

"This is it!" Mr. Hart shouted. "This is it!"

"You ready, son?" Mrs. Hart shouted.

"He ready," Mr. Hart said. "Don't distract him."

"He look ready," Mrs. Hart said.

As the boys took the field for the kickoff, the stadium dropped into a hushed tension. Legs in the bleachers jittered nervously. Knuckles cracked. Hands tightly gripped the railing in front of the stands.

"They beat 'em last time," one man said to another. "In double overtime."

Brick City shot out like a cannon ball. Its offense knifed through Mo Better's defense for 33 yards on the first two plays, blockers laying knock-down hits, runners gliding through big gaps in the middle of the field. By the fifth play, nearly every Mo Better defender had been bumped to the ground. On the sixth play, the quarterback easily scram-bled into the end zone. 6–0.

Big Oomz, who had volunteered to work the orange down marker on the sideline, looked on in disappointment. "Stop being scared," he said to the Pee Wees. "If you don't wanna play, say you scared. That's what you got equipment on for—to hit."

The kickoff sailed over Isaiah's head, and by the time he corralled the ball, the defenders had swarmed him, cutting him down at the four-yard line. The offense made no headway through three plays, and on the fourth play the defenders poured into the backfield and tackled Oomz in the end zone. A two-point safety. 8–0. Oomz slapped the ground, an anguished, frustrated look on his face.

"Get it together!" Big Oomz shouted. "It's football! Relax!"

Hart sensed the game spiraling out of control. He thought about their game against Brick City last year, as Junior Pee Wees, when he and his teammates crumbled once the breaks went against them. On his first play back on defense, he stuffed the runner behind the line with a force that knocked the boy's helmet straps loose. The hit sent a shock of inspiration though Donnie. "At the start, I was just like kinda frustrated that they was winning, but when Hart came through like that, I wasn't sad anymore about us losing, but instead I was mad about it," he said later. Donnie transformed into a bull, intense and fuming, crashing through Brick City's offense, repeatedly shattering their plays like a baseball through a window. "Donnie look like a killer out there," Coach Chris said.

The defenses owned the rest of the half. But while Brick City's offense found occasional moments of promise, Mo Better's offense was only knocked backward. Brick City defenders shook their blockers, cutting off Isaiah and Oomz before they had a chance to find an opening. For the Mo Better runners, it felt as if there were 20 blue jerseys attacking them, surrounding them, ganging up on them. In their 11 plays, the Brownsville boys had lost 14 yards and failed to get a single first down. As the team passed around water bottles and the coaches made strategic adjustments at halftime, the 8–0 deficit loomed over them like a high-rise.

Down on a knee, his arm leaning on the helmet in his hand, Hart clenched his jaw, pressed his lips together, and swallowed hard, trying to keep tears from falling. Isaiah stared at the ground, eyes wide with shock. Oomz stared ahead dead eyed. Only Donnie, it seemed, could escape the darkness. He ran over to Chris and, his voice giddy, reminded him of the $50 the coach promised him if he caused a fumble.

"Did you see it? I got back there and I almost got it! Did you see it?"

When the team huddled before the start of the third quarter, it was Donnie who declared that they would win this game, who slapped them on their shoulder pads and helmets and shouted, "Come on! We got this!" He brought belief back into the eyes of the boys who had worked so hard to get this far.

The Brownsville boys rushed out of the break with energy and hard hits. The offense nudged forward, and it seemed that perhaps the team was on the brink of a big play—they only needed one. But Brick City's defense held, as solid and unyielding as their name. Soon, Esau pulled out the trick plays he'd saved for big moments, and when they didn't work, he fanatically fed the ball to Isaiah, but that still didn't work either. Isaiah felt helpless, his powers doused like a bonfire in a hurricane.

"Yo, get my lil' man the ball!" Big Oomz shouted. He paced in a small circle, shaking his head, and then, with a tone of disgust, added, "Doin' all that damn blocking! They got him blocking all damn day and they not getting him the ball!"

Mo Better's defense continued to stuff Brick City, but each time they got the ball back, it was the same old story. Late in the third quarter, with Mo Better's offense pinned back near their own end zone, Brick City forced another safety. 10–0. A sense of inevitable defeat came over the Mo Better side of the bleachers. The parents fell quiet.

Then everything fell apart. Early in the fourth quarter, Brick City intercepted a pass and returned it for a touchdown. 17–0. Two plays later, they did it again. 24–0. The Brick City bleachers erupted in celebration. A boy raced up and down the track waving a big blue flag with a lion on it. Coach Chris and Coach Gary turned and began walking off the sideline toward the parking lot. In the trunk of Gary's van were several big garbage bags, which they would fill with helmets, jerseys, and pads and then store for the off-season in a green shed under a staircase in the Garvey projects. They knew it was over. Their faces were not pained and their voices were not angry. They had been in the game for many years and they had seen many hard losses. They looked past the disappointment of the present, to their visions for the following autumn.

"The further away it is, the more hope you got," Chris said with a smile.

"Ain't that the truth," Gary said.

"Because the closer you get, that's when it gets real, and reality don't feel sorry for nobody."

"Ain't gotta tell these boys," Gary said, glancing back at the field.

With the game decided and the clock ticking down, Esau handed the offense over to Oomz, with carry after carry. He muscled forward each time, for three or four or five yards. Then he broke through a pack of defenders and plowed ahead for eight yards.

"Told you!" Big Oomz shouted.

Those watching thought it was now a near certainty that the father would not allow Oomz to return to Mo Better. Big Oomz had big plans. But, as it turned out, they were soon upended. A month after this game, Big Oomz was pulled over while driving with a friend in Ithaca, New York, and arrested after police found $1,500 worth of heroin and crack cocaine in the car.

ooooo

BESIDE THE BLEACHERS, in a forgotten corner of the stadium, nearly every one of the 16 boys cried as they gathered around Esau after the game. Clouds had moved in and the afternoon was dreary. The stands filled up with different parents, and two different teams now collided on the field. The sizzle of the cheers and the pops of the hits drowned out the boys' sniffles and whimpers. Naz and Dorian shook as they sobbed. Donnie wiped the tears from his eyes and said, "I swear to God, I wish we could replay them." Hart buried his face in his hands. Marquis and Isaiah kept their helmets on, their visors shielding their eyes, but their tears dripped down to their chins. Chaka kept his helmet on too, but he was not crying; his face was angry and stoic. Oomz also looked angry, and through his tears he said, "They got Junior Midgets on their team!"

"We're not making excuses," Esau cut him off. "Listen, it was a hell of a season. This happens in football. This happens in life."

Just like that, it was over. Parents shook hands. Coaches collected equipment. The boys stripped off their pads and tossed their jerseys into a pile on the grass. They dropped their helmets into the big garbage bag. They found their rides and headed back home.

In his mother's car, Oomz wiped his tears and dried his face. He'd already decided to return to the team despite his father's objections. He didn't want to lose what he and the other boys had built. "Next season gon' be better," he said. "We got a good future coming." He felt his anger beginning to fade as he stared out the window at the birds gliding through the gray sky, high above the people, the concrete, and the noise.

BLESSINGS

December 2017

THREE YEARS LATER, CHRIS LEGREE STEPPED OFF THE
3 train at the Saratoga stop on a cold evening in December. His Con
Ed badge still hung from his neck. He was 61 now and walked with a
limp, his knees worn down from years of football and manual labor. The
crowd of commuters rushed past him as he hobbled down the stairs,
one hand gripping the railing, the other holding a cell phone to his ear.
A high school football coach from Canarsie was on the other end, and
Chris was hoping to send him some of his boys, to build a new bridge.

"I'm calling you not just to win championships but about opportunities for young black men," he said, his voice loud enough to rise above
the thunder of the departing train.

He paced in a circle on the sidewalk as he finished the call, then
stepped into the barbershop on Livonia, half a block from Betsy Head.
It was warm inside, fluorescently bright and humming with clippers

and chatter. The middle-aged owner slapped hands with Chris. Several of his nephews had played for Mo Better, including two—Poppa and Hakeem—who had been murdered. But Chris hadn't come by to re-hash old memories. He was here for neighborhood intel. As the barber faded up a teenage customer's hair, Chris asked whether the district's state committeeman, Anthony T. Jones, had passed through the block to campaign. He was up for reelection in 2018.

"Yeah, he been by," the man said.

"Oh, OK," replied Chris. "You know, I haven't told a lotta people yet, but I might run for that seat. *Might*."

The man nodded slowly, gave a small smile, then shifted his focus back to the cut. He'd heard Chris float political ambitions before: for this city council race, for that state assembly spot. It had never gotten further than talk.

But this time, yes, this time Chris was certain the moment was right. He did, after all, have a habit of turning to optimism in the aftermath of setbacks. The greater the setback, it seemed, the greater his optimism for the imminent future. As he stepped out of the barbershop, back into the cold night, Chris was brimming with hope.

∞∞∞

He stopped at the corner store next, to pick up sliced pineapple and a quarter-cut of watermelon, as was his routine on the way home. A strict diet and an intensified walking regimen had helped him lose more than 50 pounds in recent months, leaving him slim as he'd looked in decades. Just in time for the campaign, he thought. Beside the register, on the counter, a stack of 2018 calendars bearing Anthony T. Jones's face and name caught his eye.

"Who brought this here?" Chris asked the shopkeeper, whom he'd known for many years.

"Anthony."

Chris let out a chuckle, then said, "I might be running against him."

"Who, you?"

"Might."

"He not gonna like that," the shopkeeper said with a playful grin.

Eyes still on the calendars, Chris said, "When he bring that in, recently?"

He felt good about his chances. He was a workingman, like most of his potential constituents, and his record of community service spoke for itself—all those boys he'd helped push to success. Most recently, he'd been thrilled by Hart's achievements. After the 2014 Pee Wee season, Hart kept getting bigger and better and more serious about football. By eighth grade, he'd proven to be one of the country's top players in his age group. In January 2017, he played in a youth football all-star game at the Dallas Cowboys' massive stadium, with his mom and sister cheering in the stands. He played in another all-American game in May, this time in Virginia Beach, Virginia. His team won the game and Hart won the event's sportsmanship and academic awards.

At his eighth-grade graduation, Hart wore a white tuxedo under his shiny blue gown. Around his neck lay the gold stole given out to students who'd achieved academic honors. By Chris's memory, Hart's score on the specialized high school exam was the highest of any boy who'd passed through the program. In the fall of 2017, he began his freshman year at Poly Prep, just as Chris had envisioned. The school granted him a hefty financial aid package. Every adult who knew him believed that Hart could grow up to do whatever he wanted—lawyer, doctor, engineer, president of the United States. He was open to all those options, but in the meantime, his football dreams still seemed within reach.

Hart was the only boy from that 2014 Pee Wee team to end up at Poly Prep. Isaiah didn't apply. He preferred to choose from one of the public schools his friends were going to. He picked Erasmus Hall High School, where Curtis Samuel had gone. Isaiah had put much thought into the decision. Several high school football programs tried to win him over. Grand Street High School "was too far," he said. South Shore's team wasn't good enough. "I didn't feel I could win a chip there." As for Lincoln, where his brother had gone to school, Isaiah believed that its head coach wasn't doing enough to help his players get college scholarship offers. To Isaiah, it was all about getting that full ride. "I just felt Erasmus would give me the best chance to get a scholarship," he said.

Erasmus still had one of the best football programs in the city. The school was in Flatbush, where it shared a block with a bank and a sneaker shop, a short bus trip from Brownsville. Many of Isaiah's friends went to Erasmus. In his first high school football game, in the fall of 2016, his junior varsity team won 42–0. Isaiah scored a touchdown. Chaka joined him at the school a year later, and in September 2017, the two sophomores took the field together for the first time since their Mo Better days.

The football gods hadn't bestowed them with equal blessings. While Chaka had enjoyed a recent growth spurt, pushing him to nearly six feet just as his muscles were beginning to fill out his frame, Isaiah remained nearly the same size he was at 12 years old. He was usually the smallest boy on the field. His speed, which he had used to dominate Mo Better's opponents, was now merely a tool for survival. But he was still the fastest kid out there.

oooooo

As far as Chris knew, none of the boys on that 2014 Pee Wee team had been lost. This was what progress was supposed to look like. There were other visible signs. In the summer of 2016, the city announced that it would dedicate $30 million to renovating Betsy Head Park, where the field lost grass and gained dust each passing year. Chris was among the community leaders invited to advise on how exactly the money should be spent. A year later, the mayor's office unveiled the Brownsville Plan, a proposal to infuse the neighborhood with one billion dollars in public and private funding to build affordable homes and health-care facilities, repair infrastructure, support new businesses, and create additional public spaces and recreational centers. Cell-phone chargers would be built into park benches and new trash cans placed around the neighborhood. One rendering of the plan's vision showed a bustling street corner beneath the elevated subway tracks, with patrons sitting at sidewalk tables outside the hypothetical "Café Livonia," shoppers browsing at the hypothetical "Fashion Designs," and construction workers installing plate-glass windows into a hypothetical new grocery store called "Livonia Market." Around the corner was a hypothetical "Food Co-Op." Every person in the illustration had a brown face.

Residents were split on what this meant for the neighborhood moving forward. They all welcomed the investment, but would rents rise too high? The mayor's office assured locals that Brownsville would remain a welcoming place for working-class and low-income families. "We'll see," more than one resident said. In big cities across the country, space was becoming limited, exponentially valuable, and frequently at the center of clashes between longtime residents and new arrivals over the use of public grounds, proposals for housing developments, and the cultural insensitivity exhibited by businesses popping up to serve the gentrifiers. In one instance, the owner of a new bar in Crown Heights joked that she had left "bullet holes" in the wall to commemorate the neighborhood's violent past. To the new arrivals, that past was almost invisible. Crime rates continued to decline through Mayor Bill de Blasio's first term. In 2017, the city had its lowest tally of murders since the 1950s.

In the toughest of years, locals had found stability and solace in the neighborhood's tight-knit community, a collective investment and unspoken understanding of one another, a sense that *we're all in this together*. When the struggles got too heavy to bear for one person, there were others to share the load, watch the kids, cover the rent, fix a plate, or offer a couch to sleep on. It was this community pride that fed the current of nostalgia that ran through Brownsville. Most locals had seen too many tough years to assume any change was for their benefit.

As he strolled home on this December night, Chris liked the changes he was seeing. He walked below holiday lights that brightened blocks and passed storefronts that had sprung up over the past year or two. A chic restaurant, owned by three local women, served sandwiches named after local heroes, including the "Mr. Richard," which honored a community activist who had been one of Chris's childhood mentors. Further up the block, a fondue restaurant franchise managed by a local man shared a large, high-ceilinged, big-windowed space with the Brownsville Community Culinary Center, where 12 neighborhood residents enrolled in a job-training program cooked the food for the café at the front. Chris stopped in for a coffee and a biscuit, chatting with the manager as he waited for his order, which was on the house. Paintings hung on the walls, and white-hatted aspiring chefs darted around in the open kitchen. Two weeks earlier, Chris had hosted his mother's 80th birthday party in the building, turning the culinary center's classroom into a banquet hall, with a buffet set up and a big TV showing college football.

So many of the hopes he'd carried had become reality. More and more of his boys were doing well. Donnie was a freshman in high school, staying out of trouble, still playing football, and in better control of his anger. His brother Tarell continued to follow his lead. Their family moved out of the Castle and into a quieter apartment nearby. Chaka was passing his classes, impressing his coaches, spending much of his free time with his girlfriend, and thinking about college. Even Gio had found his way back onto a promising track. After his summer in Saint Lucia, his mother brought him back to Brooklyn. His conflict had cooled by then, and Gio, too, seemed calmer. He hadn't erased all his habits or totally cut himself off from the streets, and Chris understood that any day might bring bad news. He mostly had the same friends, but he stayed out less often and began to accept his mother's rules. He joined the football team in high school and was a good student. His motivation for acting right hadn't changed since those early months in Brooklyn: "Chasin' my dreams," he still told people.

It was often hard to tell what separated the ones who made it from those who didn't. The margin for error was smaller for black children growing up in working-class communities, and any youthful mistake could be the one that sent a boy down an irreversible path to destruction. For all Gio's troubles, and despite whatever toll all that danger and stress had taken on him, he had avoided being shot, arrested, or otherwise permanently damaged. It easily could have gone differently—if the wrong boy had access to a gun on the wrong day, or if the wrong cop came at Gio the wrong way and got angry and scared upon seeing this muscular, stone-faced boy show anything less than deference.

If there was a lesson boys got from football's violence, Chris hoped it was this: Keep your head on a swivel, your body braced, and your mind focused, because the smallest slipup often brought painful consequences—

Pop!

And there you were on your back, staring at the blue sky, ears ringing, the stakes clearer than ever.

The men who seemed to most value this lesson, and the other virtues intrinsic to football—toughness, resilience—were the men who'd clawed their way out of poverty in large part thanks to these virtues, men who understood the stakes and the historical reality that a black boy had to overcome injustice after injustice on the climb to success. Surely, there were other ways to pass on these virtues, but this was the method they knew and understood. It was a great luxury to not need these virtues hammered in, but these men had not come from places of great luxury. The stakes were too severe to stray from what they knew. In America, the cost of progress is high but inexact, and the more desperate a person, the more he is willing to risk and sacrifice.

Fewer and fewer parents were willing to have their children risk the dangers of tackle football. High schools in several states had shut down football programs. Some professional football players, even old-school tough guys like Harry Carson and Mike Ditka, had said they wouldn't let their sons play. More NFL players were retiring early, during their physical prime, in hopes of avoiding the life-altering brain damage that had become almost expected. Previously unknown risks became clear, and American society began to shift accordingly. Leagues at every level, from Pop Warner to the NFL, were banning certain kinds of hits, limiting full-contact practices, and eliminating the sorts of plays that are most likely to result in violent collisions. Nobody was quite sure whether any of it would make a difference, whether any of it could save football.

The fathers at Betsy Head heard talk that youth football was in its dying days. There were good reasons to ban the game at least until high school, if not further. It was not so much that the fathers resisted this oncoming reality. Rather, they were concerned first with what they saw around them—a world in which football talent is still an exceptionally valuable commodity, a ticket to private high schools and four-year universities. The virtues of football appealed to the fathers, but these rewards were what made the sport essential to them. Boxing, by comparison, also teaches toughness and resilience, but it is decidedly a poor man's game, reserved for those desperate enough to pay a high physical cost for modest purses and the very, very slim chance of riches. Whatever might happen to football in the future, it was here now to help their sons. The country's commitments to football and racial oppression made the sport's danger seem to them a worthwhile risk.

When the sons of these men grow to have their own sons, perhaps they will pass on the philosophies of their fathers. Perhaps football will have remained America's favorite sport, and Brownsville will have remained a hardscrabble neighborhood, and Mo Better boys will have gone on kicking up dust at Betsy Head Park. But these sons came of age at a moment of immense change, straddling eras, attuned to the shifting collective values of their society. These were worldly, modern boys, the first generation to know only the Internet age, only a black president. The fading, old world was one they never knew, a rumor. Amid discussions over the long-term prospects of football, Hart often seemed far more curious and thoughtful than the fathers at the park about the scientific research on brain injuries. Isaiah and Oomz, raised in Brownsville from birth, didn't carry the neighborhood pride common in previous generations: Oomz had claimed Fort Greene; Isaiah had repped Crown Heights. These were boys focused on escaping the expectations of the past.

ooooo

CHRIS LEFT THE café, bound for his house a few blocks away. As he passed a church, he heard somebody call his name. It was an old friend, a former police officer who now worked as an undertaker, and they slapped hands and embraced. Been too long, they said to each other. Dressed in a black suit, the old friend was on the clock for a funeral that night but had a few minutes for small talk.

"You guys still up at Betsy Head?" he asked Chris.

"Mmm, well, here and there," Chris mumbled in reply, bobbing his head but not quite nodding, before adding enthusiastically, "We got big things coming."

He didn't tell the old friend that this autumn had been the first without Mo Better football games in more than 20 years. Chris had held practices through the spring and into the summer, but by August it was clear that the program didn't have enough kids in any age group to field even a single team. The concerns about brain damage "killed the market," he said. "Absolutely. That's real." So, Chris was pivoting the program to account for the shifting sands. He now called it Mo Better Leadership Academy. Rather than limit his reach to boys who played football, Chris envisioned an expansive community organization that taught leadership and life skills through a range of activities, including sports teams for both boys and girls and music classes. He had purple hats designed and stitched up with the new name, and he wore one on this night. This was more than just an idea. Chris had already been meeting with middle school principals about partnerships, though the details were still being worked out. He hoped to have Mo Better basketball and soccer teams within a year, maybe golf, too. He wasn't sure about football. He hoped its days weren't over, but he understood he had to adjust to stay in the mix. Without any games or practices on the calendar, his autumn had been dull. "I miss the action," he said.

ooooo

BEFORE THE SUMMER was up, as it was slowly dawning on the coaches that the Mo Better season might have to be canceled, Vick left the program on bitter terms. He and his mother, Miss Elsie, joined up with the Brooklyn Saints, which had been founded in 2009 by a group of former Mo Better coaches. One of those coaches was stepfather to Curtis Samuel, and the Carolina Panthers wide receiver now sponsored the program. Vick's first season there, the program had only enough boys to form one team, in the Mitey Mite age group.

Vick felt hurt by Mo Better's decline and was upset that his youngest son, D-Lo, wouldn't play out his youth football career in purple and gold. Yet he hadn't been surprised. The previous two seasons—D-Lo's first two as a Mo Better Mitey Mite—were a debacle, with no playoff games and many forfeits across the age groups. Some weeks, the

program had no money to pay the referee, leaving parents to string together the $45 before the first quarter could start. "It really got embar-
rassing," Vick said. He laid some of the blame at Chris's feet. "Making
too many promises," Vick said. But the politicians didn't grant the funding and kids didn't come out to the park. "I remember when Mo Better
had the nicest banquet and the biggest trophies," he said. After its final
season, it had neither.

If Chris couldn't resurrect the football team, the 2014 Pee Wees
would go down as the last playoff team in Mo Better's illustrious history.
The program's final moment of glory, in Vick's mind, had been the banquet following that 2014 season. They had gathered in Brooklyn Borough
Hall on a bitingly cold Friday evening in March 2015, a lofty and elegant
scene in Vick's memory, shimmering with tall gold trophies and celebrity
appearances. Everything had been the way it was supposed to be.

ooooo

THE MONTHS AFTER the Brick City loss were stressful for Oomz. His
father's arrest upstate brought the familiar blend of shock, sadness, frustration, and disappointment. He never got used to the fear that his father would be locked up again. For those watching from the outside, Big
Oomz's latest troubles seemed to follow a familiar path. He had come
home to much fanfare and relief, only to soon collide with the cold realization that hits most formerly incarcerated people. To get some money
into his pocket, he relied on low-paid, part-time, hard-labor jobs that
came and went without consistency. Could anyone truly fault him for
turning back to his old, more lucrative business dealings?

After all, even Coach Vick had thought about resuming his hustling career. If not for how much he loved coaching a football team
of grade schoolers, Vick admitted, he probably would have. Like Big
Oomz, Vick was scraping together part-time work, in construction and
security, honest money that failed to bring financial stability but paid
the bills. He was still living in his own apartment, furnishing it slowly
and inexpensively. It was a home that gave him nearly as much pride
as his Mitey Mites did. "Wherever's there's work, I'll be there," he said.

He was as committed as ever to setting a good example for the boys who looked up to him, especially D-Lo. Vick had been stunned into a new urgency when his 24-year-old son, Donte, was sentenced to nine years in prison for his robbery conviction.

Big Oomz denied that he'd gotten back into the drug game. He said he was riding in the wrong car with the wrong person and had no idea about the heroin inside. The judge seemed to give him the benefit of the doubt. Big Oomz pleaded guilty to a minor drug possession charge and served 90 days in jail before returning home, where the status quo of part-time employment was waiting for him. "It's still a transition," his mother, Monique, said. "A lot of places don't want to hire a felon."

During those months between his father's arrest and return, Oomz struggled in school. His mother and grandmother observed that the boy was falling into the same traps at Mott Hall as he had at PS 156: too close to home, too many friends, too many distractions. Before his seventh-grade year, his mother transferred him to a middle school in Park Slope, an affluent, mostly white, café-and-brunch neighborhood in western Brooklyn. It was the most diverse school he had ever attended. His grades improved in seventh and eighth grade, though Monique still thought the boy didn't dedicate enough mental energy to school. She was encouraged that he at least maintained aspirations beyond professional sports. Instead of becoming a doctor, he now considered studying computer science and maybe pursuing a career in video-game design. He figured he'd change his mind again before college.

In the meantime, Oomz kept alive his most ambitious dreams. He wasn't sure if he wanted to aim for the NFL or NBA. During basketball season, Oomz was practically obsessed with the sport, playing on the blacktops several times a week and watching every NBA game he could catch. It was a natural development. Within his circle of friends, as well as a fast-growing share of the American population, basketball was the most popular sport, far more talked and thought about than football. Though he still wasn't tall, Oomz was talented enough to carry hoop dreams. His buddy posted on Facebook a video of Oomz crossing over an opponent so badly that the boy fell down, to the raucous cheers of all in the audience. Near the end of the 2017 NBA season, Oomz changed his Facebook profile photo to an image of him dribbling a basketball with the caption, "Just a Young nigga trying to make it out."

He still played football. At the end of his eighth-grade year, the city's education department assigned him to Samuel J. Tilden High School in East Flatbush, one of the three high schools nearest Betsy Head Park. But Oomz no longer lived in Brownsville. He stayed with Monique, who had moved two miles south to Canarsie. As summer vacation began, Oomz was having second thoughts about Tilden. He considered applying for a transfer. Erasmus Hall's football coach had reached out. "Been asking me to come play for them," Oomz said. The coach said he would be the JV team's starting running back and middle linebacker and was expected to soon help their varsity compete for a city championship. The possibility was almost too sweet to imagine: Oomz, Isaiah, and Chaka standing together at midfield holding up the trophy.

Thoughts of this potential reunion excited Oomz, pulled his mind back to that glorious, near-perfect 2014 season. Only years later did he come to realize how the rigid routine of those months pushed him through the tumult at home after his father's return, at school among his disobedient classmates, and in the streets that swallowed up Poppa.

Five months after that season ended, on that cold Friday night in March 2015, Oomz showed up late and unhappy to Mo Better's annual banquet. His father's case was pending. Uncertainty hovered over his family.

Dapper in a royal blue suit, Oomz slouched in the front row. All around him, boys sat, smiling and giggling, on cushy chairs under a big chandelier in the opulent main room of Brooklyn Borough Hall. In the row behind Oomz, Isaiah, in a black suit, looked around the room wide-eyed, at the portraits of white faces on the walls and the gold-plated moldings on the ceiling. A few seats over, Hart, in a gray suit, gazed at the tall, shiny trophies on the table at the front. This year's end-of-season banquet was an upgrade from the previous one. Chris organized a slate of speakers, including the borough president, a state senator, a state assemblywoman, a police captain, and several former players who'd gone on to impressive careers: a doctor, a principal, a professional football player, and an assistant coach on the New England Patriots. It was a sentimental evening. At one point, the lights dimmed and the former players marched down the center aisle holding candles, which they then handed—"passing the torch"—to current players. A few minutes later, players recited speeches they'd written about Black Lives Matter, domestic violence, and "being a man."

At first, Oomz took it all in with a look of indifference, but within minutes his mood began to thaw. When the trophies were given out and his name was called for the Hitman Award as the team's most brutal tackler, Oomz slowly pushed himself up and waddled to the podium, eyes on the ground but a slight smirk on his face. The boy held the big trophy with both hands. A smile grew. People were clapping. Coach Vick met Oomz in the aisle and embraced him. The coach whispered a few wise words, his purple suede suit jacket engulfing the boy.

Taking in the scene, an older man whose son had played for Mo Better years before said to the father next to him, "I recognize that name. Is that whose son I think it is?"

"They say he plays like him too," the father replied.

"Oh! Boy must be a hell of a player, then."

"You know it. Bet he ends up even better than his dad."

The older man nodded his head, watched Oomz slide back into his seat, and turned back to the father.

"We should all be so lucky."

Acknowledgments

THIS BOOK WAS POSSIBLE THANKS TO THE SCORES OF
kids, parents, and coaches who generously allowed me into their lives. I
am forever indebted to them.

I have eternal gratitude, too, for my agent, David Patterson, a constant source of enthusiasm and foresight since the day we met, and my
editor, Ben Adams, whose brilliant vision transformed this book into a
story I wouldn't have known how to write without him.

My editors at BuzzFeed, Tina Susman and Marisa Carroll, and their
bosses, Shani Hilton and Ben Smith, have been supportive through this
whole process, and taught me many of the tactics I used to report and
write this. Tom Finkel gave me my first real job when he was editor of
the *Riverfront Times* in Saint Louis. Later, as my editor at the *Village
Voice* in New York City, he dug into this story with me, editing the article that marked the starting point of my reporting for this project.

I'm grateful to Keegan Hamilton, who read a late-stage draft of the
manuscript quickly and on short notice, providing notes that proved
essential; to Adam Serwer, Jack Feeney, Joe Eskenazi, Driadonna Ro-
land, and John Tucker for reading early drafts and offering edits that
shaped the book; and to Joel Anderson, Tracy Clayton, Nico Medina

Mora, Tessa Stuart, Jesus Diaz, Camilo Smith, and Leah Faye Cooper for helping me work out ideas at the core of this book.

During these five years of reporting and writing, I have been guided by lessons passed down from editors, professors, and mentors: Dale Maharidge and Jess Bruder, who read the embarrassing work I was turning in at the beginning of journalism school, taught me how to write, and continue to provide guidance at every step; Stephen Fried, who is still the toughest editor I've ever had and a mentor generous with his time and knowledge; Sarah Fenske and Tom Walsh, who instilled an appreciation for the journalistic art of stirring shit up; Mark Schoofs, who showed me how tireless reporting can change the world; Steve Kandell, Brandon Reynolds, and Jack Buehrer, who always strove to identify and understand the bigger meaning behind a story.

I thank my roommate Alex Vessels for the comfortable environment we've lived in, and for our long conversations about our home borough. And for having listened to my drunken ramblings about this project more times than I could count, I thank Nick Philips, Alex Campbell, Katie Baker, Jessica Testa, David Noriega, Anna Roth, Ian Port, and Alan Scherstuhl.

I thank my family. This is a book about how circumstances at birth shape a life, and mine were privileged. I have been blessed with a support system of loved ones: Auntie Ging, Auntie Mae, Auntie Lyn, Auntie Alyssa, Auntie Donna, Uncle Marlon, Uncle Joey, Uncle Paul, and Uncle Chuck, who set examples of generosity, empathy, and decency; Uncle Bobby and Uncle Spanky, who taught me about responsibility and leadership; my cousins Jed, Roscoe, Mico, Mitch, Lauren, and Chris, who showed me how to dress, what music to listen to, and how to treat people.

I thank my father, Fahim Samaha, for stoking my curiosity about the world, sharing his joy for life, and teaching me the virtue of hard work.

Most of all, I thank my mother, Lucy Concepcion, who sacrificed more than I will ever know, raised me right, and always tells me she believes in me. I hope to live up to the wisdom, devotion, and love she has blessed me with.

Bibliography

A note on research: Population data is from the US Census Bureau. New York City crime numbers are from the New York City Police Department's regularly published statistics. Newark crime numbers are from the Newark Police Department's regularly published statistics. School test score numbers are from the New York City Department of Education's database. Criminal case details are from court documents. Additional information came from interviews with more than 300 people over the course of four and a half years of reporting.

Austensen, Maxwell, Vicki Been, Luis Inaraja Vera, Gita Khun Jush, Katherine M. O'Regan, Stephanie Rosoff, Traci Sanders, Eric Stern, Michael Suher, Mark A. Willis, and Jessica Yager. *State of New York City's Housing and Neighborhoods in 2016*. New York: New York University Furman Center, 2016. http://furmancenter.org/files/sotc/SOC_2016_Full.pdf.

Baerwald, Craig, Jacob Bogitsh, Mia Brezin, Erin Coombs, Rhonda-Lee Davis, Alcia Hall, Prudence Katze, Jessica Lax, Sarah Meier-Zimbler, Tariqua Morrison, Juan Carlos Quiridumbay, and Yasmine Robinson. *At Home in Brownsville Studio: A Plan for Transforming Public Housing*. New York: Hunter College Masters of Urban Planning, 2014. http://www1.nyc.gov/assets/hpd/downloads/pdf/community/brownsville-report.pdf.

Beyond Meal Status: A New Measure for Quantifying Poverty Levels in the City's Schools. New York: New York City Independent Budget Office, 2015. http://www.ibo.nyc.ny.us/iboreports/beyond-meal-status-a-new-measure-for-quantifying-poverty-levels-in-the-citys-schools-october-2015.pdf.

Brooklyn Community District 16: Brownsville. Community Health Profiles 2015. New York: New York City Department of Health and Mental Hygiene, 2015. http://www1.nyc.gov/assets/hpd/downloads/pdf/community /community-health-profile.pdf.

"Brooklyn Is the Coolest City on the Planet: An Eater's Guide." *GQ*, October 2011. https://www.gq.com/story/brooklyn-new-york-guide-food -dining.

"Brownsville Hit by New Disorder." *New York Times*, September 6, 1967.

Capperis, Sean, Jorge De la Roca, Kevin Findlan, Ingrid Gould Ellen, Josiah Madar, Shannon Moriarty, Justin Steil, Max Weselcouch, and Mark Willis. *State of New York City's Housing and Neighborhoods in 2013*. New York: New York University Furman Center, 2013. http://furmancenter.org/files /sotc/SOC2013_HighRes.pdf.

Caro, Robert. *The Power Broker: Robert Moses and the Fall of New York*. New York: Vintage, 1975.

Chadha, Nadiya, Brendan Coticchia, Harpreet Gill, Renu Pokharna, Fernando Posadas, Eva Pereira, Paula Richter, and Zoe Stopak-Behr. *State of New Yorkers—A Well-Being Index*. New York: New York City Center for Innovation through Data Intelligence and Columbia School of International and Public Affairs, 2015. http://www1.nyc.gov/assets/cidi/downloads /pdfs/nyc_well_being_index_full_report_2015.pdf.

Cho, Sang, and Alan Waxman. *Brownsville, Brooklyn Health Impact Assessment: Evaluating Social Entrepreneurship Programs by Recognizing and Promoting Local Context*. New York: Made in Brownsville, 2015. http://www .pewtrusts.org/~/media/assets/external-sites/health-impact-project/made -in-brownsville-2015-brownsville-report.pdf?la=en.

"City Asked to Extend Brownsville Houses." *Brooklyn Eagle*, December 24, 1953.

Comprehensive Housing Market Analysis: New York City, New York. Washington, DC: US Department of Housing and Urban Development, 2015. https:// www.huduser.gov/portal/publications/pdf/NYC-comp-16.pdf.

Dastrup, Samuel, Ingrid Ellen, Anna Jefferson, Max Weselcouch, Deena Schwartz, and Karen Cuenca. *The Effects of Neighborhood Change on New York City Housing Authority Residents*. Bethesda, MD: ABT Associates, 2015. https://nextcity.org/pdf/nycha_ceo_report.pdf.

Donaldson, Greg. *The Ville: Cops and Kids in Urban America*. Boston: Ticknor and Fields, 1993.

East Brooklyn Housing & Development Study 2008: Context Report. Brooklyn, NY: Pratt Center for Community Development, 2008. http://prattcenter .net/sites/default/files/prattcenter-ebk_housing_report.pdf.

Fainaru, Steve, and Mark Fainaru-Wada. "Youth Football Participation Drops." *ESPN*, November 14, 2013. http://www.espn.com/espn/otl/story /_/page/popwarner/pop-warner-youth-football-participation-drops-nfl -concussion-crisis-seen-causal-factor.

From Strengths to Solutions: An Asset-Based Approach to Meeting Community Needs in Brownsville. New York: Citizens' Committee for Children, 2017. https://www.cccnewyork.org/wp-content/uploads/2017/03/CCC -Brownsville-Report.pdf.

Glauber, Rae. *All Neighborhoods Change: A Survey of Brownsville, Brooklyn, U.S.A.* Brooklyn, NY, 1963.

Hahn, Josephine Wonsun. *Community Perceptions of Newark: Neighborhood Quality of Life, Safety, and the Justice System*. New York: Center for Court Innovation, 2014. https://www.courtinnovation.org/sites/default/files /documents/NewarkCommunitySurvey_0.pdf.

Hampton, Deon J., Ellen Yan, Bob Herzog, and Zachary R. Dowdy. "Tom Cutinella, Shoreham-Wading River HS Football Player, Dead After Injury in Game, Authorities Say." *Newsday*, October 2, 2014. https:// www.newsday.com/sports/high-school/football/tom-cutinella-shoreham -wading-river-football-player-dies-after-collision-in-game-authorities -say-1.9456831.

Hechinger, Fred. "Shanker and Lindsay Appeal to the Public." *New York Times*, November 17, 1968.

Holloway, Lynette. "Officials Say Gang Broken by 21 Arrests." *New York Times*, September 30, 1995. http://www.nytimes.com/1995/09/30/nyregion /officials-say-gang-broken-by-21-arrests.html.

Kazin, Alfred. *A Walker in the City*. New York: Harcourt Brace Jovanovich, 1969.

Kifner, John. "Echoes of a New York Waterloo." *New York Times*, December 22, 1996. http://www.nytimes.com/1996/12/22/weekinreview/echoes-of -a-new-york-waterloo.html.

Kneebone, Elizabeth, and Alan Berube. *Confronting Suburban Poverty in America*. Washington, DC: Brookings Institution Press, 2014.

Kneebone, Elizabeth, and Emily Garr. *The Suburbanization of Poverty: Trends in Metropolitan America, 2000 to 2008*. Washington, DC: Brookings Institution, 2010. https://www.brookings.edu/wp-content/uploads/2016/06 /0120_poverty_paper.pdf.

Marcius, Chelsia Rose, and Tina Moore. "Slain 1-Year-Old Antiq Hennis' Uncooperative Father: For Me, Money Talks." *New York Daily News*, September 10, 2013. http://www.nydailynews.com/new-york/slain-1-year -old-antiq-hennis-dad-money-talks-article-1.1450567.

Marley, Bill. "All About Brownsville." *New York Recorder*, October 23, 1965.

Marzulli, John, Laura Dimon, and Ginger Adams Otis. "Naked Brooklyn Woman Dragged from Apartment, Left Topless in Hallway for Minutes by NYPD Officers Who Say She Beat 12-Year-Old Daughter." *New York Daily News*, August 1, 2014. http://www.nydailynews.com/new-york /brooklyn/nypd-officers-drag-naked-brooklyn-woman-apartment -video-article-1.1889292.

New Jersey Community Capital, Joseph C. Cornwall Center for Metropolitan Studies at Rutgers University, and Center for Community Progress. *Measuring the State of Newark's Neighborhoods*. Newark: Strong Healthy Communities Initiative, 2014. https://www.newjerseycommunitycapital .org/sites/default/files/Measuring%20the%20State%20of%20Newark %27s%20Neighborhoods_2014.pdf.

New York Amsterdam News, August 18, 2014.

Ng, Alfred. "Man Killed after Brooklyn Cookout." *New York Daily News*, June 22, 2014. http://www.nydailynews.com/blogs/theshack/man-killed -brooklyn-cookout-blog-entry-1.1839602.

Paddock, Barry, Rocco Parascandola, Emily Field, and Corky Siemaszko. "Teen Charged with Murder for Killing Brooklyn Dad on Bus Admitted to Participating in the Crime, Prosecutor Says." *New York Daily News*, March 22, 2014. http://www.nydailynews.com/new-york/nyc-crime/brooklyn-dad -shot-dead-bus-leaves-family-dire-straits-article-1.1729428.

Peters, Mark G. *Probe of Department of Homeless Services' Shelters for Families with Children Finds Serious Deficiencies*. New York: New York City Department of Investigation, 2015. https://www1.nyc.gov/assets/doi/downloads /pdf/2015/mar15/pr08dhs_31215.pdf.

Pratt Institute's Programs for Sustainable Planning and Development. *Brownsville: Opportunity and Strength in the Heart of Brooklyn*. Brooklyn, NY: Brownsville Partnership, 2015. https://www1.nyc.gov/assets/hpd /downloads/pdf/community/final-report-brownsville-pratt-spring-2015.pdf.

Pritchett, Wendell. *Brownsville, Brooklyn: Blacks, Jews, and the Changing Face of the Ghetto*. Chicago: University of Chicago Press, 2003.

Proposed Health and Wellness Interventions in Brownsville and East New York. Brooklyn, NY: Community Care of Brooklyn, 2016. https://www.ccbrooklyn .org/media/file/FINAL_CCB_PAR_REPORT.PDF.

Report of the Safer Newark Council, 2016: A Call to Action. Newark, NJ: Safer Newark Council, 2016. http://www.safernewark.org/report-of-the-safer -newark-council-2016-a-call-to-action/.

Report of the Study Commission on Violence. Trenton: New Jersey Study Commission on Violence, 2015. http://www.nj.gov/oag/library/SCV-Final -Report--10-13-15.pdf.

Rivlin-Nadler, Max. "Hell on Wheels: Port Authority's Broken Promise Is Choking Newark's Kids." *Village Voice*, May 3, 2016. https://www .villagevoice.com/2016/05/03/hell-on-wheels-port-authorrys-broken -promise-is-choking-newarks-kids/.

Robert Morris University Polling Institute. "Head Injuries in Mind, RMU Survey Shows Strong Support for Ban on Youth Contact Football." Press release, November 14, 2013. http://www.rmu.edu/PollingInstitute /HeadInjuriesinMind.

Sanzone, Joy, Mindy Weidman, and Bernadette Doykos. *Needs and Segmentation Analysis for the South Ward of Newark, New Jersey.* New York: Metropolitan Center for Research on Equity and the Transformation of Schools, 2016. https://steinhardt.nyu.edu/scmsAdmin/media/users/atn293/reval /needs_segmentation_alalysis_south_ward.pdf.

Schanberg, Sydney H. "New York; Gentrifiers: The Greed." *New York Times*, May 8, 1982. http://www.nytimes.com/1982/05/08/opinion/new-york -gentrifiers-the-greed.html.

Schram, Jamie, Erin Calabrese, and Leonard Greene. "Slain Tot's Dad: I'll Talk to Press—for a Price." *New York Post*, September 10, 2013. https://nypost .com/2013/09/10/slain-tots-dad-ill-talk-to-press-for-a-price/.

Sit, Ryan, and Barry Paddock. "Brooklyn Man Brutally Beaten to Death by Group of 10 Others." *New York Daily News*, September 27, 2014. http:// www.nydailynews.com/new-york/brooklyn/brooklyn-man-brutally -beaten-death-group-10-article-1.1955346.

Statement of William P. Barr, Attorney General, Before the Committee on the Judiciary United States Senate Concerning Department of Justice Authorization for Fiscal Year 1993. U.S. Department of Justice, June 30, 1992. https://www.justice.gov/sites/default/files/ag/legacy/2011/08/23/06-30 -1992.pdf.

Stop-and-Frisk during the Bloomberg Administration (2002–2013). New York: New York Civil Liberties Union, 2014. https://www.nyclu.org/sites/default /files/publications/stopandfrisk_briefer_2002-2013_final.pdf.

Stop-and-Frisk 2012. New York: New York Civil Liberties Union, 2013. https:// www.nyclu.org/sites/default/files/releases/2012_Report_NYCLU.pdf.

"Teen Gangs Linked to 40 Percent of New York City Shootings." Associated Press, May 1, 2014.

Thompson Jr., William C. *Audit Report on the Contract of Basic Housing, Inc., with the Department of Homeless Services to Provide Shelter and Support Services.* New York: The City of New York Office of the Comptroller, 2009. https://comptroller.nyc.gov/wp-content/uploads/documents/ME09_088A.pdf.

"3 Shot Near Eastern Parkway and Thomas S. Boyland Street in Brownsville." News 12 Brooklyn, September 28, 2014. http://brooklyn.news12.com/story/34786805/3-shot-near-eastern-parkway-and-thomas-s-boyland-street-in-brownsville.

Vasquez, Emily. "Brooklyn: Two Men Fatally Shot." *New York Times*, September 11, 2006. http://www.nytimes.com/2006/09/11/nyregion/11mbrfs-001.html.

Webber, Alan M. "Crime and Management: An Interview with New York City Police Commissioner Lee P. Brown." *Harvard Business Review*, May–June 1991.

Weber, Bruce. "Greg Jackson Dies at 60; Ran a Haven in Brooklyn." *New York Times*, May 2, 2012. http://www.nytimes.com/2012/05/03/nyregion/greg-jackson-brooklyn-youth-mentor-dies-at-60.html.

Youth Justice Board. *Looking Forward: Youth Perspectives on Reducing Crime in Brownsville and Beyond.* New York: Center for Court Innovation, 2011. https://www.courtinnovation.org/sites/default/files/documents/report%20for%20website.pdf.

Index

Albert Samaha is a criminal justice reporter at BuzzFeed News. He has written for the *Village Voice*, *San Francisco Weekly*, and the *Riverfront Times*, and his work has appeared in the *San Francisco Examiner*, the *New York Observer*, and *Pop-Up Magazine*. His stories have won awards from the National Association of Black Journalists, the National Education Writers Association, the California Newspaper Publishers Association, and others. He is a graduate of Columbia's Graduate School of Journalism and lives in Flatbush, Brooklyn.

PublicAffairs is a publishing house founded in 1997. It is a tribute to the standards, values, and flair of three persons who have served as mentors to countless reporters, writers, editors, and book people of all kinds, including me.

I. F. STONE, proprietor of *I. F. Stone's Weekly*, combined a commitment to the First Amendment with entrepreneurial zeal and reporting skill and became one of the great independent journalists in American history. At the age of eighty, Izzy published *The Trial of Socrates*, which was a national bestseller. He wrote the book after he taught himself ancient Greek.

BENJAMIN C. BRADLEE was for nearly thirty years the charismatic editorial leader of *The Washington Post*. It was Ben who gave the *Post* the range and courage to pursue such historic issues as Watergate. He supported his reporters with a tenacity that made them fearless and it is no accident that so many became authors of influential, best-selling books.

ROBERT L. BERNSTEIN, the chief executive of Random House for more than a quarter century, guided one of the nation's premier publishing houses. Bob was personally responsible for many books of political dissent and argument that challenged tyranny around the globe. He is also the founder and longtime chair of Human Rights Watch, one of the most respected human rights organizations in the world.

. . .

For fifty years, the banner of Public Affairs Press was carried by its owner Morris B. Schnapper, who published Gandhi, Nasser, Toynbee, Truman, and about 1,500 other authors. In 1983, Schnapper was described by *The Washington Post* as "a redoubtable gadfly." His legacy will endure in the books to come.

Peter Osnos, *Founder*